BRECHT

BOOKS IN THIS SERIES

RONALD GRAY

Lecturer in German in the University of Cambridge
and Fellow of Emmanuel College

Brecht

THE DRAMATIST

CAMBRIDGE UNIVERSITY PRESS

CAMBRIDGE

LONDON • NEW YORK • MELBOURNE

Published by the Syndics of the Cambridge University Press
The Pitt Building, Trumpington Street, Cambridge CB2 1RP
Bentley House, 200 Euston Road, London NW1 2DB
32 East 57th Street, New York 10022, USA
296 Beaconsfield Parade, Middle Park, Melbourne 3206, Australia

First published 1976

Printed in the United States of America

Library of Congress Cataloguing in Publication Data

Gray, Ronald D.
Brecht the dramatist.

(Major European authors)
"A chronological list of Brecht's plays and of translations": p.
Bibliography: p.
Includes index.
1. Brecht, Bertolt, 1898-1956—Criticism and interpretation. I. Title.
PT2603.R397Z634   832'.9'12   75-19575
ISBN 0 521 20937 4 hard covers
ISBN 0 521 29003 1 paper back

CONTENTS

GENERAL PREFACE TO THE SERIES

The *Major European Authors* series, as the name implies, considers the most important writers of the European literatures, most often giving a volume to each author, but occasionally treating a group or a genre. The basic assumption is that the general reader and the student will be able to find information on biography and literary history fairly easily elsewhere: that what he will look for in this series is a single volume which gives a critical survey of the entire oeuvre or the most important works. Authors of books in the series are asked to keep this general critical objective in mind, to write critical introductions which will help the reader to order his impressions of the works of art themselves, to assume little prior knowledge, and so far as possible either to quote in English or to translate quotations.

It is hoped that the series will help to keep the classics of European literature alive and active in the minds of present-day readers: both those reading for a formal literary examination, and those who in the original languages and in translation wish to keep in touch with the culture of Europe.

AUTHOR'S PREFACE

This book had its origin in a much smaller one which was published in 1961 by Messrs Oliver and Boyd in their 'Writers and Critics' series, now out of print. Some fragments of that earlier book are scattered through this one, but it is essentially rewritten, and extended to cover several aspects not touched on before. Some of the chapter on *Mother Courage* appeared in the *Oxford Review*, and some of the final chapter, so far as it concerns Shakespearean productions, in *The Human World*.

Although Brecht wrote poems and novels, and was involved in several films, his work in the theatre is what has aroused interest abroad, and I have kept strictly to that; I have also not ventured into the musical compositions associated with his plays.

I thank Mr. Michael Black for many critical comments and helpful suggestions.

R.G.

1

MARXISM AND POLITICAL THEATRE

Political theatre is not, here, the same as theatre about politics or the State. If it were, it would include plays like the *Oresteia* and *Hamlet*, Shakespeare's histories, *Le Cid*, and many more. In the particular sense relevant to Brecht, political theatre is more akin to the Jesuit didactic theatre of the seventeenth century. It begins with the French Revolution, and, as we are beginning to discover, there was much more of it at that time, at least in France, Spain and Germany, than used to be supposed. This was theatre deliberately aimed at changing the attitudes of audiences, as in *Die Aristokraten in Deutschland*, published 'in the fourth year of Liberty', and mocking the pretensions of German nouveaux-riches while contrasting them with the French soldiers of the revolutionary armies.[1] It had no popular success, since it was given no place in the established theatre. More acceptable, politically, were plays like Heinrich von Kleist's *Prinz Friedrich von Homburg* (1811, though here too recognition was delayed) and Friedrich Hebbel's *Agnes Bernauer* (1851), inculcating total submissiveness to the State.

In Germany, the connection between theatre and politics has always been more prominent than in England. Though the German Jacobin theatre had no following, the revolutionaries of a later generation turned to the theatre in the same way, trade unions and political clubs producing plays of their own to educate the workers into a recognition of their situation. As early as 1847, Friedrich Engels composed a one-act play about revolution for a Brussels club-theatre (a recently discovered play of his, *Rienzi*, had been written in 1838–40), and in 1858–9 an equally prominent Socialist, Ferdinand Lassalle, wrote his unwieldy tragedy *Franz von Sickingen*, the subject of much correspondence between Marx, Engels and the author.

There were already in the established repertory several plays by the classical dramatists, Goethe and Schiller, dealing with the revolt of the Hamlet-like or Robin-Hood-like outsider. *Götz von Berlichingen, The Robbers* and *Fiesco* are all concerned with the revolt of a 'great individual' against the society of his time. But they are all defeated, and either look forward wistfully to a better age to come, or condemn themselves for their arrogance in supposing that they could ever effect reforms by their own powers. The classical tradition in Germany, taken up later by Grillparzer in Austria, tends politically to acquiescence in the long run, as does even the more radical but fatalistic theatre of Georg Büchner.

The revolutionary drama itself was still tinged with this, in the early stages. The point of Lassalle's tragedy was to demonstrate that although the revolutionary idea might be pure enough, the revolutionary leaders trying to put it into practice were certain to make compromises. Being merely single individuals, they could not grasp and realise in practical terms the new Idea – in Hegel's sense, of a force at work in all historical events – and could only buckle under the strain, and even become corrupted.

The revolutionary movement, Lassalle believed, derived its strength from its complete certainty about the omnipotence of the Idea. History was moving towards socialism, inevitably, but the revolutionary was involved in an insoluble contradiction, when his finite reason attempted to use that omnipotence: he was thus doomed to failure, and Lassalle was more inclined to trust to gradual reforms, leading by degrees, perhaps, to the ultimate realisation of the Idea on earth, rather than risk the cataclysmic changes which Marx and Engels believed to be essential. Lassalle's tragedy was meant to underline his point.[2]

Marx and Engels condemned Lassalle for continuing in the tradition of many German philosophers who saw the Idea or the Will or the noumenal world as beyond human experience, or in some other way separated from mankind. As Marx saw it, there was no such separation. 'With me', he said, 'the ideal is nothing else than the material world reflected by the human mind, and translated into forms of thought.'[3] In other words, the prime mover was not some god or demigod, as Hegel proposed, but man himself. The revolutionary ideal could be attained because man produced it; it was not falsified through using him as an intermediary.

The working-class theatre in Germany followed Marx, in this

respect, rather than Lassalle. It flourished as it did partly because the German working-classes – unlike those in England, who flocked to theatres to see sentimental melodramas about people like themselves[4] – were only recent city-dwellers, and theatre-goers scarcely at all, the city-life of the Industrial Revolution having begun much later in Germany. It also flourished partly because Socialists were more persecuted in Germany, especially after the notorious 'Socialist Laws' had been passed in 1878.

At first, however, the 'workers' drama' was largely composed of comedies, humorous dialogues, satires on contemporary figures, in which the representatives of capitalism are defeated by more resourceful employees. Jean Baptiste von Schweitzer, Lassalle's political successor, followed him also in composing a dramatic dialogue, *Der Schlingel* (The Rascal), written in 1867–8, intended to make workers acquainted with the main points of Marx's *Capital* in an entertaining way. He had great success with it, Marx himself admitting that Schweitzer had 'done his homework', and though it was not meant as a play, the dialogue was frequently performed by working men's dramatic societies all over Germany. It was followed in 1869 by Schweitzer's *Die Gans* (The Goose), a play in which a woman demands to know why she should receive less wages than a man. The employer who tries to talk her out of it is quickly put in his place by a trained Marxist.[5]

These were plays with definite points of instruction: *Der Schlingel* is concerned with the theory of surplus value, *Die Gans* with women's rights, and a third play, *Der Verunglückte Agitator* (The Accident to the Agitator) is concerned with the resolutions of the First International at Basle, on the issue of landed property. Tragedy was at first not represented, nor did working-class dramatists concern themselves with political martyrs like Paul Beutler: if tragic events occurred, they were seen in the optimistic light of a dawn that was about to break for the whole of mankind. Working-class characters were shown as brave, clever, and tough, with significant names like Roth, Fels, Stein, and Frei: Red, Rock, Stone, Free. The general motto, taken from Bader's *Das Gesetz* (The Law) was 'Fight, not weep' ('Nicht flennen, kämpfen').

All this was at a time when the English theatre, so far as it portrayed the working-class at all, either sentimentalised them as in T. W. Robertson's *Caste* (1867) or melodramatised them as in Tom Taylor's *The Ticket-of-Leave-Man* (1863). It was not that workers in England were denied what they sought in the theatre. For many years there was such a period of mob-rule in the English theatre that the pit and the gallery could dictate to the stage the matter and 'style of their entertainment. But as often as not the entertainment took the form of seeing workers like themselves, in pitiful conditions, lost in the maze of London or forced to eke out an existence under railway arches, with no thought of improvement other than the chance of some totally unexpected legacy, which often enough supplied the denouement. The 'philosophy' is that of a ruling class: as Robertson's military hero says, marrying a ballet-girl: 'Oh, caste's all right. Caste is a good thing if it's not carried too far. It shuts the door on the pretentious and the vulgar; but it should open the door very wide for exceptional merit. Let brains break through its barriers, and what brains can break through love may leap over.'[6]

The main stream of German drama was capable of such sentiments. Unlike the English, it also had a strong under-current of amateur plays of Marxist character. August Bebel, the Socialist leader, recalled in 1913 how in the 1860s there were hundreds of working men's educational clubs, many of which produced plays with their own home-made scenery and costumes, and flourished for more than a decade.[7] During the period of the anti-Socialist laws, between 1878 and 1890, it became impossible to perform or print political drama, but as soon as Bismarck allowed the laws to lapse – in the expectation that the Socialists would take enough rope to hang themselves – the flood began. The popularity of the Social Democrats, that is, the Socialists, had in any case risen despite the suppressions, and despite the brutal expulsions of Socialist politicians and agitators. The votes given to Social Democrat candidates rose during the twelve years from about half a million to a million and a half, and were to rise during the next twenty years to four and a quarter million. During the last decade of the century, more than thirty plays – little enough, compared with the hundreds of plays performed in professional theatres – were published by Socialist presses, and performed all over Germany, most of them 'agitation-plays', or didactic plays', though Scaevola's *The French Revolution, an Epic Dramatic Poem in 12 Living Tableaux* was highly popular. At the same time, the didactic element squeezed out the more humorous tone that had been present before 1878. The idea of the theatre as a place of political education rather than amusement began to take hold in a way that has no parallel in English theatrical history.

During the 1890s, acknowledged literary figures adopted working-class or revolutionary themes. Friedrich Bosse, who introduced both factory-workers and class-conscious agitators into his plays, is scarcely known today. Gerhart Hauptmann's *Die Weber* (The Weavers), on the other hand, is still widely known, and accounted one of the best plays of the German Naturalist movement.

Hauptmann had no revolutionary intent. The document on which he based his play, a report by Wilhelm Wolff on an uprising in Silesia in 1845, explicitly called for 'a refashioning of society on the principle of solidarity, mutual aid and community, in a word, of justice'. The play, though it was held up at first by censorship, and hailed by Socialists as a work calling for revolution, carefully withholds itself from any such political statement. It is factual, a statement rather than a manifesto, like the dreary picture of Berlin working-class life in Holz and Schlaf's *The Selicke Family* (1890), though less crudely naturalistic. Dramatists who were not at all Naturalists also remained politically uncommitted, though Sternheim and Wedekind, in *Bürger Schippel* (1912) and *The Marquis von Keith* (1900) respectively, were satirical about middle-class characters. Even Georg Büchner's *Woyzeck* and *The Death of Danton*, written in the 1830s and first resurrected by Hauptmann in the 1890s, were fatalistic and oppressive in tone, despite the fact that one was the first play ever to take a common soldier as its main character, while the second concerned the possibility of successful revolution.

The genuinely political drama, in the sense being used here, meanwhile devoted itself to documentary reports on the many widespread strikes which took place during the 1900s, or offered entertainment of a political kind to crowds at election meetings. The distinctive feature remained, as before, a cheerful optimism, such as none of the 'literary' dramatists, to whom the established theatres were still open, thought possible or desirable.

Before Brecht began his career as a dramatist, at the end of the First World War, there was thus a long-standing tradition of political drama in Germany such as no other country has to show. It was all ephemeral; none of it is likely to be revived on the stage today. But the recognised dramatists, unlike Brecht, had taken no active interest in politics, and it was his role to bring political theatre to a level not hitherto achieved.

The complexities of the task were large. Marxist thought is not easily given dramatic life, and Brecht did not generally manage to give it any: where he is most Marxian he is least theatrical. Basically, however, there were dramatic potentialities in Marxism. One of Marx's chief contentions against Hegel was that he sought to crystallise and apotheosise the existing state of things, and thereby maintain the political *status quo ante* as the highest achievement yet attained by the Idea, in its historical self-manifestation. The opposite view, which 'regards every historically developed social form as in fluid movement . . .' and 'lets nothing impose upon it, and is in its essence critical and revolutionary'[8] ought at least to lend itself to the flux of drama. Again, the fact that Marx, like Hegel, conceived of the whole world in terms of a dialectical play of complementary opposites, constantly circling round and interpenetrating one another, could easily supply the conflicts and confrontations that are the stuff of plays.

The economic aspects of Marx offer less dramatic potential, though they too exploit the dialectic. The broad pattern of history, as Marx sees it[9] is one of opposition between the expropriator and the expropriated, between the capitalist and the worker whose property-rights in his own labour the capitalist exploits. As a pattern, it is extremely simple: the capitalist first gathers together in one factory the various skills which formerly belonged to individuals, and establishes under one roof the industry that had formerly been scattered widespread. Unknowingly, he sows in this way the seed of his own destruction, since the unified control of labour becomes a first step on the road to socialism. The 'opposite' whom he has thus incorporated into his own system does not remain content within it, but recognises, if properly instructed, the fact that he has been expropriated. With the necessity of a living organism, the worker must then take back his property. But in doing so he takes it back not as an individual, but as an integral part of the mass, the community, to which he belongs. Thus a paradoxical situation arises: the ex-

propriator has been expropriated, but there is no return to a
simple individualism. Rather, the opposites come together in a
permanent fusion of individual and corporate rights. To quote
Marx himself:

The capitalist mode of appropriation, the result of the capitalist mode
of production, produces capitalist private property. This is the first
negation of individual private property, as founded on the labour of
the proprietor. But capitalist production begets, with the inexora-
bility of a law of Nature, its own negation. It is the negation of
negation. This does not re-establish private property for the producer,
but gives him individual property based on the acquisitions of the
capitalist era: *i.e.*, on co-operation and the possession in common of
the land and of the means of production.[10]

There is nothing a dramatist can do with that. The potential is
entirely in the dialectical tradition, which Brecht shares with
Thomas Mann, Nietzsche, Goethe, and many other writers whose
sole connection with Marx is that they thought 'in opposites'. The
distinctively Marxist feature is the vision of a society in which
not only individual property will have disappeared, but all other
forms of division, the family, the national State, political parties,
and every line of demarcation whatsoever. Negation will cease
to exist, once it has itself been negated, and there will remain
only an undifferentiating affirmation of all existence. Echoes of
this can certainly be found in Brecht, though they are not always
what Marx made of them.

Equally relevant to an understanding of the political background of the plays is the Marxist debate on how the classless
society was to come about, or be brought about. Lassalle had
supposed that the individual must corrupt the absolute reality by
limiting it to himself. How was the discrepancy between the
ideal and the real to be overcome? Since each individual mind
must reflect reality in its own way, how was the distortion of the
ideal, which Lassalle foresaw, to be avoided? Or was the ideal
only the reflection of the material world, an exact copy of it?

Marx and Marxism have two answers to this. On the one hand
Marx claimed to have discovered a law of Nature, to have demonstrated by reference to historical and economic facts that
human society must progress as he predicted. This part of the
claim was, however, an absolute one: it was as though history

could be predicted precisely, while still continuing to change incessantly.

The other part of the claim advanced by Marxists concerns the role of the Communist Party, and this is a more flexible, fluid one. The Communist Party is not in the position of Lassalle's private individual, attempting to achieve the ideal, it is a corporate body, and though of course it is not the totality of all humanity, it may claim more than a purely individual authority. In addition, the Party, though it assumes or is *prima facie* convinced of the truth of Marxist doctrine, is not rigidly bound to any one view of the course to be adopted. It realises the truth of Marx's assertion that every affirmative recognition is also accompanied by a negation, that there is continual flux, and it continually revises its plans in accordance with this. It adapts itself to the passing moment in order to bring about the ultimate moment. But in this dual role, grasping the Absolute or the Ideal with one hand, as a given fact, and the passing moment with the other, as a manifestation of the material world, there is always the possibility of confusion and ambiguity for the Party. When the ideal and the real are not clearly separated from one another, when one can be the reflection of the other, and when a group of individuals known as the Party is held to be in the right yet constantly adapting to change, false claims are certain to be made.

It was out of this situation that the German Marxist parties were created.[11] Although Lassalle died in 1864, his influence continued in the programme of the Sozialdemokratische Partei Deutschlands (S.P.D.), as crystallised in the Erfurt Programme of 1891. On the one hand, the Erfurt Programme continued to assert, in a Marxist spirit, that the Communist programme had the force of a natural law, which nothing could hinder in the long run. It also asserted that only the working-class could bring about the necessary change – the working class was the element through which alone change could function. (This was a doctrine which had serious effects on Brecht, who seems from his plays to have thought of himself as born outside the working-class, and so rather in the position of a convert to, say, Judaism. The idea of a 'chosen people' may well have influenced Marx, as a Jew, in making this kind of emphasis.) But on the other hand the Erfurt Programme was not strictly revolutionary, or not immediately so. It held that the time for the advent of Communism was not yet, and accordingly planned for a number of ameliorations which were, in some cases, not so much socialistic or communistic as radical – votes for women and abolition of capital punishment were included in the aims of the S.P.D. And in general the history of the S.P.D. from 1891 until quite recent times was more often empirical and pragmatic than theoretical: it held to the flux, rather than to the principles of Marxism (if the two can properly be distinguished), and this was to lead to a sharp division, coming to a head between 1914 and 1919, a time when Brecht was in his final years at school, and first going out into the world.

For the main body of the S.P.D., the war of 1914 presented a dilemma. They had sworn repeatedly in the preceding years never to fight against their socialist brothers in France and else-where, and appeared to be entirely opposed to any war fought in the interests of Imperial Germany and Austria. Yet when war was declared, it was represented as a defensive war against Tsarist Russia, an enemy of socialism even greater than the Germanic Empires could be. For this and other reasons, German Marxists found themselves pledged to fight in a war which seemed in some respects to be fought against their socialist com-rades in other countries, and as it went on they found themselves at the mercy of almost any pretext that could be thought of. It was necessary to fight the war because it was a defensive war against Tsarist Imperialism. When that no longer appeared true, it was necessary to go on fighting because a defeat of Germany by foreign capitalist powers would mean also defeat for the strongest socialist party in Europe (which the S.P.D. was, up till the Russian Revolution of 1917). Even a German war of con-quest, which the S.P.D. had at first abhorred, could be justified on the grounds that a purely defensive war was more likely to lead to defeat than an aggressive one. And even when Ger-many was defeated, and the S.P.D. took over the government from the German Emperor's temporary successor, it still found itself unable to make radical changes. Order had to be main-tained, if only to keep up food-supplies, and the only order maintained was the old one.

In contrast to this were the revolutionary voices, only a few of them at first, led by Karl Liebknecht and Rosa Luxemburg.[12] From the beginning of the war, these urged that no compromise be made, and that the international solidarity of the working-class be maintained. The changes of pretexts for continuing to support the war, such as the S.P.D. continually had to make, looked irresponsible in comparison with the insistent, unchanging demand by the extreme Left that the system itself be changed, though in fact the centre and Right wing of the S.P.D. were acting with a great deal of careful thought, within their own frame of reference. For Liebknecht and Luxemburg, capitalism was responsible for the war; all compromise was useless, and could only lead to more and more compromise; nothing but a revolutionary change had any value, and only the party of the working-class could bring this about. After the Russian Revolution they could claim that their case was stronger, for there was no possibility of maintaining, now, that the war was being fought against the Tsar, whereas the refusal of the Russian working-class to fight for the fatherland was a model for Germans to follow. The first stage of the international revolution had begun, and Germany had only to continue it for a world-wide eruption to take place, as Marx has predicted.

The attempts at establishing this revolution which were made in Berlin and in Munich, where there was a short-lived Soviet Republic in 1919, were unsuccessful, not least because Luxemburg and Liebknecht were assassinated. So far as Brecht is concerned, they matter because this was the world into which he was born. On the one hand, compromise, going with the flux of things, adapting to circumstances; on the other, a complete break with the capitalist system, realising the ideal if not at one stroke, then at least very swiftly: both points of view could claim Marxist ancestry, and both were to find a place in his dramatic work.

Just as important for understanding Brecht are the apocalyptic expectations of many Germans in the years immediately after the armistice of 1918. The 'last fight' in the words of the 'Internationale', had begun, and the war was the Armageddon which announced it. If Germany were to follow the Bolshevik example, victory for the international working-class might be imminent.

The importance of drama was quickly appreciated by the Bolsheviks themselves. Lenin had announced the programme that all literature must be party-literature. 'Literary activity must become part of the general proletarian cause, a cog in the one great unified social-democratic mechanism set in motion by the whole politically conscious avant-garde of the whole working class.'[13] Though this literary activity was also to be free, it was so only in the sense of the word known to Lenin. All newspapers were to become organs of party organisations. All writers must belong to such organisations, and all publishing concerns, bookshops, reading-rooms, libraries must be subordinate to the party and answerable to it. Under such conditions, Lenin announced that everyone was free to write or say whatever he liked, without the least limitation, but the party would be also free to turn out anyone of whom they disapproved. The face of totalitarianism had begun to show itself, and the path lay open for Stalin and his censors to crush the slightest breath of opposition, with Lenin's full authorisation.

For a while, the real import of Lenin's words seems not to have been felt. The Russian theatre became, for a few years, the most freely experimental in the world. It had good cause: there was more savage repression in Russia than there had been in Germany even in the latter years of Bismarck's regime. As the Russian dierctor Meyerhold wrote to Chekhov in 1901, soon after witnessing the brutal suppression of a student demonstration by the police and the military:

I want to burn with the spirit of the times. I want all servants of the stage to recognise their high destiny. I am irritated by those comrades of mine who have no desire to rise above the narrow interests of their caste and respond to the interests of society. Yes, the theatre is capable of playing an enormous part in the transformation of the whole of existence![14]

On the other hand, like Chekhov himself, Meyerhold did not attach value to plays which 'force the spectator to rack his brains over the solution of all manner of social and philosophical problems'. The theatre was for him a world of marvels and enchantment, of breathless joy and strange magic. This remained his way of thinking right up to the revolution of 1917, and it was the same with the so-called 'Academic Theatres' in Moscow, which had by 1920 still not produced one Soviet play. As Tairov said, 'A propagandist theatre after a revolution is like mustard after a meal.'[15]

In the amateur theatre things were very different. In 1918

theatrical groups performed agitatory shows everywhere in Petrograd, while in Moscow a mass spectacle was provided, the *Pantomime of the Great Revolution*. New amateur groups sprang up all over Russia, acting events from recent revolutionary history; railway trains were used for whistle-stop productions, and another mass spectacle involving over 6,000 performers re-enacted the storming of the Winter Palace. In 1920 Meyerhold was recalled from military service to take charge of theatrical activity in the entire Soviet Union, and the intense excitement he was able to engender can be gauged from his production of Verhaeren's play of world revolution, *The Dawn*. Mass enthusiasm was carefully stimulated by a claque of actors, and the result could be highly emotional:

At a fixed point in the play the character of the Herald would enter and deliver a bulletin on the progress of the real Civil War in the South. Meyerhold's highest aspirations were gratified on the night when the Herald announced the decisive break into the Crimea at the Battle of Perekop and the entire theatre rose in a triumphant rendering of the *Internationale*. Such unanimity of response did not occur every night, but usually only when military detachments attended *en bloc*, as they sometimes did, complete with banners flying and bands ready to strike up.[16]

This was a long way from Chekhov, and from traditional theatre, but it was popular in the extreme, and widely known abroad, though Meyerhold was not granted permission to go on tour outside the U.S.S.R. till 1930. The inspiration afforded to other political theatres can be imagined, and although nothing truly comparable to Meyerhold's spectacles was staged in Germany, the possibility of using theatre in order to change the world began to look much more real.

While Brecht was still making his first attempts at drama, political playwriting in post-war Germany was becoming a profession to which he might well turn his hand. In 1920, at Leipzig, for instance, a reconstruction of the revolt of slaves in ancient Rome, led by Spartacus (whose name had been used for the Communist uprising in Berlin the previous year) was performed at the race-course by 900 actors before 50,000 spectators. Like the more recent events it ended depressingly, as the local newspaper[17] complained, and the zest of the Russians was not shown. Next year at Leipzig there was a spectacle of 'the great peasant uprising in the eighteenth century', though again the newspaper complained that the idea of the revolution did not go well with a Dance of Death. A pessimistic note was still present in 1922, when a small audience at the same arena saw a spectacle of the French Revolution, after drenching rain, with words specially written by Ernst Toller, most of which could not be heard.

Toller was the best known of the 'literary' Communist dramatists at that time, though his earliest plays were more religious than political. He became a Minister in the Soviet republic of Bavaria in 1919, and was sentenced to five years' imprisonment for it; his convinced belief in Communism could hardly be doubted. Yet his work is deeply despairing. In *Die Wandlung* (Transfiguration, 1919), he autobiographically shows a character who returns from the war to give up his faith in nationalism for the cause of socialism. In *Masse Mensch* (Mass, Man, 1919) he faces the dilemma of a revolutionary who is at heart a humane idealist, but who seems obliged to adopt barbaric methods to achieve her goal. She sees no way to persuade her comrades to give up bloodshed and violence except by sacrificing herself, but the play ends with no certain conclusion, and Toller has not seen his own proper course with any clarity. In his later plays, *Der deutsche Hinkemann* (Brokenbrow, 1923) and *Hoppla! wir leben!* (Whoops! we're alive!, 1927) he despairs of any realisation of the brotherhood of mankind. Even his more factual, less autobiographical plays, *Feuer aus den Kesseln* (Draw the Fires) about the Kiel naval mutiny of 1917, and *Die Maschinenstürmer* (The Machine-Wreckers), about the English Luddites of the early nineteenth century, are entirely without the kind of conviction that the Russians were showing at this time. Toller was crushed by the inhumanity which revolutionaries seemed to take in their stride, and by his exile after 1933. His play *Pastor Hall* (1939), about the Nazi concentration camps, was the last to be published before his suicide.

Brecht was also confronted with these issues of humanity and revolution; he found them easier to solve, in fact even in his earliest plays brutality is portrayed without a qualm, and by his thirties he was allowing characters in his plays to advocate it without contradiction. Even in the milder period of his forties and fifties he could still unleash a spurt of violent hatred without obvious political necessity. He was, in fact, the only one of the German and Austrian 'literary' dramatists of his day to do so. Karl Kraus and Hugo von Hofmannsthal, though opposed to each other, were too conscious of a humane tradition to contemplate it, and even dramatists with a more experimental turn of mind, like Georg Kaiser, Ernst Barlach, Fritz von Unruh, Reinhard Goering, tended to concern themselves with personal matters even when social problems seemed to be their topic. None of them wrote Communist plays, with the exception of Friedrich Wolf and Gustav von Wangenheim, neither of whom bears comparison with Brecht or Toller.[18]

The cinema also reflected the trend of the dramatists: though highly experimental, it produced films dealing with the division between capital and labour, like Fritz Lang's futuristic *Metropolis* (1926) and, in Pabst's *Kameradschaft* (1931), the breaking down of the hatred dividing French and German miners. (Pabst's filmed version of Brecht's *Threepenny Opera*, much altered from the original text, appeared in the same year.) Yet on the whole it was more involved with the forces of the supernatural, demoniac possession and the like. Murnau's *Satanas* (1919) and *Nosferatu* (1922), and Wiene's *The Cabinet of Dr. Caligari* (1919) represent the preoccupations of the non-commercial film better than the political films do, and even these were not didactic or exhortatory.

The amateur, or, more strictly speaking, the party theatre was much more productive of that kind of work. In 1922 the recently formed German Communist Party decided to give special support to theatrical pefformances with a political purpose. A play caricaturing the new German Parliament, which, for the first time in history, had just come into existence as a truly democratic institution with universal suffrage, was promoted. The 'Revue Roter Rummel', using a text by Erwin Piscator, supplied satirical songs, films, sketches, acrobats, in aid of the Party cause at the elections of 1924. In the following year a 'historical revue', *Trotz Alledem!* (In Spite of All That) surveyed the period from 1914 to 1919 'in 24 scenes with interspersed films', and so popular did such revues become, that the Communist Youth of Germany instituted a series of them, known as 'Rote Rummel'.

The tone was merciless. Nothing that Brecht wrote matched this song by Erich Weinert, the music for which was by Brecht's collaborator Hanns Eisler; it was sung by the Agitprop troupe from Wedding, Berlin:

> Links, links, links, links! Die Trommeln werden gerührt!
> Links, links, links, links! Der 'Rote Wedding' marschiert!
> Hier wird nicht gemeckert, hier gibt es Dampf,
> Denn was wir spielen ist Klassenkampf nach blutiger Melodie!
> Wir geben dem Feind einen kräftigen Tritt,
> Und was wir spielen, ist Dynamit
> Unterm Hintern der Bourgeoisie.[19]

> Left, left, left, left. The drums are beating.
> Left, left, left, left. 'Red Wedding' is on the march.
> No bleating here, full steam ahead, because
> What we are playing is class-struggle to a bloody melody.
> We give the enemy a hefty kick,
> And what we are playing is dynamite,
> Under the backside of the bourgeoisie.

Yet in 1929, when the song was first sung, it became one of the most popular pieces of the whole Communist movement. It was sung, according to the author, at processions and demonstrations throughout Germany. Children playing in the street sang it; he heard it in Vienna, in Basle, and a comrade who had been in the Ukraine was asked to sing it there.

The relish in these lines gives a slight taste of the atmosphere in which Brecht's indisputably Communist plays were written. These did not begin until the late 1920s, by which time the hatred fomented by such songs and the plays related to them had reached a fanatical pitch. The song, it needs to be remembered, was directed not even at a wartime enemy but at Germans not of the working-class. The Nazis had still not established themselves as a dominant party, though street-fights between them and Communists were a regular occurrence. Brecht came comparatively late onto the scene, at a time when factories throughout Germany were used to seeing lunch-time performances of revolutionary propaganda. If his own work in the late 1920s and early 1930s reflected something of that mood, it is not altogether surprising. It remains true, all the same, that no other writer of distinction lent himself to such performances. It also remains true that Brecht seldom permitted himself the crudities of the Agitprop theatre at its most intolerant.

EARLY PLAYS

Brecht's first plays[1] were written in the chaos of post-war Germany. When he returned to civilian life in 1919, after serving briefly in a military hospital, two literary movements seemed to the *avant-garde* to matter most, Expressionism and Dadaism, and he responded to them at the same time as he rejected them.

The Expressionists saw in the final months of the war an Armageddon from which a new human race was to arise. The four years of trench warfare, together with the Bolshevik Revolution of 1917, made it appear that a great turning-point in history had been reached and that society, as Marx had predicted, was about to be transformed. The result turned out differently. But for a short while hopes continued: there was an abortive Left-wing uprising in Berlin immediately after the Armistice, a Soviet Republic was briefly established in Munich, and others were expected soon in other great cities.

Within a year, the chief Communists had been assassinated and the German Soviets put down by right-wing paramilitary groups, with some connivance from the Weimar government. Expressionist works went on, expressing belief in the 'New Man', spreading a message of love and brotherhood, and of a more intense Dionysian existence: there was in them an incompatible combination of Marxist ideals for society and Nietzschean ideals for individuals, total integration and total self-realisation. They were also, and this is where Brecht withdrew his sympathy, ludicrously melodramatic. Serious treatises are written about Expressionism these days, which argues a large amount of tolerant sympathy in the writers of them, though, as Brecht saw, very few of the plays are not absurdly inflated. There is a fervid desperation about them: skeletons go on parade like soldiers, and roll heads by numbers; a severed head in a sack talks to the man to whom it used to belong; a woman bleats to a billy-goat, expressing Dionysian ecstasy; a father horsewhips his son, and the son chases his mother round the table, after which he joins a Society for the Brutalisation of the Ego. A man earns a living by eating live mice. A crowd of pitiless spectators exult over the exhausted riders in a seven-day cycle-race. The German Navy sinks splendidly at Scapa Flow. The straining after effect is equally apparent on the positive side. Having demonstrated how seriously they took disaster, Expressionist authors felt entitled to indulge in exhibitions of fervour. A radiant sun floods the landscape with light. Crowds of pilgrims rejoice in their freedom. A dying man spreads out his arms against a crucifix, and shouts 'I love!' There is painful contrivance, a hysterical abandonment to the wildest hopes and the unlikeliest despair.

Brecht's *Baal* (1918) is not Expressionistic either in style or purport. It has no staccato rhythms, stabbing spotlights, crazily angular sets, no 'telegraphese', which was the name given to the short, sharp mode of speech some Expressionists favoured, and it is not unintentionally comic, or melodramatic. It does share with the Expressionists, though not in their mood, a concern with a new kind of individual. Baal, not so very aptly named after the heathen god who devoured small children, is at once a lyric poet, a practical joker, a homosexual, every man's dream of a potent lover, a helper of elderly women, and the only really outspoken character in the play. He is also, conveniently for him, without conscience or self-awareness. He might be called a Dionysus. He might be said to express 'a passionate acceptance of the world in all its sordid grandeur'.[2] In fact, that is what he does not do. It was the Expressionists who used that kind of language. *Baal* has more subtlety.

'Passionate acceptance' would suit the play which gave rise to Brecht's, the romanticising tragedy by Hanns Johst, *Der Einsame*, (The Lonely Man). Johst's play, published in 1917, is a series of episodes from the life of a nineteenth-century dramatist, Grabbe. Influenced by the current vogue for Rimbaud, it glorifies the poet's uninhibited life. Grabbe shudders fairly often, in ecstasy; he weeps, and is unfaithful to his dead mistress. He is ruthless, egotistical, misunderstood, lonely, but inspired:

Oh! This feeling! Not for a throne would I exchange it! This God-the-Father feeling! Heaven and earth dependent on my favour! I am the Cosmos![3]

Being the cosmos was fashionable; so was accepting the world, and declaring oneself free of all moral and social ties. Brecht's play, written as a retort to Johst's, actually shows Baal enjoying pleasures about which Grabbe only talks. Again, Baal is a murderer, not merely an ungrateful son, or a faithless lover, and the dramatic quality is enhanced by that fact alone. Yet the extremeness of Baal's lusts and instinctive reactions is linked with a lazy, laconic indifference, providing continual surprises, changes of front. In his dying moments, Baal says nothing passionate, though he does express a reflective appreciation of life in general, in his final grunt. He is not heroic, or stoical, but amused and analytical, without self-pity. His 'acceptance' is expressed in paradoxes like 'The world is God's excrement'. ('Das Exkrement des lieben Gottes' – the familiar use of the name of God, not possible in English without over-emphasis, softens the violence of this. Baal could mean that the world is that much more acceptable, on these terms.)

Brecht establishes his play by the way he uses words, more than by any other means. Any dramatist who could write as he did ought to have won attention by that fact alone. There are lyrical passages, for instance, in which he gropes for words at a level where the sound carries as much of his meaning as the literal sense, and this poetic concern, not always so much in evidence later on, occasionally overrides everything else, as in the scene where Baal talks to a tramp on Corpus Christi Day. Brecht roots himself here, as he seldom did later, to a language that is not international, nor readily translatable, but dependent for its real meaning on an understanding of the German.

The central symbol derives from a custom peculiar to Catholic parts of Germany, where on this feast-day young birch-trees are placed as decorations on the walls of houses. Brecht sets the scene against such a background, and takes the graceful shape of the trees – known in England as Lady-trees – not only to suggest women's bodies, but also crucified bodies. Baal and the tramp weave associations of sound and sense round both:

BAAL. Wer hat die Baumleichen an die Wand geschlagen?
STROLCH. Die bleiche elfenbeinerne Luft um die Baumleichen: Fronleichnam.
BAAL. Dazu Glocken, wenn die Pflanzen kaputtgehen!
STROLCH. Mich heben die Glocken moralisch.

BAAL. Schlagen dich die Bäume nicht nieder?
STROLCH. Pah! Baumkadaver! *(Trinkt aus einer Schnapsflasche.)*
BAAL. Frauenleiber sind nicht besser!
BAAL. Who nailed all those tree-corpses on the wall?
TRAMP. The pale, ivory air round the tree-corpses: Corpus Christi.
BAAL. And ringing all those bells, when they're killing the trees!
TRAMP. I get moral uplift out of those bells.
BAAL. Don't the trees get you down?
TRAMP. Pah! Tree-carcases. *(Drinks from a gin-bottle.)*
BAAL. Women's bodies are no better.

The language here is not typical, though the inconsequentiality of these random associations is like the random pattern of the play. But the words do enact the spirit of *Baal*. The line about the pale ivory air, though it sounds odd, coming from the Tramp, is in the German full of heady alliterations and assonances; like Rilke's, it evokes a confused perception, in key with the confusion between the birch-trees, dead bodies, Christ's body, Corpus Christi, women's bodies. All through this scene, there are hints of correspondences between the world of Nature and the human world, self-sacrifice and the intoxication of alcohol and necrophily, corresponding in turn to the lack of clarity in the direction of the whole. All through the play there are linked images: whiteness, clouds, suggestive shapes with no definite meaning. For much of the time Brecht is in the mood of Rimbaud's *Bateau Ivre* (to which he alludes): slipping downstream in a drunken ecstasy, not distinguishing clearly between sensations. This is the mood of some of his lyric verse, too, in the 1920s. It was to disappear, along with the local colour, after some years. What survived better was the laconic tone, audible even in this conversation.

In structure, *Baal* is episodic, like the later plays. The scenes are loosely strung together, in no compelling sequence. What Baal dies of is not at all clear; his death is merely the point at which there is no more play. A kind of climax occurs when Baal kills Ekart, but it is not a sequel to any earlier happenings: Baal becomes angry at his friend Ekart for flirting with a prostitute, sticks a knife in him, and passes on to the next happening. His freedom from scruples is inhuman, and Brecht does nothing to set him in a light where the real consequences of his actions can be seen. On the contrary, he allows Baal a comparatively easy ride: he tricks nobody but compliant girls and stupid farmers, is never obliged to defend his conduct seriously. The play is a kind of day-dreaming; Baal himself does not escape a degree of Romantic sentimentality. 'Schweig still, meine liebe Seele', 'Be mute, my beloved soul', is not the language one would expect him to use.

The common theme that does unite the scenes up to a point is that a complete realisation of his personality is essential for Baal, and must involve evil as well as good actions – a post-Nietzschean idea. More important is the foreshadowing of Brecht's later dramatic practice, and the play's position in a long tradition. *Baal* deliberately alludes to Rimbaud, and includes a scene recalling the ending of Büchner's *Woyzeck*. In tone, Brecht is closer to these two authors. In structure and theme he follows in the wake of Ibsen's *Peer Gynt*, and so ultimately of Goethe's *Faust*, little as Brecht would have cared for the comparison. Both these plays show attempts at self-realisation in an episodic structure, without necessary interlinkings, and both explore conscienceless egoism, though with more appraisal of its possible consequences than *Baal* shows. Perhaps the episodic quality is directly linked to the theme – it seems more appropriate to treat a life as a whole in a rambling, inconsequential way. At all events, episodic treatment is a presage of what Brecht later called 'epic' theatre, theatre in which there is not the logical progression of *Macbeth* or *Othello*, but rather a collection of scenes not necessarily related to one another, as in *Henry IV* or *Henry V*.

In this respect *Baal* is seminal. It is also central to Brecht's personal concerns: there is more than a hint that Baal represents a projection in drama of Brecht's own *alter ego*, not least in the comparison of Baal with an elephant, a favourite self-image of Brecht's; and Baal-like figures reappear throughout Brecht's lifetime, in Macheath, Mother Courage, Puntila, Azdak, perhaps Galileo. For a Communist playwright, Brecht poses issues surprisingly often in the form of problems akin to those he experienced personally, rather than those of society as a whole.

Yet in some ways *Baal* is separate from all Brecht's other work. Not only does it have a more poetic concern with language and locality, it has no concern at all with poverty or with criticism of capitalism. It seems the glorification of naked egotism, though Brecht later defended it against this charge. Curiously enough, however, even this egotism is not at variance with Brecht's later social concerns.

In defending the play, Brecht said that Baal was 'antisocial (*asozial*) in an antisocial society',[4] and he does something towards showing this in the opening scenes where Baal meets his middle-class admirers. For Brecht, in fact, capitalism and anarchy were in one sense indistinguishable. In a capitalist world there was nothing but the glorification of naked egotism, and as time went on he increasingly opposed it on these grounds. Yet he also had some regard for the idea that each individual needs to develop every propensity in himself to the fullest possible extent, rather as Goethe's Faust says: 'And what all mankind must undergo, I will enjoy within my own sole self.' At the time he wrote *Baal*, Brecht was even prepared to state this in a form that owes more to Nietzsche than to Goethe:

> Alle Laster sind zu etwas gut
> Nur der Mann nicht, sagt Baal, der sie tut.
> Laster sind was, weiß man was man will.
> Sucht euch zwei aus, Eines ist zu viel!
>
> All vices are good for something or other,
> though not the man, says Baal, who does them.
> Vices are something, if you know what you want.
> Get yourself two—one is too many.

The deliberate ambiguity of this, coupled with the apparent incitement to viciousness, are typical of Baal's irresponsible individualism. He kills Ekart in just such a nonchalant mood, that is too nonchalant even to want to justify itself in serious terms.

In saying that Baal was antisocial in an antisocial society, however, Brecht seemed to be saying that Baal was no better, but no worse, than the society which made him – a not obvious argument, when Baal is so alien to all forms of society shown in the play. Very likely, Brecht was doing no more than whitewashing his early work to make it more acceptable in East Germany after 1945. Yet there is a sense in which Baal is a kind of ideal figure even in terms of a Brechtian Marxism. In so far as he is an anarchist – and he is at any rate anarchical – he is the prelude to a kind of humanity which Brecht as well as Marx saw as the ultimate goal of human progress. Anarchy is, strictly speaking, the Marxist vision of the future, the type of society which is to succeed the present dictatorships of the proletariat, if that is the right name for them, in various so-called Communist countries. In the anarchy which follows after the State has 'withered away', each man will live in total self-fulfilment, total enjoyment of all his potentialities. Baal may be a first adumbration of such men: he can be seen, with hindsight, in that light. He reappears, modified, and with fewer repellent characteristics, in the judge Azdak of *The Caucasian Chalk Circle*, who, though not the finally liberated Man, is a step on the way to him. It is during Azdak's brief spell of authority that people have a foretaste of the Golden Age, and the affinity between him and Baal suggests that Brecht put more into Baal than he realised at the time.

Of the other early plays which rapidly followed, all take some cognisance of society, whether to accept or reject its claims. *Drums in the Night* is mainly concerned with the reactions of a returned prisoner of war to the abortive left-wing uprisings of late 1918 and early 1919, and is surprisingly different from *Baal*, in taking so much notice of contemporary events. Yet it takes notice only to reject any responsibility for them, or so it appears.

To understand Brecht here, more about the nature of the German Revolution needs to be known. It had been a damp squib. Whereas in Russia, a year or so before, revolution had unleashed tremendous enthusiasm, in Germany, which had been singled out by Marx as the nation in which the proletarians were most likely to revolt, none of the three main socialist groups could agree, and none could carry the others with it. The party to which Brecht belonged – the U.S.P.D., or Independent Social Democrats – wanted a Marxist revolution without bloodshed, whereas the S.P.D., or Social Democrats, were more content with the reforms which coincided with the abdication of the Kaiser. Only the Spartacists, the forerunners of the K.P.D. or Communist Party, wanted a revolution on the Soviet model. As a result, the first uprising on 9 November 1918 was, as A. J. Ryder says, 'a bitter victory which the haggard working population of Berlin celebrated at the end of a lost war and in face of a future as sombre as the November weather.'[5] The second, properly called the Spartacist uprising, of January 1919, was a desperate effort to recover the lost revolutionary momentum, and was brutally put down by the right-wing 'Freikorps'. The sequel was half-hearted acquiescence in a parliamentary democracy headed by a President whom many on the Left believed to be already hand-in-glove with the reactionaries. The refusal of Brecht's ex-prisoner of war, Kragler, to have anything to do with the Spartacists is in key with this general mood of disillusionment: 'Do you think I'm going to rot in the gutter so that what you call the Idea can keep on the up and up? What's the matter with you, drunk?'

Attempts have been made, preserving Brecht's orthodoxy, to maintain that he was writing here ironically, pointing at Kragler's desertion of his true duty. If he was, he did nothing to indicate the irony, and the autobiographical element suggests a more straightforward attitude. Brecht's first marriage coincided with the writing of the play, and was surely reflected in Kragler's final decision in favour of taking his girl off to 'the big, broad, white bed'. On the other hand, as Kragler leaves the stage with her, cries are heard from the buildings where the revolt is still going on: they must stick in Kragler's conscience as Spartacus probably did in Brecht's. But Brecht is writing a play, not a thesis on revolutions, and he merely 'shows', at this stage in his career. Pointing a moral is far from his mind.

There is a presage of later developments in the insistence that what the audience is seeing is a play. When Kragler rejects Spartacus he knocks down the moon, which is really a Chinese lantern, and the moon 'falls into the river, which has no water in it'. There is a rough reminder here, that the events on stage are not the revolution anyway. But this is still far from being a piece of 'alienation' technique: it is more in keeping with Heine's self-ironies, and carries no political weight.

Closer to the later 'alienation' for which Brecht became known is the scene in which a heated argument in a restaurant is interrupted by a waiter, who then retails the whole thing over again for the benefit of a new arrival. By this means, Brecht introduces a pause which can be reflective, as he did later in a variety of ways. Events seen a second time, or narrated as though they had happened before, take on a different look. There is something ironical in the mere fact of the repetition, and absurdities show up which might otherwise not have been apparent. Whether they lead, as the 'alienation' theory later maintained, to any further thought by the audience, let alone to Marxist solutions, is another question. For the moment, all that matters is Brecht's presumably intuitive use of this device, at a time when he can scarcely have thought out its implications.

The New Man and Revolution were the themes of the first two plays. For the third, *In the Cities' Jungle*, Brecht echoed yet another contemporary theme, Dada, or the vogue for nonsense with serious implications. Though the play has none of the special hallmarks of Dadaism – '*bruitisme*', or the cultivation of noise, 'simultaneity', or the coincidence of incongruities and dissonances as in real life – it has the same rejection of logic, psychology and verisimilitude as not only Dadaists but Futurists, Vorticists and the French followers of Apollinaire and Jarry cultivated. It is grotesque, and incomprehensible, giving a fantastic caricature of American capitalism, and making no attempt to interest the spectator. Characters with names like Shlink, Garga, Skinny and Manky appear and vanish; the spectator is instructed in an ironical preface not to worry about their inexplicable motives but to share in their human endeavours, to sum up impartially the form of the competitors, and to concentrate his attention on 'das Finish' – a horseracing term, which suggests that the only important part is the ending. Brecht confessed to having been influenced formally by reading Rimbaud's *Une Saison en Enfer*, of which there are several reminiscences, and J. Jensen's novel about Chicago, *The Wheel*. Some characters have the same names as Brecht's friends, George recalling George Grosz the artist, and John recalling John Heartfield, known for his photographic montages and political posters. 'George Garga', with its repeated initial, reminds one of Galy Gay in *A Man's a Man*, and of the fact that Brecht often referred to himself as 'B.B'. But such clues to personal involvement are no help in making out the sense. For the moment, Brecht had renounced meaning as he had renounced form. Not only society but everything else was in the melting-pot.

In later life, Brecht suggested that *In the Cities' Jungle* was an attempt at describing a struggle between two men in social conditions which did not allow a real struggle to take place. 'More and more it became a play on the difficulty of bringing such a struggle about.' It was comparable to the shadow-boxing of a boxer training for a real match, which in this case was the

class-war. 'I had an inkling then of the fact that in late capitalism the enjoyment of struggle is only a savage distortion of the
enjoyment of competition.'⁶ As Schumacher says, however, there
is no hint of a class-struggle within the play, and Brecht's comment does not refer to anything that he put into the play at the
time of writing. Like all the earliest plays, it is Marxist only with
hindsight.

Another work in which aimless casting about for themes and
topics unexpectedly leads to a resemblance to a later play is *Das
Elefantenkalb* (The Elephant Child). This is presented as sheer
absurdity, a kind of Goon Show, in which the audience is explicitly instructed not to look for any sense, although at the end
a character says that the pure truth has been told. Looking back
from much later in Brecht's life, it seems that that remark may
have been more than half serious.

Galy Gay, from *A Man's a Man*, to which this is a kind of
otherwise unconnected epilogue, is here the 'elephant child',
accused before a court of having murdered its mother. (Brecht's
frequent association of himself with elephants may have something to do with this.) Bets are invited as to the outcome of the
trial. The moon hears the case, and the mother herself is present,
though alive, as evidence *against* the elephant. Polly, as a banana
tree, then declares that the mother is not the true mother, and to
prove this she has a chalk circle drawn on the ground by the
moon, places a rope round the mother's neck, and says that if
the elephant's child is really the son of this mother he will be
able to pull her by the rope out of the circle. When Galy Gay
succeeds, as the elephant's child, in pulling the mother out of
the circle, Polly declares this to be proof that he is not the son
of this mother, as no true son would have strangled his mother
as Galy has just done. By attempting to prove himself the son,
Galy has proved he is not the son, but he has also committed the
very murder of which he was accused.

When the audience demand their money back, Galy Gay
challenges them to box him for it, and all go off to see the fight.

The parallel with the scene in *The Caucasian Chalk Circle*,
where Grusha and the Governor's wife tug at the hands of a
child to decide which of them is the true mother, is self-evident.
In the later play, the point is unambiguous, and has none of the
psycho-analytical shadows of *The Elephant Child* – the 'Oedipal

truth' of which seems to be that a true son will prove his sonship
by doing the very thing a true son would not do. Yet the earlier
work, playing with the uncertainty of the meaning of actions in
an almost Pirandellian mood, first threw up the idea which Brecht
developed into a plain message twenty years afterwards: the
true mother will do the very thing true mothers do not do.

If there was little political matter in these plays, it was largely
because Brecht was still questioning himself, still trying to understand himself, and experimenting with all the new ideas in
vogue. For the most part they were Romantic in implication:
surprisingly often Brecht comes to an uncommitted standpoint,
closer to Buddhism than to Marxism, though expressed in his
usual laconic way, rather than ecstatically. He drifts, changes
like a cloud, lets himself drift with the tide as the drowned girl
does in one of his poems.

Keats had spoken of the chameleon poet, who has no personality of his own, no views or opinions, but adapts to every situation
with camouflaging colours. Thomas Mann and Hugo von Hofmannsthal used the idea of the writer as a seismograph, recording
but passing no judgement on the convulsions of his day and age.
There is something of a similar attitude in Brecht's lines, from
the poem 'Vom armen B.B':

> Bei den Erdbeben, die kommen werden, werde ich
>   hoffentlich
> Meine Virginia nicht ausgehen lassen durch Bitterkeit.
>
> In the earthquakes to come I shall, let's hope,
> not let my cheroot go out, in bitterness.
> [A 'Virginia' is not a cigarette: Brecht
> intended to imply a certain modest luxury.]

The equanimity that these lines express does not exclude the
awareness of bitterness, and the causes for it. But it is a surprising sentiment for a revolutionary poet, and at this stage in his
life – in the 1920s – there was more of the chameleon in Brecht
than of the revolutionary.

The early plays are more an attempt at coming to terms with
his own personality than an attempt at changing society: they
are increasingly concerned with the way society can change individuals, but the fundamental issue is what a man can make of
himself. In this, Brecht was influenced by Rimbaud, and so by

the whole tradition of the nineteenth-century *poète maudit*, the 'accursed poet', who rejects no experience, however ecstatic, however diabolical, and who actively encourages himself to pervert and invert normal experience. Rimbaud and Verlaine have more to do with the conception of Baal than has Ibsen's Peer Gynt.

A short story published by Brecht in 1921, though at first sight untypical of him in every way, shows more of the personal dilemmas which Brecht faced than the plays themselves do. 'Bargan läßt es sein' ('Bargan lets it be') is Romantic in spirit, and uses religious ideas in a way that Brecht never allowed himself openly, later on. But it is a valuable key to understanding the plays of the 1930s and 1940s, a precursor of developments which at the time could scarcely have been suspected.[7]

Bargan, who like Baal has Brecht's initial letter, is a pirate captain of complete ruthlessness who is inspired with a fatal attraction for a worthless pariah, Croze; for the sake of this murderer he allows himself to be degraded (there is an analogy here with Shen Te's love for the worthless airman Sun, in *The Good Woman of Setzuan*), and to lose the vigorous zest for living which had won the respect of his crew. In Bargan and Croze, Brecht polarises two aspects of human personality, while at the same time he explores the motives of common humanity which lead the one to seek out the other and attempt some kind of union with it. The 'complete man', 'total man', to use an early Marxist concept, must know both sides of human nature, as the traditional view had it, and Brecht heavily underlines the implications of the tale by the Romantic device of providing Croze with a club-foot, to suggest a devilish nature. Dimly in the background of the story can be sensed something of the spirit of Goethe's Faust: Bargan deliberately widens his knowledge of human nature by committing himself to a devil.

At length Bargan is allowed to leave with Croze in a small boat, and a sailor who watches them go reflects on the story in surprisingly religious terms. He sees Bargan as something of a Christ-figure who sacrifices himself for the sake of the other:

. . . suddenly I understood God, who could, for the sake of a fat, mangy dog, not worth hanging, and better starved to death than slaughtered, sacrifice an incomparable man like Bargan, a man absolutely made for conquering Heaven. . . . I'll be hung, drawn and quartered if he didn't enjoy ruining himself with that small dog he'd

set his eye on, along with everything he had, and gave up everything else on account of it.[8]

The Romantic allusions to conquering heaven, and to welcoming
total ruin on account of one man, have little superficially in common with the political plays. They seem more related to the
accounts of homosexual love in other plays: one of the themes of
Baal is the relation between Baal and the worthless parasite
Ekart, whom he kills, and the epithet 'devil' is used between
them. In *In the Cities' Jungle,* which quotes liberally from *Une
Saison en Enfer,* the relationship between Rimbaud and Verlaine
is echoed in the love–hate of George Garga for the Chinese
Shlink, his 'diabolical spouse', as he is called in reminiscence of
Rimbaud's 'époux infernal'. Beneath the surface there is an ob-
scure working-over of a conflict which never comes into full consciousness.

In the 1920s Brecht associated with Paul Samson-Körner, German heavy-weight champion in 1924, about whom he wrote in a
short story, 'Der Kinnhaken' ('The Uppercut', published in
Scherls Magazin in January 1926), and the various references to
boxing or wrestling in the love–hate relationship between Shlink
and Garga seem at times to be related to his own life, at least
to his imaginings. Homosexual themes are prominent not only in
Baal and *In the Cities' Jungle,* but also in his next play, *The Life
of Edward II, King of England,* adapted from Marlowe, and
largely concerned with the downfall of a ruthless king on account
of his sexual fascination for a worthless favourite, Piers Gaveston.
The Bargan theme is echoed here again. All through these early
plays, Brecht is partly dramatising a personal sense that fem-
ininity is lax and despicable, that hardness and even harshness
is demanded of a man, and possibly some sexual attraction to
men might account for the sudden predilections for violence
shown by his characters, as in *The Good Woman of Setzuan*
where the heroine feels obliged to adopt the mask of a man in
order to exercise the harshness she believes to be necessary. Certainly, homosexuality and violence are prominent themes of *Edward II,* though here Brecht's personal concerns are also reflected
in Mortimer – a single character instead of the two in Marlowe's
play – here presented as an intellectual revolutionary whose chief
care is the welfare of working people.

Mortimer is opposed to the bishops and barons, who seek war against the King solely because of his idolisation of Gaveston. This is as trivial a reason for bloodshed, to his mind, as the rape of Helen of Troy. Yet Mortimer is no highminded idealist, but a cynic, who adds that but for the rape of Helen we should have no *Iliad*, and this cynicism is reflected in his later behaviour towards the King.

Determined to save the people from Edward's folly, but also inspired with personal ambition, Mortimer captures the King and subjects him to the series of degradations and mental torments which history and Marlowe record. But whereas in Marlowe these are gratuitous acts of cruelty, in Brecht Mortimer seeks to justify them in the light of his social aims. After Edward's murder, which Mortimer himself ordered, he demands to know from the peers, and from the young Edward III, whether they can possibly manage without such ruthlessness as his. If they avenge Edward II, will not the whole kingdom be plunged into war?

> Fragt euch, ob jetzt die Stunde ist,
> Den Fall des toten Eduard zu klären.
> Oder ob, von einem Mord gereinigt, in Blut
> Wegschwimmen soll die ganze Insel.
> Ihr braucht mich . . .
> . . . wenn eure Hände nicht
> Befleckt sind, sind sie noch nicht befleckt.
> So kalt abgetan sein schmeckt nach Moral.

> Ask yourselves whether this is the time
> To go into the case of the dead Edward,
> Or whether, purified of this murder,
> The whole island is to float away in blood.
> You need me . . .
> . . . If your hands are not
> Dirty, they are not dirty yet.
> Being so coldly averse smacks of morality.

Mortimer is executed, but not before the cold-hearted justice of the new King Edward has been castigated by his mother, in terms similar to Mortimer's own, as inhuman. The argument may be meant seriously – it has since been used seriously by many revolutionary terrorists – and is close to the similar arguments of the Marquis de Sade, among others, defending personal cruelty and opposing dispassionate, impersonal justice. It introduces a further non-Marxist element into the web of the early plays.

The language in the passage just quoted is typical of the play in its inconsequential use of blank verse. Brecht is not at home here, and the absence of any convincing rhythm in the speeches indicates that: his real purpose, as in his *St Joan*, is to mock at all such forms of highfalutin speech.[9] On the other hand, Mortimer's speech is reminiscent of the 'Chorale' in *Baal*, where it is said that 'every vice is good for something,' and of several similar utterances in later plays. Although *Edward II* still has no definite political purport for Brecht's own times, the idea that, in politics, those who have clean hands have merely not yet dirtied them is echoed, for instance, in *Galileo*. The remarkable thing is that in the earlier play Brecht still seems to be experimenting, in the wake of de Sade, with the idea of diabolical practices as realisations of total man, whereas in the later plays he occasionally advocates brutality or cruelty only as unfortunately necessary evils. (Women who send their sons to fight for the Tsar, says Pelagea Wlassowa in Brecht's *The Mother*, deserve to have their wombs ripped out: here as elsewhere, the violence sounds vindictive.) When Mortimer says 'You need me', he calls to mind the harsh counterpart of Shen Te, in *The Good Woman of Setzuan*: Shui Ta, whose disregard of normal humanity is agonisingly painful to Shen Te, yet who, so the play argues, must behave as he does if there is to be order.

Brecht was, then, engaged on a dual path. In one sense he was aiming at complete self-realisation, even if this involved what had till that time been accounted inhumanity. In another he was beginning to experiment with the belief that social change requires such inhumanity. The exploration of what humanity means was the theme of his next play.

A Man's a Man (1924–6) is the fantastic account of an extremely adaptable character, Galy Gay, who is beguiled by three British soldiers (inspired by Kipling's *Soldiers Three*) into taking the place of a comrade in the Indian Army. Step by step, he is transformed from a peaceable citizen into a ferocious warrior, armed to the teeth and thirsting for blood. The play presents a case of brain-washing, achieved by means of a subtle undermining of the sense of personal identity, with the difference that it is carried out not by trained interrogators but by the hirelings of imperialism, and that the mood of the whole is one of prolonged extravaganza and farce. Bitter farce: as the title indicates, men are men, a man is a man, and any one man can be turned into another and still remain 'man'; once the full potentialities of 'man' are realised, they can be channelled in any direction. Shaw attempted with great success a more light-hearted treatment of a similar theme in *Pygmalion*. Brecht was unwittingly foreshadowing transformations that were to change all Germany within a few years. But, for the first time, his bitterness had the shadow of an ironical purpose. The earlier plays had been complex presentations of human nature, ascertainings of its range, and they had been offered without comment, except in the form of an ironical preface outside the acting-text. It is true that there were already indications of 'alienation', as in the restaurant scene in *Drums in the Night*. Until *A Man's a Man*, however, Brecht had never interrupted the course of the play as abruptly as he does now in the interlude where the Widow Begbick comes forward and explains to the audience with deliberate over-simplicity of rhythm and rhyme what they have already seen and what is to follow:

> Herr Bertolt Brecht behauptet: Mann ist Mann.
> Und das ist etwas, was jeder behaupten kann.
> Aber Herr Bertolt Brecht beweist auch dann
> Daß man mit einem Menschen beliebig viel machen kann.
> Hier wird heute abend ein Mensch wie ein Auto ummontiert
> Ohne daß er irgend etwas dabei verliert.
> Dem Mann wird menschlich nähergetreten
> Er wird mit Nachdruck, ohne Verdruß gebeten
> Sich dem Laufe der Welt schon anzupassen
> Und seinen Privatfisch schwimmen zu lassen.
> Und wozu auch immer er umgebaut wird
> In ihm hat man sich nicht geirrt.

Herr Bertolt Brecht maintains that a man's a man, and that's something anybody can maintain, but then Herr Bertolt Brecht goes on to show that you can make anything you like of a human being. This evening here we take a man to pieces like a car, and change the parts, without him losing anything in the process. We come up to this man and ask him very seriously, without annoyance, to accom-

modate himself to the way of the world, and let his private fish float
by itself. And whatever he's converted into, we shan't have made
any mistake about him.

The last line is a statement of what the earlier plays had already
brought home to Brecht, and the history of the next two decades
proved true, that a true appraisal of human nature would show
how easily a pacific man might become bloodthirsty. At the same
time, the passage as a whole reveals Brecht's own earlier preoccupations: adaptation to circumstances, and the possible requirement to yield self-interest to the demands of society. It is still
possible to read it in fluidly ambiguous terms. The remainder of
the interlude, however, introduces the new note of criticism
which was perhaps responsible for the interruption being made
at all. It continues:

> Man kann, wenn wir nicht über ihn wachen
> Ihn uns über Nacht auch zum Schlächter machen.
> Herr Bertolt Brecht hofft, Sie werden den Boden, auf dem
> Sie stehen
> Wie Schnee unter Ihren Füßen vergehen sehen
> Und werden schon merken bei dem Packer Galy Gay
> Daß das Leben auf Erden gefährlich sei.

If we don't watch over him they can make a slaughterer of him
overnight. Herr Bertolt Brecht hopes you will see the ground you
are standing on disappear like snow under your feet, and will observe from the stevedore Galy Gay that life on earth is very dangerous.

It is not clear who are meant by the 'we', who need to take care
of Man in order to prevent him from being debauched by imperialism (as might be the role of the Communist Party), nor
does this comment become developed any further in the play.
On the contrary, the final lines slip back into a comparatively
neutral statement: the audience is asked to do no more than
observe how mutable man is, and how dangerous life can be –
was Brecht warning himself as much as anyone? In so far as the
comment continues at all, it is in the refrain repeated several
times by the Widow Begbick, as though pointing a moral to the
play:

> Beharre nicht auf der Welle
> Die sich an deinem Fuß bricht, solange er

Im Wasser steht, werden sich
Neue Wellen an ihm brechen.

Do not stay with the wave that breaks over your foot, so long as it
stays in the water other waves will break over it.

and this, without closer definition, might equally well refer to a
mystical transcendence of change as to a political transcendence
of class-ridden society; it might also be taken as advice, not to
be attached to any particular manifestation of life, but to accept
each as it comes, without regrets or hopes. As a whole, however,
the play reveals a deep Pirandello-like anxiety at the fluid imper-
manence of human personality, an anxiety which can be met only
by a feverishly exaggerated depiction of it, and the working
of a desire either to escape from the flux or to canalise it in a
particular direction. Brecht is still indeterminate, wanting the
vivid intensity of varied life, but perceiving also how, in present
society, it can be immensely dangerous. As yet, he foresees no
future society in which the variety and intensity might become
safer.

Social conscience is at work in all these plays, with a varied
intensity that is never very strong. It does not appear in them
with anything like the conviction to be heard in the refrain to
the 'Ballad of the Child-Murderess Marie Farrar':

Doch ihr, ich bitte euch, wollt nicht in Zorn verfallen,
Denn alle Kreatur braucht Hilf von allen.

But you, I beg you, do not yield to anger,
For all creation needs the help of all.

Brecht's concern with the condition of the poor appears only
dimly in the earlier plays. In the *Threepenny Opera* it found an
opportunity to express itself more vigorously, for one of the main
themes of Gay's *Beggar's Opera*, from which it was adapted, was
poverty. Yet here also, the cynical mood of the day did not
allow of a direct appeal to charitable sentiments. Brecht took
over the eighteenth-century text, modified it considerably, was
helped considerably by Kurt Weill's music, but aimed at his audience's heads rather than at their hearts. The opera was conceived
in terms of parody: it went with the current in so far as it appeared to give the public what it wanted, but it did so in such

outrageous fashion as to make it deliberately unpalatable. Brecht, in the usual forthright mood of exaggeration which made him paint the faces of soldiers in *Edward II* chalkwhite, to represent fear as their only emotion, went the whole hog with the conventions in this work also. It was one more instance, and for the time being almost the last, of the violent caricature which was meant to force the audience into demanding a contrary.

'The *Threepenny Opera*', he was to say later, 'concerns itself with bourgeois conceptions not only in its subject-matter, representing them, but also in the way it represents them. It is a kind of report ['Referat'] on what the spectator in the theatre likes to see of life.'[10] The finale, borrowed from Gay, in which the highwayman Macheath is fantastically and extravagantly pardoned on the scaffold at the last instant, served this purpose well, in so far as it parodied a sentimental attachment to villainous heroes.

Yet the opera as a whole still suffered from an ambiguity not to be found in Gay. Gay's Macheath had been recognisable as a caricature of Walpole; other characters also had had their counterparts in the politicians of the day. Brecht's figures had no particular relevance to his own times. Macheath in the *Threepenny Opera* was the 'representative of a declining class',[11] the bourgeoisie, a general formula whose applicability was not always apparent to audiences. He becomes such a representative on the basis of Proudhon's dictum, 'Property is theft', for, if this is so, the bourgeois is best represented by the thief, and the bourgeoise love of thieves (on stage at least) is accounted for by this fact. The difficulty with Macheath was that he did not look in the least a bourgeois. His debonair, unconventional, independent and amoral mode of living (including a kind of homosexual relationship between Macheath and 'Tiger' Brown) had more affinity with Baal and other of Brecht's 'originals', and attracted a measure of sympathy accordingly. In the film version of the opera, it was sought to remedy this by allowing Macheath not only to compare robbery with the founding of a bank, but actually to found one himself. The device remained unsuccessful, for the reason that Macheath was irrevocably committed to being not only the representative of the bourgeoisie, but also the mouthpiece of its opponents. He not only speaks the line which was generally taken to present the main point of the play, 'Erst kommt das Fressen, dann kommt die Moral' ('Eats first, morals after'), but also sings the ironical song in which he begs forgiveness from all and sundry, including the police –

> Man schlage ihnen ihre Fressen
> Mit schweren Eisenhämmern ein.
>
> Smash their jaws in with heavy iron hammers.

as he suddenly declares in uncontrollable anger. He inspires revolution as well as being in himself the cause of revolution.

Brecht caused some confusion by placing these lines of comment in the mouths of the characters themselves. In a text so full of irony, it becomes difficult to see what is being ironised. In one aspect, Brecht appeared to have written a work demanding a social revolution; in another, he appeared to have satirised the revolution itself. This is reminiscent of what Thomas Mann called his own 'irony in both directions': it seems to require a stance completely outside the affairs of this world, an absolute viewpoint from which all temporal phenomena are equally worthless.

On the other hand, there is a note of compassion running through the opera which contrasts with all that has been said of it and of Brecht's work so far, a note that is announced at the outset by the employer of professional beggars, Peachum:

Something's got to happen. My business is too difficult, you know why? – because it's my business to awaken human sympathy. There's a few things that shake people, a few, but the worst of it is, once you've used them a fair number of times, they don't work any more. Because people have this terrible faculty of making themselves feel nothing at all, more or less when they like. For instance, if a man sees another man with one arm standing at a street-corner, he'll want to give him a shilling the first time out of sheer fright, but the second time it'll be sixpence, and the third time he'll hand him over to the police in cold blood. It's just the same with these religious gimmicks. [*A large placard with the words* 'IT IS MORE BLESSED TO GIVE THAN TO RECEIVE' *descends from the flies.*] What's the use of the most attractive placards, when they get used up so fast? There must be four or five texts in the Bible that touch your heart; once you've used those, there's nothing in the kitty. . . You have to give 'em something new all the time. The Bible will have to fish something out again, but how long is that going to last?

With this there enters a note which also recurs in the later plays a number of times: the statement of a religious standpoint expressed with such irony as to seem an attack on religion. On closer inspection, however, it is seen that this is a device serving to introduce the demand for compassion in a roundabout way. Peachum regards misery as a means of making money; at the same time his words have a ring of truth. And one of the most effective scenes in the opera is that in which Peachum parades his beggars in order to criticise the turn-out in which they hope to melt the public's heart and open its purse. The beggars are seen first in their normal appearance, a set of healthy rogues, and are transformed in front of the audience into cripples covered in sores, dressed in filthy rags, and holding placards declaring that they have suffered for Queen and Country. Nothing but perfection will do for Peachum, however. He points out that there is a difference between melting the public's heart and frightening it out of its wits: only a nicely calculated poverty will produce financial results. By this means, the audience is tacitly invited to reflect on the condition of the genuine poor who have no such expert as Peachum to instruct them. Here the technique of 'alienation' has been developed a further step: the scene depends for its effect not on the direct participation of the audience in the happenings on stage, which are deliberately 'acted out', but on their reacting from them and remembering more forcefully the true state of things.

The cynical recognition of facts, already observed in Brecht's earlier plays, thus acquires a new edge in this opera. Each of the finales rounding off the three acts applies it more sharply, affirming first that the world is poor, that man is bad, and that nothing can be done about it, then that crime is the basic condition of human life:

MACHEATH. What does a man live by? By resolutely
　Ill-treating, beating, cheating, eating some other bloke!
　A man can only live by absolutely
　Forgetting he's a man like other folk!
CHORUS. *[off]*: So, gentlemen, do not be taken in:
　Men live exclusively by mortal sin.[12]

The lines spoken by the chorus here might have been spoken by Baal; thanks to the 'alienation' devices, however, they have a different ring. They are now clearly meant both to be an objective appraisal, and also to arouse a reaction through shock. The brief glimpse of what human nature might be, in contrast to what it is, that appeared in *A Man's a Man*, becomes a longer look. It still does not, however, provide insight into the theme of the opera as a whole, which retains a dual aspect, partly amoral, partly charitable, as a brief glance at the last finale will show.

Here, Macheath is saved from execution, as he is in Gay, by a last-minute pardon from the King, which is greeted with exaggerated relief as the sign of a 'happy ending', and the irony is apparent enough. Villains are pardoned in real life as well as on the stage, 'capitalist villains' in particular, and by providing the public with its favourite entertainment Brecht comments cynically on its taste. Yet the sung finale itself, in which the whole cast advances to the footlights, is not so plain in intention. Free pardons from the King, Peachum has just declared, very seldom come when the downtrodden masses have risen against their masters, and thus, he implies, Macheath and his like will not evade justice so easily in future. 'Therefore', he adds, 'we should never be too eager to combat injustices.' Thus far, we still know where we stand, the irony is still apparent, from a Communist point of view. And even when the chorus advances, accompanied by the organ-music which Brecht used to lend a note of false solemnity, the implications remain clear for a moment:

> Combat injustice but in moderation;
> Such things will freeze to death if left alone.

Yet in the last two lines of all, Brecht seems to evoke again the compassion that was ironically aroused in earlier scenes of the play:

> Remember: this whole vale of tribulation
> Is black as pitch and cold as any stone.

This can scarcely be taken in a contrary sense without making nonsense of those earlier scenes.

With this, a considerable weakness of Brecht's text emerges. Not merely is it difficult to relate his characters to the prototypes they are meant to satirise; Brecht's still 'all-embracing' attitude allows him to move at will from one standpoint to another completely contradictory one: at one moment he seems to aim at arousing a general compassion for the condition of all men, at another he allows his characters to advocate extreme brutality, and the oscillation from one to the other renders every reaction uncertain. It is not surprising that his audiences, for whom he had meant to write a 'report' on the kind of entertainment they liked to see, seized on those aspects which took their fancy and ignored the rest. There was grist in the text for everybody's mill.

Apart from the failure, *Happy End*, of 1929, which was taken off almost immediately after the first performance, Brecht was to write one more opera, *The Rise and Fall of the Town of Mahagonny* (1928–9) – for which once again Kurt Weill wrote the music – before turning to a completely different style and subject-matter. In a sense, *Mahagonny* is a transitional piece, for the attack on money-centred appetites is more direct than it had ever been before, and the single-minded propagandist works are to that extent foreshadowed. Yet the mood is still bitterly ironical rather than moral or didactic, as in the crooning lullaby (in English in the original) with its meaningless rhymes:

> Oh, moon of Alabama
> We now must say goodbye
> We've lost our good old mamma
> And must have whisky
> Oh, you know why.

The plot is still laconically thrown together, but there is a more binding theme and a comprehensible sequence of events.

Mahagonny is a gold-rush town where anything can be had for money. A Biblical doom seems to threaten it with destruction, as reports come in of a hurricane sweeping towards the town, the original 'permissive society', whose motto is 'Du darfst' ('you may'). But in suitably climax-breaking manner the hurricane swerves aside, and the chorus of Mahagonnians sings with relief:

> Erstens, vergesst nicht, kommt das Fressen
> Zweitens kommt der Liebesakt.
> Drittens das Boxen nicht vergessen
> Viertens Saufen, laut Kontrakt.
> Vor allem aber achtet scharf
> Dass man hier alles dürfen darf.

> First, remember, comes stuffing yourself,

Second comes the act of love.
Thirdly, don't forget the boxing
Fourthly boozing, as per contract.
But above all remember this
That here you can do whatever you like.

This is more or less Baal's philosophy, put in harsher terms. It is
not at all certain that the play goes against what Baal represented; what is clear is that it could never be realised in the
world of Mahagonny. The hero, Paul Ackermann, now lives
through the four kinds of enjoyment referred to in the song, and
is finally brought to trial by the hypocritical citizens for indulging
in exactly the same pleasures they fancy themselves. In the crazy
proceedings, recalling distantly *The Elephant Child*, Paul is condemned to various penalties for murder, seduction, and singing
songs during the hurricane, but sentenced to death for the one
crime unforgivable in Mahagonny, not having money to pay for
his whisky.

Out of the whirlwind of events, this ironical ending points a
clear moral. The confusion increases: processions tour the stage
with placards reading 'For the Struggle of All Against All', 'For
Commercial Love', 'For the Unjust Distribution of Earthly Goods',
'For the Freedom of the Rich', while each procession ends up
with 'For the Continuance of the Golden Age'. Girls bring in
Paul's watch, revolver and chequebook on a linen cushion, singing with what is now revolting sentimentality the 'Moon of Ala-
bama' song. Finally, his corpse is brought in, with more placards,
and a general chorus concludes that there is nothing to be done
about anything.

Though hankering after a Baal-like existence still remains in
the background, this was a much more straightforward piece of
Communist pleading than anything Brecht had written before.
It did not make any Marxist analysis, or supply any realistic motivations: it was a deliberate and successful caricature, vigorous,
and painful to accept. Perhaps for that reason it had less success
than *The Threepenny Opera*, which had been welcomed by
middle-class audiences without making an effective point. This
attack on the attitudes of the Weimar Republic – to be more ac-
curate, one should say 'of parts of Berlin' – aroused opposition not
only from the Nazis, who had to be ejected from the second performance, but also from spectators of no party commitment.

It made its point by not making its mark. It was the last of Brecht's plays to use such an oblique method.

The situation was growing more desperate day by day. The peace which had followed the war had been a devastating blow to German hopes. The Reich had vanished in 1918 after only forty-six years of existence. Heavy penalties had been exacted from Germany: the colonial empire was shared out between the victors under trusteeships, millions of pounds of reparation were demanded, the wartime blockade continued, there was a fantastic inflation of the currency, destroying many lifetimes' savings; foreign garrisons occupied German cities. In the immediate post-war years there were still serious fears – and hopes – of a revolution comparable to that of the Bolsheviks in 1917. Marx had predicted that an industrial nation like Germany would be the first to throw off capitalism, and the fact that Russia, a largely agricultural nation, had taken the first step did not seem to contradict the prophecy in an important way: it almost made the German revolution more probable. Given that Marx had spoken of a world-wide revolution taking place simultaneously, more or less, in all countries, the Russian success of only two years before seemed to promise equal success everywhere before long.

Brecht had thus reached his twentieth year at a time when the old order had almost completely vanished, and when the new was quite undetermined. The chances of a parliamentary democratic regime were not insignificant—the parties which desired one were numerically strong – but the extremes of Left and Right were not prepared to offer such a regime a breath of hope. The extreme left wanted a dictatorship of the proletariat; the extreme right, which also called itself socialist, wanted a dictatorship of one man. Both claimed that their section of society, or their man, was the authentic representative of the trends of the age. Both were intolerant of opposition, and street-fighting between rival factions became increasingly widespread. Together, they made the moderate parties seem helpless, and there was some excuse, in politics, for a man who decided to plump for one or other of the dictatorial parties.

For a dramatist, a wrong choice was less excusable, though a defence of Brecht can be offered. One of an artist's main concerns is with truth, and to sacrifice this for a temporary advantage can only be justified in terms of a conviction that some synthetic, comprehensive theory of universal development is over-ruling. Up to the time of *Mahagonny*, Brecht was still uncertain about where his allegiance ought to lie. By 1929, he had made up his mind: only Marxism could provide a solution, and the propagandist works of the early 1930s were the result.

The time of chaos was drawing to an end. Germany had barely emerged from the inflationary period after the war into relative economic stability when it was plunged again into disorder by the world depression of 1929. This in itself, as a clear sign of the irrationality and wastefulness of the capitalist system, was enough to turn Brecht's thoughts more strongly to the Communist offer of a solution. At the same time, capitalism seemed to him and to many other Left-wing intellectuals to be entering on its ultimate stage, in the growth of Nazism. The Nazi Party, with the support of financiers and press-magnates, took advantage of the depression to capture the imaginations of millions of supporters with the promise of an organised society which should be self-supporting, thoroughly German, and no longer subject to the vicissitudes that had oppressed the nation for the last decade and a half. It first emerged as a power in the land when it gained 112 seats in the Reichstag election of 1930. Whether these factors in fact influenced Brecht it is impossible to say: it seems likely, but there is no concrete evidence at present to show for it. (Indeed, in the absence of any fully-documented biography,[13] all accounts of Brecht's life must be regarded as provisional.) What is certain is that his own explicitly Communist plays date from just this period of economic depression and the threat of a tyranny such as Germany had never known before.

PROPAGANDIST PLAYS

> Ach, wir,
> Die wir den Boden bereiten wollten für Freundlichkeit,
> Konnten selber nicht freundlich sein.
> Ihr aber, wenn es soweit sein wird,
> Dass der Mensch dem Menschen ein Helfer ist,
> Gedenkt unsrer
> Mit Nachsicht.

We, who wanted to prepare the ground for kindness, could not be kind ourselves. But you, when the time has come when Man can be a helper to Man, think of us with forbearance.

These lines from one of Brecht's last poems, 'To those born after me', make a comment on his didactic plays. He would have liked to be wise, he says here, to have kept aloof from worldly conflicts, to have got by without violence, and to have rewarded evil with good, but could not: 'truly, I live in dark times'. The lines are close in literal meaning, though not in tone, to these from *The Threepenny Opera*:

> Wir wären gut, anstatt so roh,
> Doch die Verhältnisse, die sind nicht so.

> We'd like to be good, instead of so rough,
> but its' the conditions, they're not made like that.

The tone, it is true, makes a difference. When Brecht seems to speak in his own person, in the poem, he is solemn almost to the point of self-indulgence: two short lines of verse bring about at the end a pause, dwelling on the thought much more than the briskness of prose would allow. The tone in *The Threepenny Opera*, where the lines are sung by Peachum and his family, is mocking; the rapid rhyme and raucous music make for jauntiness here, and the effect is to make the excuse seem ironical: the Peachums may believe in it, but the listener is not expected to.

In both cases, the reasons given, why goodness cannot be achieved, are economic. Peachum cannot be good because he is in competition with others who have to make profits. The Marxist cannot be good because he lives in a profit-making world which can only be improved by means evil in themselves. But once the evil has been grasped – once Bargan has come to terms with Croze, to put it in terms of Brecht's early story – a millennium will follow. Kindness will be possible when men no longer need to compete for profits.

This argument ignores the fact that other impulses besides profit-making lead to self-assertion and conflict. Vanity, sexual jealousy, ambition for power are not removed by abolishing capitalism, and they are not made less likely to arise. The arguments that could be made against Peachum – that the imperfections of present society do not justify unlimited licence – apply equally well to Brecht, who seems to imply, in his propagandist works, that any degree of violence is proper in ridding the world of capitalism, whether or not the particular circumstances of the moment leave open a less violent alternative.

That Brecht should have made such an over-simplification is the more intelligible when the history of Germany in his time is considered. From 1914 onwards it had been the Communists (or rather, in the war-years, the revolutionary Socialists) who had most consistently opposed the militarist policies of the Reich. Every other party had yielded, first to the Imperial demand for war-credits, then to the connivance whereby the worst features of the old system were perpetuated under the Republic. The rising Nazi Party was supported and financed by powerful industrialists, a fact which readily allowed it to become identified by Marxists as the last phase of capitalism. And that party was prepared to use every form of deceit, violence and inhumanity in order to attain power. Brecht's attitude towards Nazism was that of many Western democrats today towards Soviet Communism: it had to be prevented from extending its influence by whatever means came to hand.

In Brecht's advocacy, however, there was still a tendency to speak not only openly and frankly, but in such extreme terms as to cause a reaction in an opposite direction. In the didactic plays, of which there were nine or ten written between 1928 and 1934, there can be no doubt at all about his intention to convey in dramatic form the lessons of Communist doctrine. Yet they are so forthright and uncompromising that both 'bourgeois' and Communist critics have felt a need to withhold assent.

In turning to purely didactic plays, Brecht made a complete break. Instead of going along, parodistically, with the theatrical forms which were, as he felt, 'produced by capitalism' he now began to strike out on his own. But he still claimed to represent reality, and to teach the lessons of Communism as derived from the study of reality. As the final words of his didactic *The Measures Taken* put it:

> Nur belehrt von der Wirklichkeit, können wir
> Die Wirklichkeit ändern.
>
> Only when instructed by reality can we change reality.

The question still remained, whether reality was as he saw it. Brecht assumed that it was, or that at least his way of seeing was justified and correct because it was associated with the Communist Party. But there is something more than an assumption in the phrase 'Only when instructed by reality': it suggests that there is no mere assuming, no element of subjectivity, in the process. 'Reality instructs' means something different from 'experience teaches', and Brecht is prepared to omit any mention of subjectivity so long as the corporate 'we', that is, the Party, is substituted for the individual 'I'. The Party, to judge by the words of the four Communist agitators in *The Measures Taken*, is a unity which achieves true judgement by transcending the individual. It 'thinks in your head', and lives in your house, and fights when you are attacked, and each individual can show it the way, but if any individual goes his own way, separated from the Party, he will be wrong, *extra ecclesiam*. The dogmatism is thus at one remove from the crudest kind, which asserts a single view once and for all: it is open to correction, but not indefinitely, as there is always the limit imposed by adherence to Marxist doctrine.

So far, at least, the theory. In practice, Brecht's plays of this period make so much of the Party at the expense of the individual that total submissiveness seems the only recommended course of action, however unpersuasive the argument may seem. In the *Baden-Baden Cantata* the situation is that four airmen, in some ways supposed to be representative of all airmen, have achieved Man's great ambition of flying, but have now crashed, and are asking a crowd of people for water and help to save them from dying. The leader of the chorus, however, steps in to put questions to the crowd, and so prevents any help being given. Why he should do this is not explained. It seems that before anything else can be done there is a problem to be thrashed out, and the whole situation needs to be outlined in simple terms to the crowd. First the airmen themselves describe what has happened, and conclude, in over-explanatory fashion:

> Aber wir bitten euch
> Zu uns zu treten und
> Uns Wasser zu geben
> Und unter den Kopf ein Kissen
> Und uns zu helfen, denn
> Wir wollen nicht sterben.

But we ask you to step over to us and give us water and to put a cushion under our heads and to help us, because we do not want to die.

Hardly has this point been made, when the leader of the chorus makes it yet more laboriously:

> Hört ihr, vier Menschen
> Bitten euch, ihnen zu helfen.
> Sie sind
> In die Luft geflogen und
> Auf den Boden gefallen und
> Wollen nicht sterben.
> Darum bitten sie euch
> Ihnen zu helfen.
> Hier haben wir
> Einen Becher mit Wasser und
> Ein Kissen,
> Ihr aber sagt uns
> Ob wir ihnen helfen sollen.

Do you hear, four men are asking you to help them. They have been flying in the air and have fallen to the ground and do not want to die. Therefore they ask you to help them. Here we have a cup of water and a cushion, but first tell us whether we are to help them.

The crowd reply to this bluntly and straightforwardly: 'Ja'. But the matter is not so straightforward as they suppose. Have the airmen ever helped the crowd, the chorus asks, to which the reply is a simple 'Nein'. The airmen have after all only just crashed. Whereupon the chorus concludes, implicitly, that the airmen had better be neglected, while a new subject is broached, whether it is normal for men to help other men.

And in fact the airmen never do get their water or their cushion. Whether they die as a result is not clear: the pilot, who insists that he has done something worthwhile by flying, is eventually told to go away, which he does; the other three, who turn out to be mechanics, are told to die their own deaths, but are suddenly required to mend the aeroplane and march in company with the chorus, which they may or may not do: the situation at the end is obscure.

This is not a play that demands close attention except in so far as it reflects two of Brecht's preoccupations. First, like some other didactic plays, it takes a concrete situation in order to pursue an abstract argument, and the concreteness of the situation works against the argument: instead of the crowd helping as human beings normally would help in such circumstances, there is a debate on the question of whether it should do so. Second, Brecht urges, as he does in *Galileo*, the point that only work which is directly beneficial to 'the people' is worth doing. The pilot (based on Charles Lindbergh, who had recently made the first solo transatlantic flight) is condemned without taking any account of his pioneering courage, the technical lessons of his flight, and its ultimate value to world transport. Later, Galileo will seem to be condemned despite his achievements, on similar grounds, though the earlier play is much the cruder both in structure and in language. The condescending simplicity of tone seems to reflect Brecht's notion of the right way of addressing workers.

The tone may, however, owe something to the extremely simple language of Arthur Waley's translation of Japanese Noh plays, one of which formed a basis for Brecht's *Der Jasager* ('He Who Said Yes'). In the original, *Tanikō*,[1] a boy who goes on a ritual mountain-climbing expedition falls ill, and is hurled into a valley by the superstitious pilgrims. (In the second part of the play, which Waley merely mentioned in a footnote, the boy is miraculously restored through the pilgrims' prayers; the mood is not so harsh as the one play taken alone might suggest.) It says something about Brecht's opposition to individualism at this time that he took the theme, with only a slight twist, as the basis for a playlet indicating the need for self-sacrifice in a common cause. The school-children, however, who were called upon to act it, protested at the fatalistic acquiescence shown by the boy, and as a result Brecht wrote a companion-piece, *Der Neinsager* ('He Who Said No'), which is sometimes thought to be a paradoxical contradiction of the first. In reality, Brecht altered the circumstances in the second play so much that no contradiction follows. In the first, the boy would, if he refused to be left to die, hinder a party taking urgently needed medicine to a town beyond the mountains. In the second there is no such urgency, and the boy's refusal to die is unproblematic.

In general, Brecht makes no such efforts as Yeats made, to write plays in the spirit of Noh, with hypnotic music, hieratic gesture, dance, and ritual as the most important elements. Apart from the language, he may well have had from Noh, however, an insight into the value of masks, and the indication of scenery by the simplest of symbols.

Plays with an Oriental setting, of which Brecht wrote several more, are also represented in another propagandist work, *Die Ausnahme und die Regel* ('The Exception and the Rule'), which again is written in the simplest of words. Like all the other 'didactic pieces', its value is open to question, since the conditions it shows are so far removed from those with which Brecht's potential audiences were concerned. But it does have a backlash irony that can be very effective. The plot is again extremely straightforward, so much so that the dialogue is spun out to great length to make a play at all. A businessman takes a coolie to carry his baggage across a desert to discover an oilwell. On the way, when they are short of water, the coolie offers his flask to the businessman, who, mistaking his purpose, imagines he is about to brain him with a stone, and shoots the coolie dead. At a trial, later, the businessman is acquitted on the grounds that the coolie had every reason to hate him, and that it was therefore reasonable to expect the coolie to be about to kill him: the businessman must have shot, the court concludes, in what he at any rate believed to be self-defence.

The moral seems to be drawn by one character who says, near the end:

> In the system they have made
> Humanity is an exception.
> Anyone, then, who acts humanely
> Has to take what he gets.

This is slightly affected as a moral by the fact that the coolie did
not offer the water out of humanity, but out of fear of what
might happen to him if he were found alive while the businessman was half-dead with thirst. Essentially, though, the point is
made, that in the circumstances humanity was not to be expected, and once this is driven home, the foolishness of the coolie
in not braining the businessman while he had the chance is obvious. Here 'alienation' works well: when it is seen how strangely
the coolie was behaving in *not* killing his boss, the need to do so
seems proven.

There remains the question, how far this parable was appli-
cable to German conditions in the early 1930s. The uncompli-
cated relationship of master and coolie was not that of the car-
tels, trusts, and trade unions of Brecht's day, for although the
attitude of employers would now be called 'paternalistic' it was
not dictatorial; industry flourished until the Wall Street crash and
the living standards of the working man had greatly improved.[2]
To inculcate a demand for a violent solution to economic problems, without even a hint at how they might be resolved afterwards, was politically unhelpful. A valid criticism of Brecht's
play is that it has no point except the need for violence in a
violent world (unless it is read without the ironic backlash, as
condoning the coolie's acquiesecnce) and that at that particular
moment in history every merely violent action helped to create
the uproar in which the Nazis could triumph.

A similar thought inspires *Die Maßnahme* ('The Measures
Taken'), written at a time when Stalin's new policy of branding
all non-Communists as Fascists was dividing the German Left
in its opposition to Nazism. Had any collaboration between the
comparatively moderate Social Democrats and the Communists
been possible in the early 1930s, the Nazis might not have
achieved their 'bloodless victory': they never achieved a majority
of votes in a free election. Brecht's play might have been written
in order to help in the Stalinist opposition to all forms of gradual-
ism. Its theme is the need for voluntary acceptance of party discipline, and it is set in China, where Gerhard Eisler, the brother
of Hanns, who wrote the accompanying music, had been sent in
1929 to destroy opposition to the Russian Politburo. Ruth Fischer,
who provides that detail,[3] describes the play as a parable on the
annihilation of the Party opposition, and sees in it a forecast of

the 'show' trials which Stalin was to stage in 1936 and later. Whether it is precisely that or not, it has been widely praised even by critics unsympathetic to Brecht's Marxism, as conveying its situation in a particularly moving way. Thus Martin Esslin writes, 'Many years before Bukharin consented to his own execution in front of his judges, Brecht had given that act of self-sacrifice for the sake of the party its great, tragic expression. With the intuition of the poet, he had grasped the real problem of Communist discipline with all its far-reaching implications. To this day *The Measures Taken* remains the only great tragedy on the moral dilemma of Soviet Communism.'[4] Much the same view is put by Walter Sokel, who speaks of the play as 'the one classic tragedy of Communism which world literature possesses'.[5] And even Peter Demetz, who disagrees entirely with this estimate, still feels it necessary to yield to the point of saying that because of the play's 'admirable terseness and controlled craftsmanship', it 'may well be the most accomplished and disturbing of the didactic pieces'.[6]

These terms suggest a greater literary quality than the play possesses. Its argument is no better based than that of the *Baden-Baden Cantata,* and the conclusions are equally unconvincing. The situation is that a group of four Communist agitators cross the border into China, presumably in the 1920s, and try to spread knowledge of Marxism in preparation for a revolution. One of their number is swayed by pity for the workers, and instead of adhering to a policy of relying on the workers' dissatisfaction over a long period, he either attempts to improve their condition temporarily, or to stand up for justice here and now, or to denounce selfishness, or in some other way to prefer the immediate righting of a wrong to the long-term planning which will abolish all wrongs. As a result, on each occasion he brings the other agitators into danger, until he becomes altogether too much of a liability. So, at least, the general drift of the argument is taken to run. Thus Mr. Esslin writes of the softhearted agitator: 'Instead of exploiting the hardships of the coolies pulling the rice-boats on the river, he found a way of alleviating their plight and thereby delayed their revolt.'[7] A closer look at the play shows that this misrepresents the facts: the intention of the agitators was in any case to alleviate the coolies' plight. Seeing a group of them on a slippery towpath pulling a barge by a rope, they instruct the youngest agitator to approach the coolies and tell them he has seen shoes nailed with wooden slats, which gave a better footing, and to urge them to demand these collectively, though the agitators also warn him not to fall a prey to pity. The young agitator carries out his orders precisely and the coolies do make their collective demand, but the only result is that the overseer whips them, whereupon the young agitator, out of pity, places stones on the towpath to help the coolies each time they fall. At length it is he who is exhausted, but the coolies merely laugh at him, and the overseer has him arrested.

In short, the orders of the other agitators are followed, except that afterwards the young man does act out of pity, and this needs emphasis because in the stage-discussion that follows this short scene the point is ignored. The 'Kontrollchor' or 'Supervisory Chorus', for whose benefit the scene is re-enacted, put the question whether it is not right to help the weak, and receive the reply that the young man did *not* help the weak, though he did prevent the agitators from spreading their propaganda further in those parts. And the moral based on this misrepresentation is that the young man had separated feeling from reason'.

It might be argued that separating feeling from reason is precisely what the agitators required when they excluded pity from their considerations. But leaving that aside, the question still remains whether Brecht's exemplary scene has the sense given to it in the subsequent discussion. The policy of the agitators is clearly shown not to work: the coolies laugh at the agitator when he urges them a second time to make a collective demand, and they are either too cynical or too fearful of the whip to respond to his theoretical approach. In these circumstances, some display of pity for them might have gained their confidence. Again, the laying of stones might well appear to the coolies as a less useful way of helping them, but the encouragement to demand better shoes might equally well seem to them to be inspired by pity.

Such objections are never contemplated in the play. The discussion is over in a flash, and takes no account of why the agitators, for their part, were endangered. It was not, after all, because their younger comrade showed pity. He might have drawn attention to himself because he had urged collective demands or because he helped individual coolies; what counts is that while he was being pursued by the overseer, he happened to meet the other agitators, who were then pursued along with him – this accident in his flight endangered them, rather than any policy for the coolies. All his mistake (if mistake it was) lay in making himself known as a man working in the interests of the coolies, and this might have come about in any event, if he was to operate at all. Brecht's loaded interpretation, conveyed through the 'Kontrollchor', shows no open mind: he has simply decided to construct a scene and inform his audience that it proves the point he wants to make.

The final illustration is similar. True, the youngest agitator does this time behave indefensibly. The others tell him to persuade the unemployed workers to join in the 'Revolutionary Front', in the name of the whole Party. The young agitator refuses this, preferring to act individually and to do 'the only human thing', as he puts it. Accordingly he rips off his mask, and declares that he and his friends have come from Moscow to help the Chinese. He does not actually call for a revolution, and he has no success, for the Chinese merely observe that the agitators are foreigners, and refuse to have anything to do with them. Since the young man goes on shouting, the other agitators knock him on the head and escape with him. He has, of course, been extremely rash, in imagining he could start a revolution by shouting that he was from Moscow, and might think himself lucky to get away with a knock on the head. It is much less clear that he deserves the execution by shooting which the others decide on for him.

The situation at this point is that there are disturbances in the town; unarmed workers are roaming the streets. The pursuers, presumably police, are ten minutes behind the agitators, who have to decide on the spur of the moment what to do with the young comrade, after he recovers consciousness. Their thoughts are as hasty as one might expect them to be in such circumstances, but that is not the view taken by the 'Kontrollchor'. In the first place, the agitators think of getting the young comrade over the frontier; they reject this course because 'the masses are on the streets', and they must get them into meeting-halls to hear the lessons of Marxism. Why this task was so urgent that not even one agitator could be spared, or the youngest one allowed to try to cross the frontier on his own, no-one explains. The agitators consider further whether the young comrade might be hidden. Or rather, they put the rhetorical question, what would happen if they hid him and he were found, to which one could reply that he might not be found, and that even if he were he might not be executed. Finally, the agitators add that gunboats and armoured trains are on the lookout for them everywhere, and would attack 'if any of us were seen there'. The 'Kontrollchor' round off this section, saying that wherever Communists reveal themselves people rise against the ruling classes (which we have just seen to be untrue), and therefore Communists must not be found. What all this has to do with hiding the young comrade so that he is not found, or with getting him to safety across the frontier, is one more of the obscurities in this account. And last of all, the agitators have to persuade the young comrade not only to accept being shot without protest, but also that his body will have to be thrown into a nearby lime-pit, so that it vanishes completely.

He does agree to this too, but is unable to take on the shooting himself:

DIE DREI AGITATOREN. Wir fragten: Willst du es allein machen?
DER JUNGE GENOSSE. Helft mir.
DIE DREI AGITATOREN. Lehne deinen Kopf an unsern Arm. Schliess die Augen.
DER JUNGE GENOSSE. (unsichtbar)
    Er sagte noch: Im Interesse des Kommunismus.
    Einverstanden mit dem Vormarsch der proletarischen Massen
    Aller Länder.
    Ja sagend zur Revolutionierung der Welt.
DIE DREI AGITATOREN. Dann erschossen wir ihn ... [etc.]

THE THREE AGITATORES. We asked. 'Will you do it yourself?'
THE YOUNG COMRADE. Help me.
THE THREE AGITATORS. Lean your head on our arms. Shut your eyes.
THE YOUNG COMRADE. (invisible)
    He said – for the sake of Communism, in agreement with the advance of the proletarian masses of all lands. Saying Yes to the revolutionizing of the world.
THE THREE AGITATORS. Then we shot him.

And with this consent from the principal person concerned (rather like the consent to his own execution offered by Kleist's Prussian Prince Friedrich von Homburg), the case against him is concluded.

It is not really a case at all. The young comrade is not even shown to be guilty of the faults of which he is accused, and the reasons for shooting him could scarcely be less persuasive. For the 'Kontrollchor', though, the point is established. 'It was not you who pronounced sentence on him', they say to the agitators, 'but reality'. Never having discussed the issues, the 'Kontrollchor' may well believe this to be true, that the agitators have done no more than let themselves be guided by the realities of their situation. On the other hand, the whole conclusion falls to the ground at the first prod any interested spectator cares to give it. And for a conclusion so repugnant to human feeling and so smugly stated in those final lines, this is even more astonishing than the fact that the conclusion was reached at all.

Ernst Toller would never have brought himself to write such a work. How did Brecht manage to? It is difficult to think that he sat down with a pre-established conclusion, merely inventing a few crude illustrations to make it look acceptable, yet he does not seem to have been driven step by step, through the remorseless logic of his political thinking, to the point where to kill the deviating comrade was the only feasible course to advocate. He may have been playing at politics, putting forward on paper, for the theatre, conclusions he did not expect to see realised in actual life. In some moods one is tempted to write off *The Measures Taken* as a piece of anti-Communist propaganda, pointing to the absurdity of the totally anti-individualist position, and that is not a thought to be dismissed out of hand. The flimsy argument may be directly related to Brecht's frank impetuosity, which could drive him to extreme positions held only, perhaps, experimentally and tentatively.

The thought that *The Measures Taken* might be a parody is interesting, if only because it echoes Brecht's own remarks about *The Threepenny Opera* and *Mahagonny*. There seems sometimes to have been a compulsion in him to write so adaptively that the line between acquiescence and parody, ironic imitation and identification, going with the stream of things and indicating what is wrong with the stream, becomes very hard to draw. Rather as Marx's distinction from Hegel is in some respects hard to discern, since the one is a reflection of the other, so Brecht's position even in propagandist works can look ambiguous. As Brecht said, approvingly, of Hegel, 'He denied that one equals

one, not only because everything that exists is continually turning into something else, namely its opposite, but because generally nothing is identical with itself.'[8] Many of the plays are continually about to turn into their opposites.

This is more evident than ever in a play that Mr Esslin
calls one of Brecht's masterpieces, one of his 'greatest and most
characteristic works'.[9] 'Like all his best plays' Mr Esslin writes
of *Die heilige Johanna der Schlachthöfe* (St Joan of the Stockyards) 'it moves on several levels. On one of those levels it is a
devastating parody of German classical drama; above all, of one
of the silliest plays in the German classical canon, Schiller's *Maid
of Orleans*, and of Goethe's *Faust*. The meat-packers of the Chicago stockyards talk in the bombastic blank verse of Schiller's
romantic heroes . . . [here a passage of verse is quoted] . . . It is
also an attempt, and rather a naive one, to look behind the
scenes of big business and stock-exchange operations. And thirdly, *St Joan of the Stockyards* returns to the question of ends
and means. The capitalist Pierpont Mauler is shown with the
hardly concealed admiration that Brecht, like Shaw, had for
the ruthless millionaire operator. In fact *St. Joan of the Stockyards* combines features of Shaw's *St. Joan* and *Major Barbara*'.[10]

These are slender reasons. There is no great merit in parodying a play as silly as *The Maid of Orleans* (though it was still
being performed at leading theatres and on television in the
Bundesrepublik in 1974), and in any case there are only one
or two scenes in which this, and Goethe's play, are parodied:
to say that these represent a movement on one of several levels,
which sounds impressive, is to inflate their importance. The con-
cession that the attempt at portraying big business is 'naive', and
that the play unexpectedly shows Brecht's sympathy with the
capitalist Mauler (the name is derived from Pierpont Morgan)
weakens the case originally made. For a masterpiece, this is not
claiming much, and there is no further account in Mr Esslin's
book of the dramatic qualities of this play.

As for the theme, Esslin convincingly describes it as the account
of a reluctant conversion from religious quietism to political
activism: 'The horror at the violence of war, which had led
Brecht to despair, turned into the willing acceptance of violence
as part of the workings of necessity. The little Salvation Army
girl of *St Joan of the Stockyards*, driven to despair by the

human suffering before her, tries to relieve suffering by kindness. But in the hour of her death she comes to the conclusion:

> For only violence helps, where violence reigns,
> And only men can help where there are men . . .

It is easy to see [Mr Esslin concludes] how this austere, poetic
version of the Marxist creed corresponded to the subconscious
needs of a young man of deep sensibility whose world had been
shattered by the spectacle of horrible human suffering.'[11] That is
not untrue, though a certain callousness may also show itself, and
'poetic' is perhaps used too freely: what Joan says here is not
unorthodox Marxism.

The portrayal of suffering in *St Joan of the Stockyards* is
grotesque to the point of self-parody, rather than simply moving,
or relevant to any political message. In showing the condition
of the working-class in Chicago, Brecht makes use chiefly of an
episode which he read in Upton Sinclair's novel, *The Jungle,*
where an employee of a canned meat factory falls into a boiling
vat, and is canned with the rest of the meat. The story, though
no doubt taken from real life, already has something grotesque
about it, to which Brecht adds a note of almost black humour.
The name of the employee turns out to be Luckerniddle, a humorous German version of a 'typical' English name rather as
Slossenboschen might be if the circumstances were reversed.
Brecht then shows how an employee who covets the cap and
overalls of Luckerniddle is allowed to have them only on condition that he sits down beside Frau Luckerniddle, wearing
them, while she is eating her dinner, and tells her how he comes
to have them on. Under the depraving influence of capitalism,
the man agrees to do this. Frau Luckerniddle, for her part,
though she has a shrewd suspicion of why her husband has vanished, agrees to make no fuss in return for twenty free meals in
the factory canteen. When she learns *how* he vanished and
appreciates, in effect, that she may start eating him at any moment, she is duly sick, but promises to return for the remaining
meals the following day.

There is a similar episode in which a character called Gloomb,
whose fingers have been cut off in a machine because of the excessive speed at which he is made to work, forgets all about
his protests the moment he is offered the job of foreman: from

this new position he actually encourages Johanna to work on the same dangerous machine herself. But the point of this and the Luckerniddle scene is not to portray the 'Lumpenproletariat', that selfish section of the working-class which, according to theory, makes Marxism hard to put into practice. The scenes are there, as Johanna says, not to show the badness of the poor, but their poverty. It is because the poor are completely dependent on the capitalist for all employment that they can be so degraded.

This mechanical, purely economic view of human nature seems hardly meant seriously. The intention is the more difficult to come at, since it is in inflated language that Johanna makes this point, the last two lines being pompous enough to make one doubt again where the real parody lies:

> Nicht der Armen Schlechtigkeit
> Hast du mir gezeigt, sondern
> *Der Armen Armut.*
> Zeigtet ihr mir der Armen Schlechtigkeit
> So zeig ich euch der schlechten Armen Leid.
> Verkommenheit, voreiliges Gerücht!
> Sei widerlegt durch ihr elend Gesicht!

> It is not the badness of the poor that
> you have shown me,
> *but their poverty.*
> If you showed me the badness
> of the poor, I show you the
> suffering of the wicked poor.
> Degeneracy, thou precipitate rumour,
> Be refuted by their wretched faces!

This explanation removes all possible humanity from the workers: if poverty can actually oblige them to act in this ruthless way, they are automata, scarcely worth consideration. But the form is as much worth noting as the content. 'Degeneracy, thou precipitate rumour' has a flourish more reminiscent of Schiller than of Brecht, yet Brecht does not seem to be ironical in his use of the phrase for Johanna, who at this point seems to have been converted to a 'proper' view. As before, the irony is ambiguous.

The scenes of factory life might, then, be a parody of how a Communist might regard the working-class and its corruption by capitalism, although Brecht's general tendency makes this seem extremely unlikely. He is much less likely to be ironical here than he is to behave like Azdak in *The Caucasian Chalk Circle*, entering into the situation, whatever it happens to be, with such chameleon fervour as to give it some air of the ridiculous. Brecht seems to be ambiguous in his portrayal of factory life, as though he were revealing unheard-of depths of iniquity and at the same time laughing at them. Similarly his picture of the operations of the capitalist Mauler is either, as Mr Esslin says, rather a naive one, or else a caricature of a very crude Communist view.

That Brecht may have admired Mauler is understandable in a certain sense. Mauler in fact resembles nothing so much as a capitalist as caricatured in the Soviet humorous paper, *Krokodil*. He is not viciously presented: though the caricature is gross it is not drawn with hatred or contempt, like the cartoons of Jews in *Der Stürmer*. He has, rather, a certain expansiveness, a sly humour, even a boyish zest, as well as a powerful sexual drive. Traces of Galileo and Azdak are obvious: he comes out of the same mental mould. His most unusual characteristic, though, is his combination of two extreme attitudes, which generally gives him the appearance of hypocrisy. On the one hand, he is squeamish to a fantastic degree when it is a matter of killing cattle, though his whole livelihood depends on that. On the other hand, he is ruthlessly unfeeling when it comes to crushing human opposition to his plans. And in much the same way, though everything he touches turns to money, he is secretly an ascetic who has no use for it. So far as the play concerns him, rather than Johanna, it is concerned with this polar dichotomy, reduced to the simplest terms, and the conclusion, parodying well-known lines from Goethe's *Faust*, draws a moral:

> Mensch, es wohnen dir zwei Seelen
> In der Brust!
> Such nicht eine auszuwählen
> Da du beide haben mußt.
> Bleibe stets mit dir im Streite!
> Bleib der Eine, stets Entzweite!
> Halte die hohe, halte die niedere
> Halte die rohe, halte die biedere
> Halte sie beide![12]

Man, there dwell two souls within your breast. Do not seek to pick
one only, since you must have both. Always be in conflict with yourself. Remain the One, always divided. Keep the high, keep the low,
keep the vulgar, keep the upright, keep them both.

It could well be that this too is meant ironically, that it represents
the foolish attitude of a Mauler, spinning round in the dialectical
dichotomies of capitalist society, whereas in the ultimate, classless society there will be no need for divisiveness. Or it may be
that Brecht has the necessity for continuing dialectical motion in
mind.

In the final passages, when Johanna is dying, convinced that
her religious mission has been mistaken, the point of Mauler's
polarised character becomes clear. He reflects, in fact, something inherent in Brecht's plays from early days onwards, the
combination of emotional humanitarianism and brutal activity.
Just as the young agitator in *The Measures Taken* is prompted
by extremely strong fellow-feeling, while the other agitators demand rigid adherence to doctrine, so Mauler (an early Puntila)
is sentimental about animals and merciless with human beings.

The confusions of the play arise from the fact that Mauler's is
the same dichotomy that Johanna experiences. She, for her part,
begins by feeling nothing but sympathy for the workers, a sympathy that is made to look almost as foolish as Mauler's for the
oxen. In the course of time, Johanna learns that sympathy is out
of place, and concludes with her notorious speech, demanding
that anyone who preaches religious belief must have his head
smashed on the pavement till he dies. But in this way she
learns only the truth of what Mauler says, that any action must
cause harm to someone, 'Handelnd musst du, ach, verwunden!'
('In acting, alas, you must wound.') The Communist cause, as
she adopts it, will be involved in the same contradictions as the
capitalist one, the sole difference being that she hopes, through
her kind of violence, to put an end to the dichotomies.

A contrast is afforded by a third play written in these years,
The Mother, based on the internationally famous novel of Maxim
Gorki. In form alone, there is a remarkable change: there is no
'argument' here, whether in a theatrical or a logical sense. Unlike
St Joan of the Stockyards and *The Measures Taken* the play
does not set out to persuade, nor do the events portrayed in it
lead on from one to another, except on one or two occasions and

in the simplest chronological sense. Instead, the lessons to be derived are set out in sequence, and directed to the already converted. Pelagea Wlassowa, the mother, is shown first in her poverty and ignorance, then in the role of a woman who has been persuaded of the rightness of the Communist cause. She distributes pamphlets, takes part in demonstrations, argues with strikebreakers, taunts the comfortable middle-class, gets up from her sickbed to help the Party in the hour of need, and is seen finally holding the Red Flag aloft in the revolution of 1917. To the unconverted, this may seem to promise a dull work of didacticism, and it is true that Wlassowa, as Brecht portrays her, is a model revolutionary. Psychologically, she has been streamlined to suit his purpose: the religious faith which partly inspires her prototype in Gorki has been ironed out, and she becomes an orthodox revolutionary in every respect. She has no hesitations, never doubts for an instant once she has heard the Party's argument set forth; every action she undertakes is correct, and meets with appropriate success. Yet perhaps because she has been played principally by Helene Weigel (whom Brecht married at about the time the play was written), and partly also because she shares the vitality of so many other of Brecht's leading characters, the play is capable of coming to life nevertheless. There are no other figures in it with her vigour: the 'Brechtian' personality that shows through in Baal, Macheath, Azdak, Puntila, Mother Courage and so on seldom allows of others standing alongside it. Yet the best scenes are those in which Brecht shows the native humour and cunning with which Wlassowa goes about her work. It is the same kind of humour and cunning that were to appear later in Azdak, and it may seem incredible that a woman who has it should follow the party line so closely as Wlassowa does here. Certainly, a good deal needs to be discounted by non-Communist audiences if the play is to be appreciated. At times the conversation of the revolutionaries sounds prim and self-conscious, and it is difficult to produce convincingly a scene like that in which Pelagea learns to read from a disillusioned teacher. Her insistence that he write up on the board – where the audience too can see them – such words as 'Worker' and 'Class War', have a touch of false naiveté, as does her request to be taught how to spell 'Exploitation'. Critics who found a patronising condescension in the play[13] were not wholly wrong.

Against such tendencies, however, there are the scenes where Brecht's ironical devices are allowed play. There is the occasion when Wlassowa speaks to her son in prison, and while playing the part of a pious mother for the edification of the warder, succeeds in extracting information on useful party-contacts. Or the similar one where Brecht makes use of his talent for presenting a case so forcefully that its defects are observed. Here, Wlassowa stands in a queue of women bringing metal vessels in aid of the 'war-effort.' Seeing the unreasoning patriotism of the rest, she begins her Bolshevik propaganda in these terms, the ironical thrust being once again very clear:

EINE FRAU. Das ist wirklich schön, dass unser Krieg so vorwärtsgeht!

PELAGEA WLASSOWA. Ich habe ja nur ein kleines Becherchen. Das gibt höchstens fünf, sechs Patronen. Wie viele davon treffen schon? Von sechs vielleicht zwei und von den zwei höchstens eine tödlich. Ihr Kessel da ist schon für mindestens zwanzig Patronen, und die Kanne von der Dame da vorn, das ist überhaupt eine Granate. Eine Granate, die nimmt gleich auf einmal fünf bis sechs Mann. [*Zählt die Geräte.*] Eins, zwei, drei, vier, fünf, sechs, sieben, halt, die Dame hat ja zwei, also acht. Acht. Da kann man schon wieder einen kleinen Sturmangriff bewerkstelligen. [*Sie lacht leise.*] Ich hätte mein Becherchen fast nicht hierhergebracht. Begegne ich da zwei Soldaten, die sollte man ja anzeigen, sagen die zu mir: "Ja, liefere dein Kupfer mir ab, alte Ziege, damit der Krieg überhaupt nicht mehr aufhört!" Was sagt ihr dazu? "Ihr", sage ich, "gehört glatt erschossen. Und wenn ich mein Becherchen", sage ich, "nur dazu hergebe, dass man euch euer dreckiges Maul stopfen kann, dann ist es schon nicht umsonst gegeben. Für zwei Patronen wird es noch langen." Denn warum gebe ich, Pelagea Wlassowa, meinen Kupferbecher her? Ich gebe ihn her, damit der Krieg nicht aufhört!

A WOMAN. It's really grand that we're doing so well in the war!

PELAGEA WLASSOWA. It's only a very little mug I've brought. They won't get more than five or six bullets out of that. And how many of those will be on target? Two out of six perhaps, and only one out of the two will kill anyone, at the outside. Your kettle there will make twenty bullets at least, and that can the lady has in the front, that'll be a whole shell. A shell, you know, that does for five or six men at a go. [*Counting the vessels.*] One, two, three, four, five, six, seven, wait, that lady's got two, that's eight. We could start up a real raiding-party with that. [*Laughing softly.*] I nearly didn't bring my mug at all. Met two soldiers on the way

here, ought to tell the police I ought, one says to me, 'Yes, you
go and hand in your copper, you old bitch, then the war'll go on
for ever.' What do you say to that? Terrible, isn't it. 'You', I
said 'you want shooting, you do. And' I said, 'if I only hand this
in so they can shut your dirty mouth', I said, 'I shan't have had my
trouble for nothing. There's enough there for two bullets at any
rate'. Because what do you think I'm giving up this mug for? So
the war can go on, that's why.

An accumulation of such scenes, helped by the mobile intelligence of Weigel's acting, which could express successively the extreme of resigned poverty, furious indignation, peasant slyness,
a humorous enjoyment of even desperate situations, and a bold
commonsense appreciation of human characters, saved the play
from the moralising primness of some Communist drama. Yet
the impression given by Brecht's Wlassowa is rather of an exceptional character than of one who can be imitated: she is a model
in the sense that she exemplifies proper activities such as pamph-
let-distributing and taking part in demonstrations, not in the
sense that others could readily adopt her original methods. Like
the 'good soldier' Schweik, in the novel of Jaroslav Hašek which
Brecht was later to adapt, she arouses sympathy for a certain
mood of humorous matter-of-factness; she does not thereby necessarily persuade anyone of the rightness of her cause. A good
deal of the sympathy she arouses is due to the fact that she is not
required, as are the characters in the other didactic plays, to
perform any of the obnoxious actions listed earlier among the
virtues of Communism. She is not called upon to break her
word, or to concoct deliberately lying propaganda, nor is she
asked to exterminate an erring comrade or take any part in the
bloodshed of revolution. The play ends, in 1917, on a triumphant
note as the revolution is about to begin. It is significant of its
avoidance of most of the grimmer issues of Communism, however, that it stops at this point, leaving the impression that from
now on all will be well, as though there were no liquidation of
Kulaks or political terrorisation to follow. The didactic and fal-
sifying element in the play establishes itself in this ending at the
expense of the one vividly drawn character it contains.

The Mother, Brecht noted in 1936, was 'written in the style of
the didactic plays, but required actors'. That is to say that unlike *He who said Yes, The Baden-Baden Cantata, The Measures*

Taken, The Exception and the Rule and *The Horatians and the Curiatians*, it was not meant primarily to be performed by schools or by proletarian amateur groups, but with the full resources of professional technique. By virtue of this technique, especially in the hands of such actors as Ernst Busch, Angelika Hurwicz, and Regine Lutz, a great deal could be added by way of comment to roles which look flat enough on the printed page. Since this comment is an intrinsic part of the alienation-effect which entered more and more into Brecht's productions in later years, and since this effect is capable of making striking differences to a work, some exploration of it will be useful before turning to the theory itself and its development. Moreover, the full significance of *The Mother* in Brecht's work is not properly appreciated without knowledge of certain alterations made to the text in the post-war years. In the original version the figure of Wlassowa is most striking: the party-members who appear in the first scene fade quickly into the background, and it is she who stands out with increasing clarity as the heroine. This idealisation ran counter to the development of Brecht's thought in later years. In fact it was likely to produce the very attitude in his audiences that he was anxious to avoid – a contented admiration for one who could perform wonders beyond the reach of ordinary folk. In the revised unpublished version, performed in Berlin in 1951, this was countered to a large extent by the rewriting of the part of one who had hitherto played a very minor role. The mechanic Semjon Lapkin, formerly an indistinguishable and unnamed figure in the group of revolutionary workers, now became a determined exponent of both theory and practice of the class-struggle, by comparison with whom the activities of Wlassowa could be seen in a more objective light. The play thus became none the less revolutionary in its message; at the same time, the comparatively individualistic heroics of the original version were toned down. No doubt Brecht created the part also for the sake of the principal male actor of his company, Ernst Busch. The intelligence brought to it by Busch nevertheless contributed to a great alteration in the spirit of the play as a whole. 'Lapkin's relationship to Wlassowa', an observer wrote,[13] 'was exhibited by Busch with great differentiation. He accepts her "inhospitable" attitude at the beginning with humor, though not at all without gravity. He realises quickly, though not immediately, that this courageous opponent conceals a courageous ally. Her mother-wit, and above all the obstinacy with which she counters his arguments for the strike give him obvious enjoyment. When she is picking up the pieces of her dripping-pot, broken by the police, how fine is the unostentatious friendliness with which he lays a hand on her arm in passing. The gesture contains also the assurance that despite her so-reasonable anger at the revolutionaries who have caused her all this trouble, she is willing to let him do it.' There was nothing of this in the earlier version of this scene, since there the revolutionaries were apparently all younger men and women: Lapkin takes over the part of Pavel here, (whose lines were in many cases adapted for him) and his maturer outlook at once puts Wlassowa in a perspective that had not been possible before. Similarly, the older man alters the playing of Pavel himself. In an earlier production, writes the actor who had taken the part of the son, 'I had acted a man . . . who put up determinedly with anxieties and dangers as inevitable consequences of his revolutionary work. Now it was a matter of showing a young man surprised by a dangerous situation, and confronting his difficulties uncertainly and somewhat helplessly. He had joined the party, but he was only at the beginning of his development into a conscious revolutionary. And in this way he made his decisions not entirely by his own lights, but under the impression and guidance of Lapkin's clear-headed purposefulness.'[14] Meanwhile, Brecht did not fall completely into the trap of replacing one idealised figure by another. Lapkin also makes his mistake, when he imagines his brother, the teacher Vessovchikov, to be an incorrigible reactionary: it is Wlassowa who finds subtler means of winning the teacher over, and who thereby becomes entitled to deliver a reproof to the too-confident plotter.

All this makes no difference to the structural qualities of the play and its still idealising conclusion. It is, however, significant of the widened focus which Brecht required in his later work, and of the humanity which his actors brought to bear on the interpretation of their parts. The still strongly individualistic conception of *The Mother* is modified by the 'ensemble' production; the pretentiousness of young revolutionaries is recognised, with charity, for what it is; a shrewd appraisal of situations, informed with a humane regard, replaces the sometimes hysterical, sometimes starry-eyed, sometimes coldly ruthless quality of much of the earlier plays.

The didactic plays contribute less than the plays of the 1920s to Brecht's reputation. Yet if, by the time he went into exile, Brecht was a famous dramatist, that was not only because of his raciness and intensity, but also because of his extreme outspokenness, which made a violent impact. Despite the comparative absence of plot, his scenes succeed each other with a ferocious insistence; blasphemies follow appeals to charity, immorality is at one and the same time advocated and castigated, a kaleidoscope of grotesque caricatures whirls over the stage in a frenzy such as only the Expressionists were capable of, while from time to time a sudden halt is called, an appeal to reason is heard and the language reverts to a laconic terseness. In some aspects Brecht's calls to mind Strindberg's demonic intensity; while in others yet again he produces knockabout farce in the manner of Chaplin. His themes show affinity with Pirandello's, his formal innovations resemble Claudel's. A crowd of apparently incompatible influences throng into his work, Nietzsche and Marx, Rimbaud, Villon and Kipling; Wedekind, the Bavarian folk-play and the Japanese Noh play; jazz and Büchner, the language of the Bible and the songs of Berlin cabaret. He conducts a running fight with Goethe, Schiller, and Shakespeare, with the tradition of grand opera, to which *The Threepenny Opera* was a counterblast, with the production methods of the best producers of his day, Reinhardt and Piscator, with the acting methods of the established school of Stanislavsky. At the same time he is continually experimenting with his own forms, thinking and experiencing in terms of theatre. Piece by piece, new elements of alienation are added; the plays change shape in answer to new requirements; nothing is fortuitous, each innovation, however radical, is intended for a purpose. The sheer profusion and vitality of Brecht's work at this time, his receptivity to influences from all sides, his ability to give expression to every reaction with swift immediacy, are impressive.

Yet this Baal-like openness still lives in a world of fantasy, is still centred on self-realisation. The characters who come alive are still the central ones: Baal, the prisoner of war Kragler, Macheath, Pelagea Wlassowa. The remainder are grotesques, types, mouthpieces for witticisms and cynicisms, objects of ridicule, models of Communist perfection. The portrayal of social conditions, even in those plays where social criticism is intended, is wildly exaggerated: the America of *Mahagonny* and *St. Joan of the Stockyards* and the England of *The Threepenny Opera* are unrecognisable, and it is only in *Drums in the Night* (and later *Fear and Misery of the Third Reich*) that Brecht gives anything like a picture of conditions in Germany. For the most part, the early plays contain no scenes where human beings enter into any relationship with one another, except in such a parodistic form as the friendship between Macheath and Tiger Brown. The audience is often invited to draw conclusions from what it sees before it, while what it sees is presented in such a form that conclusions are either undrawable or contrary to those pronounced on stage. And when Brecht deliberately turns to the advocacy of reason in his plays, he shows little regard for rationality.

It is a strange mixture, this unadorned forthrightness and lack of sentiment on the one hand, this frankness and originality, receptivity and unshrinking penetration, and on the other hand this seemingly wilful blindness, unwillingness to reason, prejudice, occasional hysteria, and preference for parody and adaptation. Brecht's openness, his 'all-embracing' attitude, was critical only on the impulse of the moment, and his dramatic unities were the largely fortuitous assemblies of these impulses, able to exist side-by-side because they left out of account the continuum of the outside world. Yet the early plays do show also the ability to observe and take account of the rest of humanity. The language of the working men in *Baal*, unlike that in *The Mother* and *St. Joan*, is full of idiomatic turns of phrase. The note of concern about the direction to be taken by human nature enters in *A Man's a Man*, and grows louder in *The Threepenny Opera*, for all that it takes so abrupt a modification into inhumanity in the propagandist plays. There are moments of genuine emotional intensity, as in Pelagea Wlassowa's grief at her son's death. Moreover, Brecht had shown repeatedly his ability to make use of the theatre: he was no armchair dramatist but one who constantly envisaged effects in terms of theatrical performance. In *Señora Carrar's Rifles*, a priest raises his hands above his head in a reverent gesture of resignation: he is held in the act by a word, and sits there, a dramatic image of a man 'surrendering'. In *The Measures Taken*, the young agitator removes his mask to declare his true identity, and the physical revelation of his human personality comes as a shock which almost in itself undoes the inhuman doctrine of the play. These, with many other devices reveal Brecht as the man of the theatre he was: a brilliant innovator, a fertile mind, an iconoclast, a man with innumerable facets, but still a dramatist more capable of momentary effects than integrated wholes.

THEORIES AND PRACTICE

From early days, Brecht was evolving not only plays, but theories of what he was doing and the effect he expected to produce. His theoretical writings now fill a large part of his *Collected Works* and, although they do not always seem to illuminate the plays, an account of them is indispensable.

The 'V-Effekt', or 'alienation technique' – 'V' standing for 'Verfremdung' – is at its simplest a means of making the events on the stage seem strange, unfamiliar. Since almost all Brecht's devices served this purpose to some degree, an account of his practice is the best way to begin understanding the theory.

He often required very strong illumination of the stage throughout, even in night-time scenes, to avoid giving the spectator any opportunity of sinking into reverie or of feeling himself linked in the darkness with those around him. Similarly, in early days he required the spotlights and floods to be actually visible on stage. 'Nobody would expect the lights to be hidden at a sporting event, for instance a boxing match. However much the presentations of the new theatre may differ from sporting ones, they do not differ on the point where the old theatre finds it necessary to hide the sources of light.'[1] In fact, Brecht did not as a rule adopt this practice with the Berliner Ensemble, just as he withdrew from sight the gramophone which produced sound-effects, when he found it merely aroused amusement.

The action was commented upon or announced by intervening or accompanying projections, a practice which Brecht continued in all his productions, although it has been felt at times to be an affectation.[2] He also used a low curtain masking only half the height of the stage, behind which the movements of actors and stage-hands could easily be seen. In *Puntila* a mountain is made out of chairs. In *The Horatii* the sun is represented by a spotlight carried across the rear of the stage by a technician. At the Berlin production of *A Man's a Man* the figures of the actors were projected on to large boards during the performance. The British soldiers in the same play appeared as enormous figures with padded chests, hideous faces, and walking on stilts. Those in *Edward II* had their faces made up completely white, to indicate – or rather to make the audience suddenly grasp at – the fear with which they entered the battle. Something of this grotesqueness remained even in the later productions, especially in the masks with protruding eyeballs worn by the soldiers in *The Caucasian Chalk Circle*. On the whole, however, the later productions forwent many of the more surprising features of the earlier practice. In the twenties, Brecht was still concerned to avoid anything beautiful, lyrical, or directly moving. He denied emotion, as he denied beauty, as an indulgence that could not be afforded while suffering still existed. Only rational thought would serve to change the human situation as he saw it.

The 'V effect' was not, however, merely a matter of production technique. The style of acting also required a radical change. Brecht conceived the bourgeois actor (to the dissatisfaction of, for instance, Michael Redgrave, but the point may have been more valid for German than for English acting of the time,[3]) as giving himself up to his part completely, so that the highest praise he might wish to hear would be, 'He didn't merely *act* Lear; he *was* Lear.' Brecht required his actors to maintain the same distance from the characters they were portraying as the audience was expected to adopt. 'He has merely to show the character, or better, not merely to experience it; but this does not mean that when he has to act passionate people he himself must remain cold. It is only that his feelings should not be fundamentally the same as those of his character, so that the feelings of his audience do not become fundamentally those of his character. The audience must have complete liberty here'.[4] The basic function of the actor is thus to 'show', just as a person in conversation may break off in order to demonstrate in pantomime a part of his story. (In a provocative image, Brecht sought to stress this point by recommending to the actor the attitude of a man who lays down his cigarette for a moment in order to act out the scene he is describing.)

The methods by which this attitude was inculcated were numerous. In *The Elephant Child* the actors walked off the stage to order drinks at the bar within the auditorium. Actors were encouraged at rehearsals to translate their speeches into the third person, preceding them with the words 'He said', or to describe their actions in the past tense as they performed them. They spoke the stage instructions, indicating mood or gesture, along with their own words, and exchanged parts with one another. Brecht wrote 'practice-texts' to be used at rehearsals, especially those of plays from the classic repertory. In one of these, intended for rehearsals of *Macbeth*, the porter's wife lays the blame for a theft of her own on another person, in much the same way as Lady Macbeth 'gilds the faces of the grooms' to plant guilt on them for Macbeth's murder of Duncan. An actress playing both these parts at rehearsals is unlikely to have any illusions left about the tragic grandeur of the heroine she portrays.[5]

The effect of such acting can be seen in the war-dance of Mother Courage's son Eilif, as performed by the outstanding actor Ekkehard Schall. The exultant savagery here is at once brutal and restrained. The dancer leaps high in the air, his sabre clasped between both hands above his head; but the head leans to one side, and the lips are pursed as though in an effort to recall the next movement. Eilif is 'shown' here as a young man who dances the war-dance because he believes it the right thing to do, but who is not wholly at home in it. The denial of a part of his humanity becomes evident, and the contemporary relevance of the action dawns through.[6]

The 'V' effect is written into the structure and language of the plays themselves. A frequent structural device is the repetition or duplication of characters or events. Herr Puntila in his drunken, generous mood comments implicitly on Herr Puntila in his sober intolerance. The 'good woman' Shen Te assumes a mask of harsh oppressiveness and turns into the businessman Shui Ta, so that each of her twin personalities recalls the possibility of the other: neither is fixed and unalterable. *He who said No* repeats almost identically the plot and situations of *He who said Yes*. A similar device of repetition in *Drums in the Night* has already been mentioned (p. 23 above). Similarly, in *The Exception and the Rule* the events which the audience has just seen on stage are summarised and partly re-enacted in the trial at the end. Indeed, the trial-scene, which affords obvious possibilities of vividly presenting occurrences which are no longer actually happening (are 'in the past tense', happening to other people, as in Brecht's rehearsal methods) is one of his most often-used devices.

Equally distancing is the scene in *The Mother* where workers explain to the audience how they acted in a recent demonstration at which they came into conflict with the authorities, and go through the motions once again. Brecht does not supply a scene portraying the demonstration itself, but encourages the audience to look back upon it as the characters themselves are doing. Much the same effect is achieved in *The Measures Taken*, where the agitators preface each scene as they narrate it to the chorus with the words 'We will show you how it was', and in *The Good Woman of Setzuan*, where Mrs Yang steps out of her part to tell the audience of a past event which is then enacted in her presence. Alternatively, Brecht used film-strips and newspaper headlines to remind audiences that what was happening on stage was in fact very different from the reality, or very like it.

Different, yet similar in effect, is the scene in *Squire Puntila*, where the chauffeur Matti pretends to make love to Puntila's daughter in order to provoke her fiancé, the diplomatic attaché. Here the action is entirely in the present. Matti goes through the motions of making improper suggestions, while it is perfectly clear that he does not mean them seriously and, since neither character is properly in his role, the audience once again is able to watch with detachment. In the same play, Puntila's daughter looks forward to the future when she will be Matti's wife, and tries to act out the situation of a working-class woman welcoming her husband home from work. With her wealthy background, she makes blunder after blunder, while each correction from Matti brings out the discrepancy between the harder life of a poor woman and her own. Thus a world of poverty which is never directly presented is conjured up by reaction from the events in the play itself.

Brecht frequently abandons the complexities of exposition. Characters do not sustain the Ibsen-like illusion that they are unaware of the audience's presence and must reveal themselves and their relationships by carefully dropped hints which must still preserve the appearance of being natural ingredients of their conversation. In *The Mother*, Pelagea Wlassowa begins the play by directly addressing the audience, explaining who she is, and what her problems are. The same simple opening is found in

The Threepenny Opera and *The Good Woman of Setzuan*. Alternatively, the audience is placed in possession of the necessary facts of the situation by a narrator who sits at one side of the stage throughout, as in *The Caucasian Chalk Circle*, or the story of the next scene is written on hanging boards. And in most of the plays the action is interrupted by songs which summarise, comment on, or predict the action. In all these ways it becomes inevitable that whatever method of acting or production is used, some element of alienation will make itself felt.

In its widest sense, however, Brecht claimed, alienation is not a matter of special techniques, but a bringing-to-consciousness of a normal procedure of everyday life. 'The alienation effect', he wrote, 'occurs when the thing to be understood, the thing to which attention is to be drawn, is changed from an ordinary, well-known, immediately present thing into a particular, striking, unexpected thing. In a certain sense the self-evident is made incomprehensible, although this only happens in order to make it all the more comprehensible.'[7] This, he adds, is a matter of everyday occurrences. A man realises more vividly that his mother is the wife of another man when he becomes a stepson. A car is alienated, made strange, when we have been used to driving a modern one and suddenly find ourselves driving a Ford model T. We hear explosions again and realise that the engine is a combustion engine: we begin to be surprised that a vehicle can be drawn along without horses, 'in short, we comprehend the car by conceiving it as something strange, new, as a successful construction, and thereby to some extent as something unnatural'.[8] Any device which introduces this strangeness produces an alienation to some degree, even such simple words as 'actually' and 'really', whereby we seek to impress our hearers more vividly with what we are saying.

The kind of theatre which these devices would produce was called by Brecht 'epic' theatre, in contrast to the earlier, 'bourgeois' theatre, which was 'dramatic'. The word 'epic' here, translating the German 'episch', is unfortunate. 'Episch' has, in this context, none of the associations with heroism and greatness that 'epic' often has, as in 'an epic tale'; it is merely a literary category, and in German this category includes not only narrative poetry, but also novels, and is often used to distinguish these from the lyric and the drama. In speaking of an 'epic' theatre,

Brecht meant to imply a theatre which would not be exciting, 'dramatic', full of tensions and conflicts, but slower-paced, reflective, giving time to reflect and compare. He lists the qualities in the formula he produced in 1931 – rather over-schematic, as he later confessed, but useful all the same:

Dramatic Form of the Theatre	*Epic Form of the Theatre*
active	narrative
involves the spectator in a stage-action	makes the spectator an observer, but
consumes his capacity to act	awakens his capacity to act
allows him to have feelings	demands decisions from him
experience	view of the world
spectator drawn into something	he is confronted with something
suggestion	argument
feelings are preserved	feelings driven into becoming realisations
the spectator stands inside, experiences with the characters	the spectator confronts and studies what he sees
man is assumed to be known	man is an object of investigation
man unalterable	man alterable and altering
suspense in awaiting the outcome	suspense at the process
one scene exists for another	each scene for itself
growth	montage
linear progress	in curves
evolutionary inevitability	sudden leaps
man as fixed	man as a process
thought determines Being	social Being determines thought
feeling	reason[9]

As Brecht observed, these are not absolute opposites, rather a matter of emphases. However, he gave the impression at the time, a justified one in view of his propagandist plays, that he discountenanced all emotion, and was obliged to correct this explicitly at a later stage.[10] Again, it is not easy to see how complete detachment can give the impetus to action: only by being 'involved' in some way can the spectator gain the emotional force necessary to make his reaction more than the working-out of a syllogism. Some of Brecht's items are obscure: there is no telling what he means when he says that, in the 'dramatic' form, man is assumed to be known. No dramatist who matters ever assumed that. Nor is man generally supposed to be unalterable: dramatists have depicted a wide variety of developments of character reaching as far as superlative wisdom. What Brecht had in mind here, however, was the tragic outcome of so many plays: this, which he regarded as fatalism, he refused to accept.[11] Man must be shown as capable of avoiding tragedy.

Again, the way in which Brecht associates 'Aristotelian' with 'bourgeois' theatre needs comment. Brecht suggests that before his day theatre audiences were passive, hypnotised by the performance, ready to accept whatever the actors gave out as the truth. That may be true so far as the political content of plays, if any, was concerned. But by and large the theatre has been far from the holy of holies that Wagner tried to make of it at Bayreuth. The audience in many epochs was not necessarily interested in the play at all. In the eighteenth century it was common practice in some theatres to supply blinds or curtains for the boxes, inside which actresses could provide better entertainment than they could on the stage. In the same period, riots in the audience might be provoked in order to obtain a change of play, or in protest at the price of tickets: at Drury Lane, the actors, far from being regarded as beyond reach, had to be protected from assault from the pit by spiked railings. The 'battle of *Hernani*', when Victor Hugo's play was subjected to violent interruptions and fights between spectators, indicated no spirit of acquiescence, nor did the productions of Naturalist plays in the late nineteenth century, the time Brecht might have had most in mind. The story of the pair of forceps thrown on the stage by an outraged doctor during a scene in Hauptmann's *Before Dawn*, when a childbirth was supposed to take place just offstage, may be legendary, but the protests were not. Similarly, at the Abbey Theatre, the Irish audience stood up as one man when Synge's *Playboy* referred to Irish women standing in their shifts. These reactions were conservative, but they were vocal. If anything, it is modern audiences that are acquiescent: theatre riots and even gallery protests are not the fashion in serious theatre.

What these practical matters do not reveal is the vast philosophical structure that has been thought to lie behind the theory. Whether Brecht's '*Ver*fremdung' derives from the '*Ent*fremdung' of Marx and Hegel is not certain. Brecht himself, at any rate, never maintained it did. But again it is at least worth seeing what the question of derivation is about.

'*Ent*fremdung' (or 'Entäußerung') seems to be a translation of the word 'alienation' as used by English economists of the eighteenth and early nineteenth centuries, that is, 'transference to another owner', though the word existed before those times, and Brecht's usage has also been thought to be derived from the similar *ostrannenie*, used by Russian Formalists.[12] In Hegel's philosophy it comes to mean the way in which each individual becomes separate from the Whole, or Spirit: there is an all-embracing cosmic Self, which is manifested also in each separate individual Self, and this latter Self is 'alienated' from the cosmic Self when it is transferred, so to speak, to an individual. This is, in Hegel's system, a part of a universal pattern. Everywhere a dialectical process is under way, whereby something that is initially whole, united, at one with itself, is disrupted, forced to become a duality instead of a unity, a separate individual rather than an integrated part of a whole, which may be, for instance, society, or may be the Spirit that transcends all duality. It is equally part of the process, however, that that which is divided seeks to become united again, and each reuniting is a miniature model of the reuniting which is the ultimate goal of all history. As Hegel sees it, history is the separation of the Spirit (or in Christian terms, the Holy Ghost), from itself, the process by which it turns into the world of phenomena as we know them, while history is also the increasing awareness of its own nature which the Spirit thereby acquires. When the Spirit has both individualised itself, that is separated itself out to the fullest extent, and fully come to know itself, the fullness of time has arrived. This self-knowledge by the Spirit is the purpose, or perhaps one should say the nature, of creation. Yet, paradoxically, this goal is continually being reached, not only on such occasions as the Incarnation of God in Christ, when an exact mirroring of the Spirit took place on earth, but at every instant. Hegel's system is a set of Chinese mirrors that continues the Incarnation at each instant into infinity on both sides, but which also declares that Incarnation does not take place completely till infinity is reached.

Hegel applies this dialectical system also to the processes of thought. To assume unthinkingly that an object is as we assume it to be, he says, is a very common form of self-deception. Only when an object is removed, 'alienated' (*entfremdet*), is it possible for it to be known. The aim of all analytical thinking, he continues, is to annul the form in which an object is represented to us as something known (*das Aufheben der Form ihres Bekanntseins*). Yet, in thus analysing and separating the object into its individual parts, the thinker produces at first merely a chaos of dissociated elements: he has set a dialectical process in motion but has reached no farther than that. What was known (or was assumed to be known) has been alienated from the original impression it made; a first 'negation' has been made.

The true recognition of an object hitherto mistakenly seen is only reached when this 'negation' is itself negated, in the 'negation of negation', and it is at this point, so it is argued, that Brecht comes nearest to Hegel's mode of thought. He does in fact use Hegel's word, '*Ent*fremdung', rather than his own '*Ver*fremdung', on one occasion in a passage from a piece written in 1936, where he writes of his refusal to allow spectators to yield themselves up uncritically to an empathetic self-identification with the characters on stage:

'Die Darstellung setzte die Stoffe und Vorgänge einem Entfremdungsprozeß aus.' 'The presentation [of the play] subjected the contents and events to a process of alienation.' And as Brecht goes on to say:

Es war die Entfremdung, welche nötig ist, damit verstanden werden kann. Bei allem 'Selbstverständlichen' wird auf das Verstehen einfach verzichtet.[13]

It was the alienation that is necessary in order that there may be understanding. Wherever things are 'matter of course' [lit. 'self-understood'], the attempt at understanding has simply been given up.

Such a formulation is clearly a Hegelian one, and it seems very likely that Brecht did have Hegel in mind at that moment. His own term, however, may have been deliberately devised to distinguish it from Hegel's. 'Verfremdung' is not 'alienation' in Hegel's sense, it has been argued: it is not simply 'negation', but implies also the second step in the dialectic, 'the negation of negation'. Brecht's intention is not merely to make the familiar unfamiliar, to 'estrange' it, but to lead on to a fresh vision of reality in a more real sense. It is either, as one writer puts it, a matter of 'Verfremdung der Entfremdung' – 'estrangement of alienation' – or 'Verfremdung' can sum up the whole process,

which is 'alienation of alienation'.[14] In either case, the theory
runs, reality not only ceases to be taken for granted, but is seen,
reconstructed, with new eyes.

It is quite possible that Brecht did have such a process in
mind. The complex jargon of Hegelianism, naive as it often turns
out to be in the end, had permeated a good deal of German
thought, and could easily have coloured his own. That does not
account for a certain hiatus in the thought, it is true. To see one's
wife or one's car with fresh eyes is not necessarily to begin a process of seeing the truth about them, and if merely 'making
strange' has this effect, then any writer worth reading is likely
to have employed the method long ago. On the other hand,
Brecht's clear statement that alienation leads to understanding
suggests that he envisaged a dialectical process. As he saw it,
earlier theatre—Shakespeare, for instance—was bourgeois in the
sense that it saw reality as a still unbroken unity. Thus, perhaps,
he saw his own technique as comparable to that of Marx in
breaking up that unity, taking the spectator out of his supposedly
naive unawareness, and so beginning the development which
would no doubt end with the spectator seeing the truth in
Marxist terms. It is difficult to imagine any other way in which
Brecht could have thought the 'V effect' would lead to understanding.

'Entfremdung' also occurs in Marx, with a meaning related
to Hegel's. As Marx uses it in his early work, it refers to the
situation of modern man, deprived of, robbed of, alienated from
the totality of human nature which should be his. It is no longer
a matter of the Spirit becoming alienated from itself. Marx will
have nothing to do with Spirit: the process is rather one in which
Man becomes increasingly alienated from that complete realisation of all his humanity which is his by right, or was his in a remote past. As this process goes on, so the pressure to reverse it
becomes more intense. There is once again something akin to
theological ideas in this: just as for Luther the true Christian
faith could only be held by one who had suffered Christ's complete dereliction on the Cross, one who knew the full sense of
the absence of God expressed in the cry 'Why hast thou forsaken
me', so Man for Marx could only become complete again when
totally alienated from himself. (The link was not in fact with
Luther, or not directly: Marx's theological echoes derive rather

from Hegel, whose theory of alienation, modified by Feuerbach and Hess, he took over.) As Marx developed the traditional ideas of this kind, he began to see in the proletariat the truest visible manifestation of Man in his alienation from his own self. Where Hegel had seen Man as alienated from God, and most alienated of all in such men as Christ, so Marx, at all events in his early work, saw Man as alienated from Man at his fullest, from true Man, total Man, and saw him most alienated of all in the proletariat. For the proletariat in an industrialised society is, Marx held, increasingly reduced to performing a very limited number of functions. Instead of spending the days in hunting, fishing, cooking, or sowing, reaping, threshing, in a series of tasks that varied with the seasons and the times of day, the industrial proletarian was virtually obliged to spend all his working hours from year's end to year's end doing one small job, turning a screw or putting a cap on a bottle. In this sense, the proletarian represented 'the complete loss of Man', as Marx put it. It could regain itself only 'by the complete resurrection of Man'.[15] And since the proletariat was no mere class, but the dissolution of all classes, it had universal significance; it could not emancipate itself without at the same time emancipating all other spheres of society.

In short, the proletariat, in this very early work of 1844, when Marx was 26 (the first volume of *Capital* did not appear till 1867) is seen metaphorically acting in a way not unlike that of Christ, suffering total loss, going on to resurrection, and thereby redeeming the world. How far the later, apparently purely economic, theories were related to the more mythical accounts is disputed. What matters here is that Marx sees the total alienation of the proletariat as a necessary prelude to all the rest, the creating of a vacuum (the non-realised aspects of self) which must be filled all the more rapidly when the revolutionary spark was ignited. Brecht had thought in not dissimilar terms in the story about Bargan, who himself appeared to have Christ-like or Promethean overtones, but was also a man who sacrificed himself for the worthless, and even diabolical Croze, though no resurrection was implied there. The echoes of Christianity never cease throughout Brecht's life.

Also related to Marx is the theory that by intensifying a situation it becomes a revolutionary one. Brecht's plays during the

1920s were notable for their extremism, and his remark about *The Threepenny Opera* in particular is enlightening in this connection. When he said that the opera was a report on what 'bourgeois' audiences liked to see, he is understandable in the sense that, by writing a work so close to being a 'bourgeois' popular success, he was intending to make such successes appear intolerable, by virtue of imitating them so closely. In the same way, 'alienation' effects are often a matter of repeating a situation so precisely (yet with some appreciable difference) that its strangeness becomes apparent. By implication, once this has become clear, once it becomes evident how far removed from the ideal situation the present one is, the vacuum is filled, and the Marxist solution presents itself overwhelmingly.

That interpretation would account for the confident expectation Brecht had, that his 'V-effects' would assist towards a Marxist revolution. The effects may not have anything like such a consequence for some audiences, but the theoretical basis at least becomes more intelligible. To understand further, one must see the circumstances out of which Brecht's theory arose.

Of the producers who dominated the stage in Brecht's early manhood, two, Reinhardt and Piscator, laid a special emphasis on the involvement of the audience in the events on stage. Reinhardt was known for the mysterious, enchanted atmospheres he was able to evoke, as well as for his devices for bridging the gap between audience and actors. In his production of Büchner's *Death of Danton*, he planted rostra deep into the auditorium and scattered actors among the seats, so that the theatre 'became' the French revolutionary tribunal. In a famous production of *Das Mirakel*, he gave the impression that all were united in a single action: the performers occupied a central area like an enclosed football pitch (the production, in London, was at the Olympia exhibition hall), and the spectators sat in raked banks of seats on four sides. 'The scene became a cathedral', wrote a contemporary observer, 'and we were imprisoned in the aisles, spectators on the stage itself.'[16] A 'mass-performance' of *Oedipus Rex* was put on in the open air at the Theresienwiese in Munich, and other productions used circuses for locations.[17] All this was too close to the heady atmosphere of other trends like Expressionism to appeal to Brecht. In his laconic way he feared the release of mass-emotions, and in this he has been supported by others, who have seen unwitting presages of later political mass-movements in these productions.

Piscator, meanwhile, also in Berlin, had a direct influence on Brecht.[18] From him among others Brecht learned several of the devices which later came to be associated with his own productions, notably the use of films or projected photographs as background to the stage action, and the use of a moving horizontal belt to allow characters to walk continuously without changing their position on stage. In theory, also, Piscator used the theatre in order to make an appeal to reason, as Brecht later claimed to do: the drama 'should not only transmit excitement, enthusiasm, passion; but rather enlightenment, knowledge, recognition'.[19] But he worked on the assumption that the inevitable result of rational enlightenment would be 'to kindle the flame of revolt among the workers',[20] and attempted to turn every performance into a public demonstration. On one occasion machine-guns were actually handed down from the stage to members of the audience, as though to arouse them to revolution at that very moment. Most telling of all, in contrast to what Brecht was doing, is the final stage direction from *Russia's Day*, the only play performed by Piscator's 'Proletarisches Theater' to have survived:

Voices. A roaring chorus repeats the battle-cry. Masses appear on the stage . . . crowds rush from every direction onto the stage, breaking down the frontier-barriers with the cry of 'Brothers, Comrades, Unite!' The German worker recites the first verse of the International, a trumpeter in Russian uniform steps forward, blows the International, the chorus on the stage join in, *as do the audience*.[21]

The main argument against Piscator's theatre at the time was that it substituted an emotional and imagined unity for a real unity in the world outside the theatre. No stronger resolve to achieve revolution was brought about by such means, Brecht maintained.

It was against Piscator's conception of the theatre, as much as against the 'bourgeois' conception of Reinhardt, that Brecht's statement of principles arose, although he was equally opposed to the theatre of Stanislavsky, which required a self-identification of the actor with his part. Brecht aimed at a theatre where there should be no self-identification either of the actor or of the audience with events on stage.

In the past, he believed, a view of the drama which he called Aristotelian had prevailed, according to which the spectator was purged of fear and pity, and rendered a harmless member of society whose feelings were 'used up' in the witnessing of purely theatrical events. Thus *The Mother*, as he later observed, was 'a piece of anti-metaphysical, materialistic, non-Aristotelian drama'.[22] The epithet 'non-Aristotelian' recurs frequently throughout his theoretical writings: it is an essential feature of his conception of the 'epic' theatre as a form of art belonging to a new, scientific age. In choosing to contrast himself with Aristotle, however, Brecht laid himself open to misunderstanding. It may well be that it was an inadequate portrayal of Aristotle's dramatic theories to which he was opposed, rather than what a different understanding would have revealed. For him, 'Aristotelian drama' was equivalent to 'pre-Communist' drama. His own form was designed for the special requirements of his own times. It

makes no such thoughtless use of the spectator's self-yielding empathy as does the Aristotelian, and has an essentially different relationship to certain psychical effects such as catharsis. It is no more concerned to deliver up its heroes to the world as though to an unescapable destiny than it is to deliver up the spectator to a suggestive theatrical experience. Seeking to teach the spectator a particular and practical attitude which aims at altering the world, it must provide him even while in the theatre with a standpoint fundamentally different from the one to which he is accustomed.[23]

Brecht does not here reject empathy out of hand, as critics have sometimes believed he did. He is opposed rather to the conception of a spectator who identifies himself with the characters on stage in a thoughtless way, surrendering himself to the illusion and thereby promoting a fatalistic acceptance of the ways of the world both in the theatre and outside it.

In a Germany where 'Schicksal' ('Fate') had become a word redolent of helpless foreboding, and where it had often been accounted the highest wisdom to come to terms with it, this opposition was only to be welcomed. Nor was it so very un-Aristotelian. In what ways his own theatre differed on the question of catharsis Brecht does not say here. He appears to have taken the word in the sense of 'purgation', and to have envisaged it as a means of expending the emotions of pity and fear within the fictional world of the theatre, so that they are no longer a hindrance in the practical world outside. Thus he says that the Aristotelian form involves the spectator in an action on stage, and thereby 'enables him to have feelings' and 'consumes his activity'.[24] Again, he observes that the various intoxicants, of which the theatre is one, whereby men seek comfort in illusions, 'are in some circumstances to blame for the fact that great quantities of energy which might be used for improving the human condition are uselessly wasted'.[25] In other words, the stage becomes equivalent in function to the church, as Brecht imagined it: it supplies an opium, drugs the spectator into unconsciousness of true reality, and persuades him that the most intolerable situations can be endured because they are endurable in the theatre. Through catharsis, the spectator is restored to health, is no longer troubled by the conditions of actual living, and ceases to have the desire to change them. 'In metaphysics', it has been said, 'everything always is all right', and the same might be said of the Aristotelian theatre as Brecht conceived it to be. It presented works in which the tragedies of the world were reflected, and pronounced them to be a justified and integral part of an unchangeable social or divine order. That is, in fact, what Hegel did make of tragedy.

Brecht certainly misunderstood Aristotle in some ways. There was nothing tragic, in Aristotle's view, in depicting either the fall of a bad man from prosperity to adversity, or his rise in a contrary direction, nor was there anything of the kind in depicting the fall of a completely virtuous man. It was in 'a person neither eminently virtuous or just, nor yet involved in misfortune by deliberate vice and villainy, but by some error of human frailty' that the material of tragedy was to be found.[26] For such a person, pity would be excited by the sight of misfortune undeservedly suffered, and fear would be excited 'by some resemblance between the sufferer and ourselves'. Aristotle did not expect audiences to drop all moral concern from the moment they entered the theatre. Nor, however, would he have tolerated the appearance of callousness, when Brecht seeks to inculcate in the spectator the attitude of the 'smoking observer'. Tragedy, and its consequent catharsis, depends on our feeling the resemblance between the sufferer and ourselves: unless we feel that his condition is potentially our own, we cannot feel fear either on his or on our own behalf. A man who sits observantly smoking while Oedipus puts his eyes out is inhuman. That attitude is appropriate for some plays, not for tragedies.

Brecht took the view, to judge both by his plays and by some of his theoretical writings, that some men, namely capitalists, are so utterly unlike ourselves that no empathy at all is possible in their case. 'Our opponents', he wrote, 'are the opponents of mankind. They are not "right" from their point of view: the wrong consists in their point of view. They may have to be as they are, but they do not have to exist.'[27] So long as this attitude towards one section of mankind is understood, Brecht's attitude towards the Aristotelian theatre can be better appreciated. In his comments, however, Brecht did not keep the distinction clearly in mind. He was displeased when the audience of émigrés at the première of *Mother Courage* spoke afterwards of 'a Niobe tragedy and the amazing vitality of the maternal animal',[28] and rewrote certain scenes to obviate the sympathy that had been aroused. His intention was to prevent any emotion that might lead away from the rational appraisal of Mother Courage as a war profiteer. He wanted no tragedy here and no catharsis, since he believed that such a purging would incapacitate the audience for political action. Yet he could not make Mother Courage the inhuman person that the theory required.

It is true that Aristotle has often been held to have meant, when he spoke of catharsis, a cleansing of the soul from those emotions that might otherwise render life more difficult to live. Yet there is something 'undialectical' about a theory of tragedy that rules out one major part of normal human responses. Just as it has been urged against Brecht that, in rejecting 'emotional socialism' as radically as he did, he ignored an essential element in Marxist philosophy, so it may be urged that in seeking to obviate sympathy for Mother Courage he ignored an essential element of drama. Unless we can recognise some kinship between ourselves and the characters we see on the stage, we can feel neither pity nor fear nor any other emotion. Unless we can recognise in Mother Courage a woman who shares our own faults and virtues in some degree, we cannot see that her blindness has any relation to our own. On the contrary, we shall see her rather as a strange monster, external to our own lives, deserving only to be destroyed, and not as the embodiment of tendencies that belong equally well to ourselves. The same applies to capitalists, of whom Mother Courage is not one.

A certain dilemma seemingly exists: either to expect a cathartic effect from tragedy, with an anaesthetising of daily life as a consequence, or to rule out any such effect, and rule out with it a good half of human personality. Yet there is no need to see the situation in this way, and the interpretation of Aristotle put forward a few years ago by Humphry House indicates a different point of view. It is not the case, House alleged, that Aristotle regarded the theatre as a kind of opiate. 'No theory of catharsis makes sense which speaks of purging away a "painful element" in pity and fear. Aristotle does not say that pity and fear have a "painful element"; he says of both of them . . . that they *are* species of "pain" or "disturbance"; therefore to get rid of the "pain" would be to get rid of the emotion altogether.' What matters in the theatre is not that we should be rid of these emotions, nor that we should luxuriate in them, but that we should feel each of them in due measure. 'Nothing is more important in the education of character', says Aristotle in House's summary, 'than training to rejoice and to feel pain rightly, at the right things and times, and to the right extent. It is not right to be afraid of nothing or to be angry at nothing: there are things the wise man should fear and be angry at.' This granted, it is then the playwright's part to present those features of human life which will arouse these emotions in the wise man. He will not do well to present only such characters as will inspire loathing and contempt, or sheer admiration, but such as will possess the same kind of mixed qualities as the wise man recognises in himself. He will also, however, present situations that are more intensely tragic than those that the audience is actively aware of in life outside the theatre at the time: he will tacitly invite the audience to live through, with a lively imagination, the kind of experience that may come to them as part of the human lot. And in this way, though the audience will enter the theatre to be entertained, not to be educated, they will, in so far as they have been alert, be the better for this entertainment. 'A tragedy', House sums up, 'rouses the emotions from potentiality to activity by worthy and adequate stimuli; it controls them by directing them to the right objects in the right way; and exercises them,

within the limits of the play, as the emotions of the good man
would be exercised. When they subside to potentiality again
after the play is over, it is a more "trained" potentiality than before. This is what Aristotle calls catharsis. Our responses are
brought nearer to those of the good man.' In other words,
catharsis means purging not in the sense of removing completely,
but of making healthy and sane; to purge the passions, as Milton
interpreted, is 'to temper and reduce them to just measure with
a kind of delight, stirr'd up by reading or seeing those passions
well imitated'.

The paradox of Aristotle's view of catharsis is that it gives what
he calls 'an innocent joy' to men;[29] it provides what Milton describes as 'a kind of delight'. That this emotion has been inti-
mately linked with tragedy for centuries past, and still has been
in recent times, is undoubted: it is 'the joy which', a recent critic
has said, 'is so strangely at the heart of the [tragic] experience'.
For Brecht, it seems, such a joy was as reprehensibly premature
as it was for Thomas Mann's Leverkühn, who sought to 'take
back' the joyful choruses of the Ninth Symphony of Beethoven.
Or rather, since Brecht himself does not speak of 'joy' but rather
of 'Rausch' – intoxication or ecstasy – any gratifying emotional response was for him as suspect a form of self-delusion as it was for
Nietzsche. Is it not in fact a betrayal of the fullest possible
human response to have any pleasure at all from tragedy? To
this, it is proper to answer that one can be too 'knowing'. A
spurious delight may well result from a spurious response, a
response which knows too well what is ultimately to be expected.
It is also proper to answer, however, that Aristotle always speaks
of a true 'mean': 'For instance', he writes in the *Nicomachean
Ethics*, 'both fear and confidence and appetite and anger and pity
and in general pleasure and pain may be felt both too much and
too little, and in both cases not well; but to feel them at the right
times, with reference to the right objects, towards the right people,
with the right motive, and in the right way, is what is both inter-
mediate and best, and this is characteristic of virtue.'[30] Just what
this rightness is can be discovered only by each individually, in
relation to particular instances, and with trial and error.

Brecht's rejection of Aristotelian drama, however well or badly
he understood what he was rejecting, is a rejection of a 'bourgeois' form of art, and the substitution of a proletarian or Com-

munist one. Was he thereby cutting himself off from the possibility of appealing to humanity in general, imposing a purely 'class-conscious' theory of drama which only the members of a particular class would appreciate, or was he nevertheless aiming at a universality which even his political opponents would in honesty be compelled to admit? Some of his utterances incline one to suppose the former. Thus he writes, in a note to *The Mother*, 'The ruling aesthetics require of a work of art . . . that it should have an effect that bridges over all social and other differences between individuals. Such an effect, bridging over class-contrasts, is attempted even today by dramas of the Aristotelian school, for all that the differences between classes are becoming more and more obvious to individuals. It is attempted also when class-contrasts are the topic of these dramas, and even when sides are taken for one class or the other. In each case, there is formed in the auditorium, on the basis of a "common humanity" shared by all the spectators, a collective entity which lasts as long as the artistic enjoyment continues. The non-Aristotelian drama of the type of *The Mother* is not interested in producing such collectivity. It divides its public'.[31]

Brecht could hardly have gone further than that in opposing common humanity to the standpoint of the Communist Party. On the other hand, he defended Communism against the charge of being exclusive, of being a mystique to be understood only by specialists. In accordance with the belief that it is the only current philosophy that is entirely in contact with reality, and in that sense the only true philosophy, Brecht held that it had a universality which was merely ignored by opponents. 'We can and must point out that our utterances are not limited and subjective but objective and of general validity. We do not speak for ourselves, as a small section, but for the whole of humanity, as the section which represents the interests of all humanity, and not a part of it.'[32] He argues in a circle here. Communism is not exclusive, because Communism is exclusively right. Opponents of Communism can be shown to lack general validity for their views by appealing to Communism as the philosophy whose views *are* generally valid. Brecht proves nothing by these means, and merely ignores the programmes of those non-Communists who are as much concerned to remove the evils of existing society as he is himself.

With time, Brecht himself came to see less sharp divisions than he had done. After the Second World War he completely reversed his attitude. By this time, it is true, he had returned from exile to live in the Eastern Zone of Germany, later the German Democratic Republic, where he may have felt, naively, that the time for persuading audiences of the need for Communism had passed. At all events, he now announced a complete change of front. In the *Little Organon for the Theatre,* written in 1948, he deliberately recalls his earlier writings only in order to reject them: at that time, he says, he had 'threatened to "turn a means of enjoyment into a lesson to be taught, and transform certain institutions from places of entertainment into organs of publicity", i.e. to emigrate from the realms of pleasure. . . . Let us now, no doubt to the general regret, recant our intention to emigrate from the realms of pleasure and announce, no doubt to even more general regret, our intention of settling in those realms. Let us treat the theatre as a place of entertainment, as a true aesthetics should, and let us find out what sort of entertainment appeals to us.'[33]

The theatre was to be neither moralising nor didactic; it was merely to detach itself from the classical models that had suited former ages, and produce entertainment adapted to our own age. In other words, it was to be a theatre scientific in mood, which was as much as to say, in Brecht's eyes, one that was Communistic in mood, since Communism represented for him the scientific way of looking at the universe. At this point in his manifesto however, Brecht ran into a certain amount of self-contradiction. On the one hand, he continued to emphasise the function of the theatre as a contribution to the political struggle – and the turgidity of his language, often found in his explicitly Marxist writings, is significant in itself: 'We need a theatre which does not merely make possible the emotions, insights and impulses allowed by the relevant field of human relationships in which the actions occur, but one which utilises and produces thoughts and feelings which themselves play a part in altering the field'.[34]

Here, Brecht is clearly thinking of the 'alienation' effect in terms of his propagandist plays of the early thirties. Towards the end of the same essay, however, he adopts a different standpoint, more in harmony with the spirit of much of his later work. In words that recall his own partly sympathetic treatment of the capitalist Puntila he writes: 'Society can derive enjoyment even from the antisocial, while it displays vitality and greatness . . . Even a river that has catastrophically broken loose can freely be enjoyed by society in all its glory if society is able to master it: for then it belongs to society.'[35]

Here already there are signs of an aesthetic attitude – for all that the antsocial is to be mastered, its qualities are recognized. This tendency becomes even more apparent later on. It is not a question of portraying successes or failures, Brecht continues: all attempts at refashioning society (not merely Communist attempts, apparently), whether they are shown in literature to have failed or succeeded, give us 'a feeling of triumph and confidence and provide us with pleasure at the possibilities of change in all things. Galileo expresses this [in Brecht's play] when he says "It is my opinion that the world is a very noble and admirable place, in view of all the different changes and generations that constantly occur in it".'[36] The criterion here is not the good of society, nor is the ultimate aim the classless society: rather, in either contemplative or enthusiastic fashion, change is welcomed for its own sake, and the highest pleasure is the morally-unmoved witnessing of such change.

The nature of the change scarcely seems to matter here. Whereas in the propagandist plays Brecht had intended to alter the structure of society for the benefit of the underprivileged, he now welcomes the sheer dynamism of the flux of life. With this conception, the effect of 'alienation' is altered. It does not teach a lesson, or at least not a political one. If anything is to be derived from the theatre it is derivable by the individual rather than by society, and in terms of pleasure rather than profit. 'It [the theatre] should not even be expected to teach, at all events nothing more useful than how to conduct oneself pleasurably, whether in a physical or an intellectual sense.'[37] The role of the theatre is to be something 'entirely superfluous', and the purpose of living is to enjoy this superfluity above all else. Indeed, there is nothing comparable to the pleasure to be derived from artistic presentations. At the play, the worker can survey at a distance the kaleidoscopic changes of life, and the ideal of a purpose underlying these changes is apparently to be abandoned. 'Let him [the worker] in his theatre enjoy as an entertainment the terrible and never-ending labours which serve to sustain him, together with the terrors of his ceaseless transformation. Here let him produce himself in the easiest way, for the easiest form of existence is in art.'[38]

Clearly, if a spectator is enjoying the representation of terrors, even in an extended use of the word 'enjoy', he is by so much the less preparing to alter them, and by so much the more accepting the prospect of a continual change that has no ultimate purpose. In these last words of the *Organon* Brecht reverts to an attitude akin to that he had expressed through *Baal*: the all-accepting, amoral delight in the dreadful as well as in the more obviously pleasurable consequences of being alive.

Brecht is, however, not exactly anti- or un-Marxist here. A similar, in fact a rhapsodic enjoyment of the 'eternal cycle' of matter is equally to be found in the principal exponents of Marxist philosophy. 'We have the certainty', writes Engels, 'that matter remains eternally the same in all its transformations, that none of its attributes can ever be lost, and therefore, also, that with the same iron necessity with which it will again exterminate on the earth its highest creation, the thinking mind, it must somewhere else and at another time again engender it.'[39] This Heraclitan welcome to the changing world, with its strange parallel in the Nietzschean doctrine of Eternal Recurrence, is paradoxically as much a part of Marxism as its eschatological vision of a classless society. Brecht does no more here than pursue the paradoxes of his masters.

The later theory, then, while it still includes a political purpose, combines with it an aesthetic attitude which it makes no attempt to reconcile with the other. Of the two trends, moreover, the aesthetic one is given much the greater emphasis, so that it is not surprising to find, in many of the later plays, a merely ostensible Communist solution to the social problems set forth. Brecht's aesthetics reveal their weakest point, however, in their complete irrelevance to tragedy, their insistence that the tragedies of the past as presented by Shakespeare and Sophocles are now to be presented as avoidable. It is all very well to speak of catastrophes being enjoyed by society in all their glory, so long as they remain potential catastrophes under society's control. Yet human history is full of catastrophes, individual and national, which could not be controlled, and tragedy has relentlessly confronted these, grasping at the worst and enduring it without pessimism or resignation. For this form of drama Brecht has no place. In theory at least, his men and women are either the misguided sufferers of the past, from whom a lesson can be drawn, or the exultant revellers in the contradictions of the present moment. For the millions who even in recent years have seen final and inevitable disaster threaten, disaster which, when it came, could only be met in the spirit and in faith, Brecht has no word to offer.

EXILE AND ANTI-NAZISM

In 1933 the Nazi Party achieved a majority in the elections to the Reichstag, not an overwhelming one, but enough to enable them to proceed with their so-called 'bloodless revolution', establishing one-party and one-man rule by degrees during a period of some months. The deputies supporting Hitler in March 1933 still numbered only 288, out of a Reichstag of 647 members. Yet the Social Democrats trusted Hitler's promise never to go outside the constitution, the Trade Unions made no notable protest in May when they were 'gleichgeschaltet', 'switched parallel' or nationalised, and in July, to the astonishment even of Hitler, a Concordat was signed with the Holy See, which brought almost all Roman Catholics into acquiescence. By August 1934 Hitler was able to claim that over 90% of the electorate supported the action of the Cabinet in appointing him Führer and Chancellor of the Reich.

The motives which led to this support being given were multifarious. Some voters were terrorised by beatings and tortures, some sent to concentration camps, some genuinely believed in a strong hand at the helm, some were not interested in politics, some wanted a reversal of the indignities and disadvantages of the Versailles Treaty, some were anti-Jewish, some were socialists who were not opposed to 'national' socialism. The intricate web has been minutely traced[1] and lends itself to no easy generalisations.

For Brecht, without the advantage of hindsight, the explanation was simple. Nazism was the final stage of capitalism. The Nazi Party, with the support of financiers and press-magnates, had taken advantage of the world economic depression of 1929 to capture the imagination of millions of supporters. Indeed, they had been supported heavily almost from the founding of their Party by one of the richest millionaires in Germany[2] and as George Orwell said, the idea that Hitler was a dummy with

Thyssen pulling the strings was accepted on all sides: 'Blimps and Left Book Club members alike swallowed it whole, both of them having, so to speak, a vested interest in ignoring the real facts.'[3] The Nazis promised an organised self-supporting society, untroubled by strikes, thoroughly German, and no longer subject to the ups and downs that had oppressed the nation since 1918, and they were without scruple in achieving their ends. To oppose them by the means of the parliamentary democracy available in the Weimar Republic was pointless, when that democracy, as it seemed to Marxists, was itself an instrument of capitalism. The only proper course was to kill the two, Nazism and capitalism, with one stone, and to establish a Communist regime in their place. Marxists were, it is true, over-ready to despair of parliamentary democracy, which had existed for barely ten years in all German history (and despaired of it even sooner, after its revival in 1949).

The urgency of the situation goes some way to explaining why the plays written between 1929 and 1933 were none of them explicitly anti-Nazi, but on the whole directed against dissentients from the Communist Party line, or against capitalism in general. But the mere fact that he was on the Left was enough to make Brecht an obvious target, and in 1933 he was forced to flee from Germany, like almost every other writer and artist of any reputation, his books already under a ban. He came nearer to worse tragedy when his two-year old daughter Barbara ran the risk of being held as a hostage within the country and was saved only by the intervention of an English welfare worker – an event which may be echoed in the slightly similar story incorporated in his later play, *The Caucasian Chalk Circle*. But although his family remained intact, his wife and both their children being restored to him, Brecht did not take the obvious step of going to Russia. Instead, after a period of moving through Austria, Switzerland, and France, he settled in Denmark, where he remained, apart from visits to Moscow, Paris and New York, made mainly in order to see performances of his plays or on similar business, from the late spring of 1933 till the summer of 1939. He did not make any break with Communism, and there could have been a variety of reasons why he chose to remain outside the central places of the movement. In fact, although he became co-editor of *Das Wort*, the refugee periodical published in Moscow, he made only one visit to the Russian capital, in 1935, and – if the report is true – explained his failure to stay there with the smiling excuse, 'I could not get enough sugar for my tea and coffee.' The sugar may have referred to sweetness of various kinds: in December 1934 large-scale political executions had been carried out. At all events, Brecht found no permanent attraction in Russia, and his later movements give rise to curious speculation. On the eve of war, Brecht left Denmark for Stockholm, and later, in 1940, for Finland. From there, almost on the Russian frontier, he applied for and received a United States visa, which he used on 21 July 1940 to enter the U.S.A. through California. He had, in fact, for what reasons can only be guessed, elected to travel across the entire length of the Soviet Union only to emerge at the other end at Vladivostok and sail to safety across the Pacific. Small wonder, then, if it has been supposed that his allegiance to Communism was less than whole-hearted. It may not have been so. Brecht may have felt he had better work to do through his contacts in non-Communist countries. More likely, with the knowledge of how writers like Mayakovsky, Bulgakov and Olesha had been stifled, he kept away from Stalin, for by this time political persecution of artists had struck close to himself: in 1936 Ernst Ottwald, who had collaborated with him on the film *Kuhle Wampe*, had been imprisoned in the U.S.S.R., where he had taken refuge from the Nazis.[4] Whatever the case, Brecht's journeyings in exile do not suggest the kind of man who was as ready to submit to Party discipline as his propagandist works of the early thirties would lead one to suppose.

There are very few German plays of the Nazi period with anti-Nazi themes, which is not surprising, seeing that no German dramatist in exile could expect to see his plays performed except to tiny audiences, and that, as some must have felt, writing political plays was not necessarily the best form of opposition to Hitler. Apart from Brecht's plays, only Ferdinand Bruckner's *Die Rassen* (The Races) and Friedrich Wolf's *Professor Mamlock* have remained memorable. What Brecht wrote, moreover, was of varying quality. Some of it is trivial, the fruit perhaps of a desperate will to go on writing even though the chances of performances, or even of a career as a dramatist at all, must have seemed infinitely remote. Some shows the genuine humane concern Brecht felt for the Germans who had been obliged to go on facing the music. None of the specifically anti-Nazi plays represents his best work. Yet since they bulk largest in the whole of the anti-Nazi theatre of the period,[5] they are worth attention. *Round Heads and Pointed Heads*, written 1932–4, is the least satisfying. Like *St Joan of the Stockyards*, it uses a rough-and-ready blank verse, of a quasi-Shakespearean kind, in order to mock the pretensions of the speakers. But there is more than imitation of Shakespearean forms. On this occasion Brecht took over the main outline of a Shakespeare play, and adapted it to a political purpose, his principal idea being, perhaps, to show that what for Shakespeare was a moral problem was in Brecht's day and age an economic one.

In *Measure for Measure* the Duke of Vienna relinquishes power temporarily to Angelo, who condemns to death for lechery the young Claudio. Angelo agrees to relent, however, if Isabella, Claudio's sister, yields to his lust. This she agrees to do, but sends a substitute, Mariana. Meanwhile a common criminal is executed instead of Claudio. In the denouement the Duke returns, Angelo is exposed, and compelled to marry Mariana, while Isabella marries the Duke and Claudio goes free.

In *Round Heads and Pointed Heads* the Duke is replaced by a Viceroy, who relinquishes power to Angelo Iberin, because, as he understands, Iberin will distract attention from the injustice in the division of property between rich and poor by dividing the people, irrationally, into those who have pointed heads and those who have round heads. During Iberin's regime de Guzman, a rich Pointedhead, is accused – much as Claudio is in Shakespeare's play – of illicit sexual relations with a young (and poor) Roundhead woman. To free him, his sister Isabella, a nun, offers to lie with Angelo, but in fact sends the same young Roundhead woman in her place, just as in Shakespeare. The father of the Roundhead girl, a poor man, consents to risk execution in de Guzman's place, in the hope of being relieved of the need to pay a year's rent. As it turns out, there is no execution, either of Roundhead or Pointedhead. In the denouement the Viceroy returns, and pardons the still wealthy Guzman. It is no longer necessary to keep up the pretence that the real injustices derive from the difference between Pointedheads and Roundheads, since the insurrectionists in a distant province who maintained otherwise – the followers of the Sickle, who held that economic differentiation was the sole source of injustice – have been defeated. The play ends as all are pardoned except the followers of the Sickle, who sing their revolutionary song just before they are due to be hanged.

The allegory is clear enough: Hitler is being allowed (at the time of writing of the play) by the capitalists and their allies in government to distract the attention of the German people from economic injustices by fomenting anti-Semitism. Once the Communists have been defeated, this decoying move can be abandoned, and the capitalists can return to their normal methods of exploiting the poor for the benefit of the rich.

As is already apparent, the political thinking is crude, and the play gains nothing from using an indirect, allegorical mode of reference to what was going on in Germany. The allusions to Shakespeare would have been obscure to many in the audiences, and serve merely to suggest an irreverence which would be the better for being grounded on something more than iconoclasm. The episodes dealing with the poor, especially their willingness to risk execution and, in the case of the young woman, to prostitute themselves, assume that only economic motives count, and – as in *St Joan of the Stockyards* – that given enough economic pressure a poor man will do anything. The anti-religious note is equally crude, and the nuns are as much at the mercy of purely monetary considerations as anyone else.

It is difficult to think what Martin Esslin could have meant by 'the many fine passages' in this play.[6] None are quoted, and it is easier to agree with him when he says that 'the Marxist explanation of Hitler's racial policies fails so lamentably that the whole play is invalidated'.[7] As he goes on to observe, if this explanation had been correct, the rich Jews would have been spared by Hitler, and in the end would have emerged as having been on his side all the time. The narrowness of Brecht's outlook in his work, his complete lack of interest in any but economic motivations, are surprising after the profusion of interests that *Baal* seemed to promise.

It is again difficult to see what Esslin means, however, when he speaks of the Marxist interpretation vitiating Brecht's *Fear and Misery of the Third Reich* (written 1935–8).[8] Here is a play which offers, by contrast, almost nothing by way of interpretation. It is entirely different from any other of Brecht's plays:

completely realistic, as far as the individual scenes are concerned (Brecht required them to be punctuated, however, with songs sung by soldiers on a Panzer), almost without alienation devices or special Brechtian effects. When it came to dramatising actual events reported to him by friends or read about in newspapers, Brecht restricted himself to a straightforward dialogue, with an occasional ironic twist. There are twenty-four scenes in all, most of them very short, all recounting some anecdotal point about Hitler's Germany. The form might almost as well have been the short story rather than the drama, but the contents are telling enough. One scene alone is typical of Brecht: a Brownshirt invites a worker to *pretend* that he is complaining against the state, and the worker responds by saying what he would have said 'if he had really meant it', so that the whole scene becomes 'alienated' – as in *Squire Puntila* when Matti persuades Eva to pretend to be a working-class wife, the better to show what such a woman's life is really like. For the rest, Brecht stays conventional. In the main, he avoids the physical horror, though there is a scene of a whipping, and another in which drunken S.S. men shoot at random in a street at night. More in keeping with the experience of most Germans at that time is the numbing feeling, accurately brought out by Brecht, of the futility of action, the sense that nobody is to be trusted, and that the slightest resistance would lead to unbearable punishment. There is the man who hears his neighbour being arrested downstairs, and who complains to his wife that 'they' ought not to have torn the man's jacket: he cannot allow himself to complain to any greater extent. There is the lawyer who realises, much against his will, that he will not be allowed to defend in court a client who was attacked by Stormtroopers, though the outward trappings of justice survive; the married couple who fear exposure by their own child, and can scarcely credit that he has only left the house to buy himself chocolate; the family that prefers not to open the coffin in which their father's body is sent home, for fear that their suspicions about the real cause of his death may become known, and bring down retribution on yet another member. There is a scene in which a Jewish wife decides to go abroad in order not to hamper her Aryan husband's career, her husband helping her to pack because 'it's only for a few weeks' – the self-deception of the husband, and his pressing need to deceive himself, are finely brought out. Perhaps most dramatically effective is the scene in a training hospital, where the surgeon going on his rounds inculcates in his students the prime need to ask questions of patients. The next patient is a worker sent back from a concentration camp, beaten to pulp. No question is asked. As the surgeon passes on, a student, who can see well enough what has happened, as they all can, remarks that this patient has an occupational disease.

The tone is clear, laconic, unemotional; the whole work has a ring of truth. It tends to credit only working-class characters with a will to resist, and though not anti-religious, it mocks at the one priest who appears, and allows nothing of the opposition of the German churches to be shown. It perhaps suggests too much that Germans were in the main intimidated by a few things – nothing is said of the active and enthusiastic support Hitler received from people who were never near to being terrorised, and so, taken as a picture of German conditions as a whole, the play is incomplete. Yet as a straightforward denunciation it has power, and when Brecht was the sole dramatist of his day, of any nation, to give any detailed picture of German conditions, it is ungenerous to ask for more. *Fear and Misery* is less remarkable as a play than as a documentary history. As the latter it still has a gruesome fascination, and deserves to be far more widely known.

The Resistible Rise of Arturo Ui was completed in 1941 in Finland, as Brecht noted at the same time as he noted the name of his collaborator, M. Steffin. It was never performed or published in Brecht's lifetime, and he never made final corrections for publication. Yet it is without any doubt the most striking and effective of his explicitly anti-Nazi plays, and has attracted several notable performances in the title-role, from, amongst others, Ekkehard Schall, Leo Rossiter, and Nicol Williamson. The deflating of Hitler's pretensions to greatness – and of any tendency in Germany to go on speaking of him as a great man – by linking his career in detailed parallels with the life of a Chicago gangster was a genial idea. Its biggest success is in the scene where the murder by Hitler of Ernst Röhm and his associates is parodied by a mass-slaughter in a garage in front of the headlights of a Ford saloon, an incident that seems to come straight out of a life of Al Capone. Equally telling in an opposite spirit is the scene, based also on Hitler's life, in which Ui receives instruction from a Shakespearean actor on how to make political speeches. The passage is a gift to actors; the ad-libbing of gestures that can be introduced into it is a certain draw at the box-office, and performances have rivalled Chaplin's *Great Dictator*.

Brecht has a more serious intention than Chaplin's, which for the main part was to ridicule Hitler by placing him in absurd situations, making a clown of him. Brecht also uses the weapons of the cartoonist and lampooner, but, as he wrote in a preface when he was considering publication, his play is 'an attempt to explain the rise of Hitler to the capitalist world by placing him in a milieu familiar to it'. This slightly cryptic remark is given further explanation in the Epilogue to the play itself, the final lines of which read:

> So was hätt einmal fast die Welt regiert!
> Die Völker wurden seiner Herr, jedoch
> Daß keiner uns zu früh da triumphiert –
> Der Schoß ist fruchtbar noch, aus dem
> das kroch.[9]

> And that's what might have nearly ruled the world!
> The nations mastered it, but let nobody
> crow too quickly about that –
> The womb it crawled from is fruitful still.

The womb referred to was interpreted in the BBC television production of 1973, as Brecht surely intended, by showing shots of Stock Exchanges, headlines about financial gains and losses, piles of notes and money: in short, Hitler was meant to be understood, as in *Round Heads and Pointed Heads*, to be the product of capitalism. He was, Brecht argued[10] in his Notes to the play, even the tool of capitalism. Hitler was not a great man; though no fool either, he had no need of outstanding qualities: 'The ruling classes in the modern State use in their enterprises as a rule pretty mediocre people. . . They have political matters looked after by people who are often considerably more stupid than they are themselves. Hitler could put Brüning out of the main stream, just as Brüning could Stresemann . . .'[11]

With this intention of belittling the Führer, and all the rest who played an important part, Brecht gave allusive names and devised the scenes so as to refer directly to historical events, accounts of which were to be projected on to a backcloth at the end of each episode. British productions which commonly omit these references give no idea of the exactness of reference Brecht intended.

'Ui' has no special meaning in German, though the sound is used to imply, comically, pain or regret. Dogsborough, however, the name of the upright innkeeper who is inveigled into taking a dishonest part in assisting Ui, is a reference to President Hindenburg. The opening scenes in which Dogsborough accepts a bribe, and so becomes Ui's most valuable supporter, are meant to recall the fact that Hindenburg was involved in the *Osthilfe* scandal of the 1920s, whereby subsidies to landowners in the Eastern provinces were diverted from their proper use, and that he was also involved in tax evasion on the presidential estate at Neudeck. Dogsborough supports Ui for fear of exposure; Hindenburg suddenly agreed to accept Hitler as Chancellor, after long having categorically refused to do so, shortly after his son had met Hitler and, it is thought, been threatened with blackmail over these very issues.[12]

The burning down of a greengrocer's shop, as a sign to other greengrocers that Ui intends to force them to accept his 'protection', is a reference to the Reichstag fire of February 1933, and the farcical trial which follows it recalls the trial of van der Lubbe, who was found guilty, though few people believed that he was anything but a scapegoat. (Until 1964 it was generally supposed that, as Brecht suggested, the fire was deliberately started by the Nazis themselves, but although they made good use of it for their own propaganda, it now appears that van der Lubbe could after all have been the culprit.)[13]

The incidents involving Ernesto Roma, who tries to turn Ui against Givola (Goebbels) and Giri (Goering), ending with his murder by Ui in the garage, parody the conflict between Hitler and the leader of the S.A., or Brownshirts, his close friend Ernst Röhm, who was shot dead at Hitler's order on 30 June 1934.[14]

Finally, the series of scenes at the end of the play, in which Ui takes over the 'protection' of the neighbouring town of Cicero, parallel the invasion of and 'Anschluss' with Austria. Ignatius Dullfeet is meant to suggest Engelbert Dollfuss, the Austrian Chancellor, assassinated by Austrian Nazis on 25 July 1934 as part of a conspiracy, with Hitler's connivance, to overthrow the

Austrian government[15], while 'Ignatius' recalls that Dollfuss's predecessor was Ignaz Seipel. Ui's flirtation with Betty Dullfeet, the widow, and his eventual marriage with her, is meant to be understood as Hitler's relation with Austria, personified.

None of the events refer to the exploits of Al Capone, but the transposition of German events to American soil, in a lower key, seems perfectly convincing. On the other hand, in so far as Brecht meant to explain Hitler, rather than lampoon him, the play is not enlightening. There is good reason to believe that Hindenburg did change his attitude towards Hitler for fear of exposure, but other factors were also at work, influencing him: his fear of the Left, the belief that the Right, to avoid chaos, could not but ally itself with Hitler, repugnant as he was, and so on.[16] Brecht's psychological picture is much simpler. More important, his play is obliged to suggest that Ui/Hitler owed his power to the fear of ordinary people, inspired by his threats of violence. There is nothing to indicate how millions of Germans, for all the hesitations they may have had, actively supported Hitler because he served their interests, and turned a blind eye to the treatment he meted out to his opponents: inevitably, given the small scale of Ui's operations, the large political issues have to be skimped. As Peter Demetz says, agreeing with Willy Haas 'by ignoring the compulsive, if not the demonic aspect of National Socialism [the play] reduces Hitler's way to catastrophe to an obsolete "Chicago gangster spectacle".'[17]

It was in fact pointed out to Brecht in 1953–4 by Lothar Kusche, that when *Arturo Ui* made clear reference to quite definite phases in German history, it omitted all references to 'the *Volk*', and Kusche might have gone on to point out that though the title speaks of a 'resistible rise', no possibility of resistance is ever alluded to. Ui is in control from start to finish: the people have no power.

Since the whole question of the seriousness of Brecht's contribution to the anti-Nazi cause is at issue, his reply to Kusche is worth giving at some length:

Ui [Brecht wrote] is a parable play, written in the intention of destroying the usual, dangerous respect for the great killers. The circle is deliberately made a small one: it is limited to the level of the State, industrial magnates, Junkers, and petty-bourgeois. That is sufficient for the purpose intended. The play seeks to give no general outline of the historical position of the thirties. The proletariat is missing, and cannot be taken account of to any greater degree, and would distract attention from the delicate posing of the problem. (How could one refer more to the proletariat and not to unemployment; how refer to that, and not to the type of work available, and to the parties, and to their collapse? One would involve the other, and what would emerge would be a gigantic work, which would not fulfill the aim desired.)[18]

This is an avowal that the play cannot, of its very nature, give that insight into the capitalistic origins of Nazism which Brecht implied in his intended foreword and in the final lines of the Epilogue. On looking closer, one sees too that the play also does not illustrate his thesis that Hitler is the mediocre tool of the capitalists. Whereas Angelo Iberin, the symbol of Nazism in *Round Heads*, is merely allowed to exercise power during the temporary absence of the 'capitalist' Viceroy, no such conditions prevail in *Ui*. The gangster is in command from the start; his methods of intimidation are all he has at his disposal, and no appraisal of any political, economic or social kind is offered. Ui wins because Dogsborough and several like him are dishonest, and because in general people are afraid of gangster methods. There is no suggestion that Ui is a puppet of superior forces, and Brecht is misleading when he suggests that he explains Hitler as a phenomenon due to capitalist self-protection. This play does nothing to illustrate his point.

The play succeeds as lampoon and caricature, but fails in any analytical account. It is no more successful in its more artistic aims.

Throughout, all characters speak a rough-and-ready blank verse, as they do in Brecht's *St Joan* – a verse which never aspires to poetry, and which makes very little use of the prosaic advantages of the form. It is simply ordinary speech slightly adapted so as to fit a line of five beats, often requiring an unnatural reading to make the beats appear to have sufficient regularity. Like Shaw's blank verse, it has no life of its own, and exists purely by virtue of its parody. But parody was Brecht's intention, for reasons which he explained.

This play, in order that the events should acquire the significance which they unfortunately deserve, must be presented in the grand style, preferably with clear allusions to the Elizabethan historical plays, that is, with curtains and rostra.[19]

And we come closer to his intentions with the remark in the intended foreword: 'the verse-speech makes the heroism of the figures measurable'.

These are still somewhat cryptic remarks, but they surely mean that the inflated pretensions of Ui/Hitler could best be cut down to size by comparing them with the Elizabethans, especially Shakespeare's heroes, for whom Brecht showed nothing but contempt at any time:

The great individuals of Shakespeare, bearing the star of their destiny in their bosom, run amok irresistibly, with futile and mortal results; they bring themselves to grief, it is life, not death, that becomes obscene when they collapse, the catastrophe is not criticisable. Human sacrifices all the way! Barbarous entertainments! We know that the barbarians have what they call art. Let ours be different![20]

Though this may overstate Brecht's case, in his revulsion from 'Aristotelian' tragedy, it is not an unfair instance of his anti-Shakespearean tenor. One often has the impression that all Shakespearean central characters alike are equally obnoxious to him, and that their speaking of blank verse is a mark of their pretentiousness rather than a means, for Shakespeare, of delineating character or creating poetry.

Such an attitude would explain why in *Arturo Ui* Brecht parodies the scene in *Richard III*, where Richard woos the widow of a man he has just murdered. There is not much gain from the parallel, and Betty Dullfeet does not in fact yield as Richard's Anne does: Brecht is not interested in the motivation for such a sudden change, and does not make Betty yield to flattery. He is simply concerned to link Ui with Richard III, which is, true enough, no compliment. The parallel, in another scene, with Goethe's *Faust*, is more cryptic. When Ui walks on and off the stage wooing Betty, while behind them come Dullfeet and Givola, both pairs repeatedly appearing and disappearing, a German audience will certainly think of the similar scene where Faust and Gretchen are followed in the same way by Mephistopheles and Frau Marthe. But there is no more purpose here than to link Ui with the devil. On the other hand, when Betty alludes to Gretchen's very well-known line to Faust in the same play:

Herr Ui, wie halten Sie's mit der Religion?
Mr Ui, what do you feel about religion?

she may well raise a laugh at the religious objections of Austrian reactionaries to Hitler.

Shakespearean verse and situation are used again in the scene where Ui recalls the murder of Roma in lines reminiscent of Richard's night before Bosworth Field:

UI. (*im Schlaf*) Weg, blutige Schatten! Habt Erbarmen! Weg!
UI. (*in his sleep*) Away, bloody shadows! Have mercy! Away!

The inflated language has no obvious purpose. Shakespeare's Richard in fact debates with himself, when the ghosts appear, whether he can find any excuse for the murders he has committed. A moral issue is at stake. Ui merely mouths a Shakespearean line, while the ghost of Roma predicts that other men will betray Ui as he has betrayed Roma: the verse has no life in it, no sense that Roma is doing more than enunciate an opinion. Worse, it sounds as false on Roma's lips as it does on those of the rest of the gangsters, so that what should have been a firm denunciation sounds merely ironical, unintended:

> Nun stehe ich in zugiger Ewigkeit
> Und du gehst mit den großen Herrn zu Tisch
> Verrat bracht dich hinauf, so wird Verrat
> Dich auch hinunterbringen. Wie du mich verrietst
> Den Freund und Leutnant, so verrätst du alle.
> Und so, Arturo, werden alle dich
> Verraten noch. Die grüne Erde deckt
> Ernesto Roma, deine Untreu nicht.
> Die schaukelt über Gräbern dich im Wind
> Gut sichtbar allen, selbst den Totengräbern.
> Der Tag wird kommen, wo sich alle, die
> Du niederschlugst, aufrichten, aufstehn alle
> Die du noch niederschlagen wirst, Arturo
> Und gegen dich antreten, eine Welt
> Blutend, doch haßvoll, daß du stehst und dich
> Nach Hilf umschaust. Denn wiss': so stand ich auch.
> Dann droh und bettel, fluch und versprich!
> Es wird dich keiner hören! Keiner hörte mich.

Now I stand in draughty eternity, and you go to dine with the great gentlemen. Treachery brought you high, and treachery will bring you low. As you betrayed me, your friend and lieutenant, so you will betray all. And so, Arturo, all will betray you. The green earth covers Ernesto Roma, but not your disloyalty. That floats in the wind across the graves, well visible to all, even to the gravediggers. The day will come, when all whom you struck down will rise again, all stand again whom you have yet to strike down, Arturo, and march against you, a bleeding world, yet full of hate, so that you will stand and look around for help. For know: thus did I stand too. Then threaten and plead, curse and make promises – no-one will hear you. Nobody heard me.

Like the rest of the blank verse in the play, this is flaccid, repetitive, over-explanatory, and without real emotion. Roma is purely rhetorical when he says that no-one heard *him;* he was shot down while shaking Ui's hand, before he could do so much as protest. The long build-up about Ui's faithlessness fluttering over the graves, visible even to the gravediggers (they are presumably mentioned as being typically Shakespearean), the repetition of the idea that the dead will raise themselves *and* stand, and not only those already killed, but those yet to be killed, is typical of the ways in which Brecht continually pads out lines to make a resoundingly hollow effect. Yet if the result is usually to make the gangsters less credible than ordinary speech might have done, in this particular case it is all the less successful, since Roma might have been allowed to make a more effective protest. The monotony and unsubtlety of Brecht's approach allows all the gangsters to be tarred with the same undiscriminating brush, and Shakespeare is brought in to add to the simple sarcasm.

The play seems inevitably incomplete, since it ends with the invasion of Austria in 1938, though the rodomontade with which Ui announces his future plans can allow an ending with a proper sense of towering menace. In the London production in which Leo Rossiter played, Ui did in fact speak at the end from a tower of scaffolding, giving the appearance of a climax if only in height. Very probably Brecht would have liked to take it further, showing Ui's defeat in further parallel with King Richard's, though the fact then becomes apparent, once the war comes into consideration, that Ui is altogether on a lower scale of horror than Hitler himself was: as Frederic Ewen says, postwar audiences could only find the analogy with gangsterism trivial.[21] Brecht did in fact complete the play, as it stands, on 29 April, barely two months before the Nazi attack on the

U.S.S.R. He may have felt that to take the story any further would be pointless, especially since the main aim of the play was to arouse opposition to Hitler. As events have turned out, it still serves an invaluable purpose in being one of the very few German works of the period to show such strong opposition, and in still being capable, through the sheer strength of its ridicule, of dealing a blow at any hopes of a revival of Hitler's claim to glory.

The remaining anti-Nazi plays are less striking. *The Visions of Simone Machard,* a play about a French girl who dreams of being Joan of Arc, and who does succeed in resisting the German invasion of 1940, is so naive and sentimental that one wonders how much of it was written by Brecht, of whose familiar techniques and devices it shows nothing, and how much by his collaborator, the best-selling novelist Lion Feuchtwanger, who, over the years, disagreed with him strongly more than once. The ending, in which Simone, instead of being burned at the stake, is handed over to the mercies of brutal nuns at a Catholic school, is, it is true, in the vein of several anti-religious pieces by Brecht.

The *Antigone,* written in 1948, is no more impressive than *Simone Machard* as an anti-Nazi work, which is what Brecht made of Sophocles' tragedy. As so often happened, the earlier work has its subtlety removed by Brecht's single-minded rewriting. In the Greek play, there is a situation of great complexity. Antigone defies the order of King Creon that all corpses of the recent besiegers of Thebes are to be left unburied, and symbolically buries the body of her brother, Polyneices. Since Creon believes it necessary for the welfare of the State that its enemies should be dishonoured, he condemns Antigone to death for her action. Only when the seer Tiresias tells him that his condemnation has displeased the gods does Creon rescind his command for execution, but it is too late. Antigone has already killed herself; her lover Haemon, Creon's son, kills himself before the King's eyes, and his wife also takes her own life. All three of the central characters are tragically torn between conflicting duties or loyalties, and all three have at least some appearance of right on their side. Brecht, however, makes Antigone's situation resemble that of a young woman living under the Nazi tyranny, so that Creon, equated with Hitler, at once forfeits sympathy. When Tiresias denounces Creon it is because of his disregard for the economic causes that have led to the war between Creon and Antigone's brothers; he calls Creon not to repentance but to a rational understanding of the connection between cruelty and determined warfare, and when Creon goes to rescind his order it is in the hope of placating his subjects, and of enticing Haemon to lead the armies on his behalf. The motives are all purely selfish and economic, and the personal issues explored by Sophocles are of no account. The real difficulty in finding profit from the play lies in the language. The text is supposed to be based on the translation by the poet Hölderlin, but in fact bears little relationship to it. Since the play has been altered so much, the acknowledgement could scarcely mean more than that Brecht had read the Hölderlin version before rewriting, but in addition the language of Brecht's play is unwieldy, pretentious, and even bombastic, as it never is in any of his other plays. It may be significant that he did not take it up into any of the collected editions of his works published during his lifetime, though works written several years later than *Antigone* were included.

Schweyk in the Second World War, however, is an amusing comedy of passive resistance through seemingly passive compliance, of a quite different order. The name in the title comes from the novel by Jaroslav Hašek about the Czech soldier fighting in the Austrian Army in the First World War, published 1921–3, and already dramatised in 1928 by Max Brod and Hans Reimann. In the original *Adventures of the Good Soldier Schweyk*, the hero is a dog-dealer conscripted into the Army who meets every act of dictatorial bureaucracy with disarming naivety and invincible stupidity. At every opportunity he declares his unswerving loyalty, carries out every order to the letter, and demonstrates as he does so the idiocy of the issuer of the orders. The book is not so much a novel as a collection of anecdotes in racy Prague dialect, but it raised Schweyk to the level of a national symbol, and today every souvenir shop in Prague has stuffed dolls for sale, with Schweyk's rosy cheeks and pig's eyes, and wearing Schweyk's field-grey uniform.

For an oppressed people there is often no other means of resistance but mock conformity. Schweyk also had the advantage, for Brecht, of demonstrating the kind of attitude that he called dialectic. It is related of Brecht himself that he adopted Schweyk tactics even as a schoolboy, when he increased the number of red ink corrections on his exercise-book and then complained to the master that he had been unfairly marked, as a result of which his mark was increased, since he had not been guilty of so many mistakes as appeared. Similarly, in his play *The Horatians and the Curiatians,* Brecht tried to convey a basic point about dialectics by stressing the scene in which one of the Horatian brothers, confronted by three opponents, appears to show cowardice, and runs away. By going to extremes, however – a tactic which Brecht used all his life – Horatius is able to entice the enemy, who run at three different speeds, into challenging him separately: faced each time by a single opponent, he is able to score a victory where the three together would have defeated him. Galileo and Azdak in Brecht's later plays have similar ideas of adaptation to circumstance, and the chamaeleon in Brecht was always prone to try them out. Schweyk proved useful material for this, and the play, really a string of dramatised anecdotes, interspersed with songs, is certain to arouse a good deal of sympathy. It is remarkable, too, for presenting Gestapo agents and S.S. men with good-humoured ridicule rather than fanatical opposition, and the tone of the play generally is light and genial, especially in the interspersed 'scenes in higher regions', where Hitler and his associates appear as it were behind the scenes. The play also contains one of Brecht's best anti-Nazi poems, 'Und was bekam des Soldaten Weib. . .' ('And what did the soldier's wife get. . .')

Brecht does not develop the 'dialectical' argument, he does not suggest that Schweyk's comic acquiescence is anything more than a *modus vivendi* by which Schweyk is able to keep up his self-respect. The lesson of the didactic play *The Horatians,* for instance, would not apply here. The final scene does, however, provide a 'historic encounter' between Schweyk and Hitler, in which a giant Hitler is lost in a snowstorm and asks his way of Schweyk, who is marching to Stalingrad. The play ends as Hitler frenziedly marches toward one cardinal point after another, only to be brought up short by blasts from Schweyk's dog-whistle: his movements grow more and more desperate until he bursts into a wild dance, and the curtain falls. There is thus some political meaning here, and when Hitler claims to have been defeated by the 'forces of Nature', Schweyk's polite reply, 'Yes, so I hear, Winter and the Bolsheviks', has the effect of indirect statement which Brecht looked for in his later plays, and particularly in this one. But *Schweyk* does not strive to make that point; it remains for nearly the whole time a series of underplayed witticisms, and Brecht is really more concerned with these than with establishing the fatalistic mood with which the play concludes. For Brecht as a Marxist there was some reason in comparing the 'Bolsheviks' with a force of Nature: world-history, he must have believed, was moving in the direction of a classless society. But the refrain of the song, sung by *all* the performers – including presumably Hitler and his generals – after they have removed their masks and so established their common humanity, is strangely unassertive:

Das Lied von der Moldau

Am Grunde der Moldau wandern die Steine.
Es liegen drei Kaiser begraben in Prag.
Das Große bleibt groß nicht und Klein nicht das Kleine.
Die Nacht hat zwölf Stunden, dann kommt schon der Tag.

The Song of the Moldau

On the bed of the Moldau the stones are rolling.
There lie three Emperors buried in Prague.
The great does not stay great, nor the small stay small.
The night has twelve hours, then comes the day.

The defeat of the Nazi armies tends to look, in this atmosphere, like a mere turn of Fortune's wheel, and indeed, reflecting on the plays in which Brecht treated of the Nazis, it is noticeable how seldom he ever makes a reference to determined opposition to them. Arturo Ui seems just as much an inevitability (despite the title) as Hitler does: the criticism by Kusche that 'the people' are not represented in it is more central to the criticism that has to be made of Brecht's work as a whole than would appear from taking *Ui* on its own. Even in *Round Heads*, the defeat of the rising symbolising the Communist opposition to Hitler is mentioned merely as a reason for the return of the Viceroy and the re-establishment of capitalism: the Communists form no part of the action, and are not heard of, except incidentally in the final scene. In *Fear and Misery* there is no portrayal of Communist or any other resistance groups. Only in *Simone Machard* is anyone shown actively combating the Nazis, and Simone's action, in blowing up a petrol station, is not warlike in the full sense of the word. In short, *Schweyk* makes the best use of an acquiescing mood that was deeprooted in Brecht; it turns the fatalism into an amusing entertainment. Schweyk entertains because he has a fundamental assurance of his own inviolability. But there is always a darker threat in the background: one is aware from moment to moment that Schweyk is saved from gruesome penalties by the skin of his teeth.

Whether *The Trial of Lucullus,* originally written as a radio-play, is more of a pacifist play than an anti-Nazi one is slightly doubtful: the two themes amount to almost the same thing in Brecht. The plot is simpler than any other he devised: the Roman general Lucullus is brought before a People's Court in the underworld, after death, and condemned to be cast into the void for his militaristic behaviour while on earth. No defence is possible: war is a monstrosity and he has made war.

The play took shape, however, in 1939, before the Soviet Union had become involved in war. When Brecht settled in the Soviet Zone after 1945, he had difficulty with the German Communist authorities, who saw in the play a condemnation of all war, whether made by the Nazis or by the Soviets – which indeed it was, as it stood. As a note in the published text drily adds: 'After the dress rehearsal arranged by the Ministry for People's Education in the Berlin State Opera House, and as a result of detailed discussions, two insertions were made.' Through the language of diplomatic protocol one senses some of the background – why, for instance, did the Ministry, rather than the producer, arrange for a dress rehearsal? The upshot was, at all events, that speeches were introduced showing that defensive wars were always permissible, and even laudable. With this, the play had nothing but platitude to offer. Brecht saved some face by printing the original text, with the additions separately (these forming, with the original text, the new version called *The Condemnation of Lucullus*) but the fundamental weakness of Brecht's position, which was that of Schweyk, was underlined. Neither of them had a trump-card. (Nor, for that matter, had John Arden when he protested vainly at the alterations made, without his consent, by the producer of his play *The Island of the Mighty.* Not only authors in Communist countries experience such interference.)

'THE LIFE OF GALILEO'

While propagandist and anti-Nazi works were among the first
fruits of Brecht's exile, he turned after a while to writing the
plays which did most to establish his reputation abroad, *The Life
of Galileo, Mother Courage, The Good Woman of Setzuan, Herr
Puntila and his Man Matti.* (*The Caucasian Chalk Circle,* belonging with these in style, was written later, from 1944 to 1945.)
These were works of a quite different kind. It is possible, though
not logically necessary, to read out of them the corollary that
only Communism can cure the ills they represent. Their general
sphere of interest and concern is not, however, directly political,
but rather one of general humanity. They are plays in which the
spectator is implicitly invited to consider the behaviour of
human beings, to understand, sometimes to sympathise, sometimes to be revolted, and always to ask himself how he might
have acted in similar circumstances. There are no incomprehensible farragos or flippant shocks for shock's sake such as occur
from time to time in the plays of the twenties, nor are there any
choruses ramming home the 'message', as there are in the plays
of the early thirties. No one is counselled to do evil so that good
may come. Instead, there is an in many ways humane theatre,
tolerant, offering comprehension rather than persuasion; though
still rigging the balances at times, ranging in mood from tender
lyricism to agony of mind, from admiration for the most insignificant details of ordinary living to a buffooning zest in wine,
women, and song, from sharp compassion with the miseries of
the poor to a not wholly unsympathetic portrayal of the pleasures
of the rich. It is the 'human comedy' that Brecht seems most of
all bent on showing in these works, and the Communist implications are at most a side-issue. What brought about this second
change in him is once again hard to determine with the knowledge at present available. Whether the grief of exile tempered
passions and increased understanding, whether the suddenness

of Brecht's conversion to outspokenly Communist views in the early thirties brought an inevitable reaction, it is impossible to say. It is also relevant that after August 1935 the Popular Front policy of the Comintern no longer favoured such uncompromisingly revolutionary works as Brecht had been writing so long as Stalin opposed all compromise with non-Communists. Though he did not conform to the official demand for socialist realism (unless in *Señora Carrar*) the works written after 1935 would have been approved by the Comintern for the way in which they presented their political points in a form palatable to non-Marxists.

In *The Life of Galileo*, written in 1937–9, but with additions made in 1945–7, Brecht curiously foresaw, without realising it, much of his own situation as it was in the post-war period in the German Democratic Republic. This was a regime which brooked even less opposition than the Catholic Church had done in mediaeval and Renaissance times. In the Soviet intervention in 1953 Brecht had a duty which he clearly could not neglect while retaining a detached critical position, as Günter Grass shows in his play about Brecht and these events, *The Plebeians Rehearse the Uprising*.

Galileo is the story of a recantation before a tyrannical threat, such as Brecht was forced or perhaps freely consented to make himself in 1953. As the play was first written, it was, however, more in the spirit of *Schweyk*: Galileo was shown as an old man who outwitted the Inquisition, refusing to become a martyr by submitting to torture, but cunningly continuing the scientific work which the Church condemned, and smuggling his writings abroad under the noses of the authorities. Had this version stood, it would have been a clear-cut defence of a man who made the best of a bad job.

The complications arise from the later additions, made in Hollywood with the help and encouragement of Charles Laughton, and under the influence of the dropping of atomic bombs on Hiroshima and Nagasaki. Brecht was convinced by these events that scientists had sold themselves to the warmongers, and sought to include an indication of this in his play.

In the final version, therefore, Galileo recants not out of cunning, not in Schweykian adaptation, but from fear at the sight of the instruments of torture. After his recantation he still goes

on with his secret investigations, but ashamedly; he thinks himself unworthy to shake the hand of a fellow-scientist, feeling he
has betrayed the cause of science. His adaptation to circumstances proves his undoing at a crucial moment. It is true that
Brecht also arouses sympathy for Galileo, even in his failure, and
the parting words of Andrea remain in the mind when the play
is over: 'I can't believe your murderous [self-]analysis will be the
last word.' As Brecht himself said, 'in view of the situation one
can scarcely be bent on either simply praising Galileo or simply
condemning him'.[1]

The difficulty about such a dual attitude is that it tends to produce an equanimity of a kind that Brecht had always bitterly
attacked. He must have feared that his German audiences in
particular would gratefully accept the idea that Galileo was
somehow right in his wrongness or wrong in his rightness: the
tradition of 'synthesising' opposite points of view dies hard. To
achieve Brecht's purpose, the play must shock, and it is not hard
to think of productions that have not shocked: the play even
lends itself to banal performance.

A Galileo who appears on stage in the first scene, as Brecht
requires him to do, to expound the Ptolemaic and Copernican
systems for the benefit of a small boy, is likely to look a ped-
agogue. His lecture takes on a different flavour when it is de-
livered as it was by Charles Laughton, with Brecht's approval, by
a Galileo taking his morning wash, stripped to the waist. Galileo's
pleasure here is not merely intellectual but physical also, in fact
his appetite for knowledge has to be shown as a part of his
appetite for all things. 'His voluptuous way of moving about',
Brecht wrote of Laughton's performance, 'and the movements of
his hands in his trouser-pockets when he was planning new researches, were all but scandalous. Whenever Galileo was being
creative, Laughton revealed a contradictory mixture of aggres-
siveness and defenceless softness and sensitivity'.[2] Galileo's thirst
for knowledge is Gargantuan; he is a colossus, but a colossus
who, in the opening scene, drinks milk. For the sake of continuing his researches he is prepared to stay in Florence during a
plague, yet when a different death threatens, from the Inquisition, he yields without a fight. He will not tolerate a moment's
divagation from complete honesty in his search for truth, yet he
is unscrupulous in presenting to the senators of Venice as his

own invention a telescope recently invented in Holland. With all this, Brecht builds up a picture of a man who would not be so creative as he is if he were not also sensuous, cowardly, tenacious, and ascetic, in short a rationalist who lives by his instincts. And thus the final scene in which Galileo appears has a strange effect of its own which yet has something in common with the other later plays. Here, Galileo has just said good-bye to his former pupil Andrea, now a grown man; Andrea is persuaded that his master's 'new ethic' is the ethic of a new age in which adherence to rigid principle will be abandoned; Galileo remains on stage to make his supper off the goose which has been sent him. He wolfs it down with a greed which it takes a Laughton to show, thrusting down mouthful after mouthful in an insatiable desire for more life, more experience, more pleasure. We, meanwhile, his audience, feel at once the excitement and revulsion which so naked a display of human appetite brings, and the awareness that it is a concomitant of the new relativistic, all-embracing attitude represented by the Galileo of this play.

Galileo's dilemma has been seen, its causes traced, and sympathy for him aroused. But, as Brecht knew, and was to discover even more intensely later on in his own dilemma, the ability to adapt to circumstances has been far too prevalent in Central European countries for centuries past. The issue of Galileo's cowardice thus takes on a sharp contemporary edge: Galileo, the play affirms, stands at the threshold of a new age, as we seem to do ourselves since 1945. If he recants, the cause of science will suffer a setback, for science depends on a relentless honesty, and cannot be associated with hypocrisy. The issue of martyrdom thus becomes acute, and Harold Hobson is partly right when he says: 'The point of *Galileo* is that men do not today live in an age of reason simply because at a particular moment in the seventeenth century Galileo recanted before the Inquisition, instead of standing firm. As in one view humanity is saved by the grace and death of Christ, so, in Brecht's, by the life and disgrace of Galileo, humanity is damned. Galileo is nothing more nor less than Brecht's Antichrist. He is the God who failed us.'[3] This point, ironically expressed as it is by Mr Hobson, is certainly a justifiable conclusion from the emotional climax reached in Scene 13, for all that Brecht sought to stress individual rather than vicarious responsibility. In his habitually exaggerating fashion Brecht does imply at this instant that a whole epoch of European history turns on one man's failure.

The confrontation of these two attitudes makes good dramatic material, despite the fundamental intellectual weakness of the play, and it provides notable moments of conflict and tension. Theatrically, there can be no question. Given a stage, Brecht came alive, and his productions were a constant flux of new ideas for presentation. *Galileo* is notable particularly for such scenes as the one in which the astronomer converses with the cardinals, each of whom carries a mask. The implied contrast with Galileo, who 'has no mask', is vividly illustrated. Similarly the long action accompanying the dialogue, during which the Pope is covered with garment after garment until his slender humanity seems smothered in pomp, is a three-dimensional portrayal of Brecht's point. The ocular demonstration that a metal object can float, despite Aristotle's denial, and the habit Galileo has of letting a stone fall from his hand, to remind people that facts are facts and that stones do not fall upwards, are also devices of the theatre, designed to work visually. The ironical effect achieved at Galileo's recantation is also remarkable. The triumphant bell which peals out is a mockery of all Galileo's disciples stood for, and of all they thought he stood for, as they wait outside like St Peter waiting for Christ outside the court of Caiaphas. The fact that the bells seem to ring in answer to Galileo's daughter's prayers to God gives a bitter atheistic challenge to the scene.

Weakness appears in the earlier scenes, in which Galileo's astronomical opponents are presented in so foolish a guise as to destroy interest in the arguments. In addition, the physical aspects of Galileo's delight in research, emphasised in Brecht's comments, appear seldom in the given action of the play; they may be brought out by actors, but the text itself gives comparatively little evidence of them. Here it becomes clear how much Brecht depended on the full theatrical effect rather than on the printed word.

One further weakness, however, does not appear remediable. In his last long speech Galileo reviews the position of science as he now leaves it, crippled for centuries by his recantation. His own failure, he declares, has been that he sought to accumulate knowledge for the sake of knowledge, without regard to the primary aim of science, the easing of human existence. He has

pursued learning outside the framework of human needs, and
left a legacy of knowledge divorced from social reality. 'You
may in time discover everything there is to discover', he asserts,
'and your progress will be merely a progress away from humanity.
The gap between you and them may one day become so great
that your cries of triumph at some new achievement will be an-
swered by a universal cry of horror.'[4]

Brecht had in mind here the dropping of the atom bombs,
together with the new age of atomic energy which they heralded,
events which he regarded as the direct outcome of science
pursued in isolation from the needs of men. But this failure is
asserted in a long and intricate monologue which relies entirely
on verbal argument, amounting to a lecture from the stage last-
ing for several minutes. This is bad drama, by any criterion, and
it is made to look worse by the irrationality of Galileo's case.
He argues, against the historical evidence, that his single failure
will reduce scientists from his time on to a race of dwarfs, sub-
servient to the wishes of monarchs and governments. Considering that the first dwarf to appear after Galileo was Newton,
born in the year Galileo died, and that even Italian science,
which might have been thought most likely to suffer under Papal
obdurateness, went on to produce Malpighi, Volta, and Gal-
vani within the next hundred years, it is clear that one defection
cannot halt so widespread a human activity.[5]

Galileo also maintains that he was at fault in not working
for the alleviation of toil – an argument which has had a considerable effect in Western Germany, where many young students today decline to do any scientific research that does not
have practical benefits, or that might be used for warlike purposes. The point might seem too obvious to labour, that the
research which led to the making of iron led to ploughshares as
well as spearheads, just as the splitting of the atom produced
energy as well as bombs, and as Galileo's telescope could be
used by warships as well as merchantmen. The scientist in any
age merely provides the technical or theoretical knowledge
which the politician and others turn to their own uses. Research
directed purely at practical ends benefiting mankind is impossible. Galileo, however, ignores the obvious, and the audience
is allowed no retort, within the play.

Similarly, Galileo maintains that he neglected his chances,

since in his day 'astronomy reached the market-places'. He clearly means that if only the people had been allowed to take advantage of his discoveries, things would have been better. In fact, the use to which the people on the market-place put Galileo's discovery is absurd. Astronomy does reach the market-place, in scene 10, but only to produce the kind of anarchy to which Brecht had been prone to revert ever since *Baal*. The lesson drawn by the people is that, since the sun is no longer thought to rotate around the earth, nobody need in future rotate around anybody, nobody needs to offer service or allegiance, and each individual can live entirely selfishly:

> Two housewives stand in the market square
> Not knowing which way to turn;
> The fishwife pulls out a loaf right there
> And eats her fish alone!
> The mason digs his plot with care
> And takes the builder's stone
> And when the house is finished and fair
> Why! he moves in on his own![6]

One might equally well have thought – if astronomical theories had any influence at all on political attitudes, which they do only in the minds of 'cultural historians' who believe that every event is reflected in every other event – that Galileo's theory would have led to the autocratic state of 'Le Roi Soleil', rather than to egotistic anarchy. But there is no need to take issue with Brecht over this. The damaging effect, in the play, is that the way the 'people' are shown to behave does not bear out what looks like an important pronouncement by Galileo at a climactic moment.

Thus, as in much of Brecht's work, the theatricality is largely vitiated by the lack of any realistically thought-out content. There is entertainment, up to a point, in seeing the Pope laden down with garments, though the humble attitude of certain Popes, in seeing themselves as bearers of a glory that was not their own, is ignored. Similarly, the action has its vivid moments, and the scene on the market-place with its carnival atmosphere is one of the most vivid, but the relevance of this to the central theme is not merely obscure, it does not exist.

Yet *Galileo* remains one of the riper plays. It is riper in one sense, as many East Europeans know, in that it shows with great imagination the alternating self-condemnations and self-reassertions of all who live deviously under a stifling regime. In this respect it has something in common with *Schweyk*. But it is riper in other ways. The fairness with which Galileo's opponents, the cardinals, are treated (not the Aristotelian scientists, who are grotesquely caricatured), and the hearing which is given to the unanswered arguments of the little monk, who asks what simple Christian believers are to make of their harsh lives if they are deprived of the rich comforts of religion, are signs of the complexity which raises *Galileo* above the purely propagandist works. The effect of the play is incalculable – while it is possible to come out of the theatre feeling that an intense demand for heroic courage has been made, it is also possible to see what is gained by taking an adaptive course. The new unwillingness to impose or suggest single answers was the essential mark of the Brecht who emerged in the late 1930s.

'MOTHER COURAGE'

'About the genuinest bit of dramatic tragedy, English, since Shakespeare' was D. H. Lawrence's opinion of Synge's *Riders to the Sea* in 1911, and that opinion has established itself widely today. Yet only fourteen years later Lawrence was to say: 'To me, even Synge, whom I admire very much indeed, is a bit too rounded off and, as it were, put on the shelf to be looked at. . . . An author should be in among the crowd, kicking their shins or cheering on to some mischief or merriment. That rather cheap seat in the gods where one sits with fellows like Anatole France and benignly looks down on the foibles, follies and frenzies of so-called fellow-men, just annoys me.'[1] This is almost Brecht-like in its attitude to the drama, especially to tragedy.

Ideas of tragedy had changed during the First World War, perhaps because of the war. Synge was still writing in traditional terms. He took particular care, in *Riders to the Sea,* to make the brief story of the Aran Islanders of his own day resemble in atmosphere and telling power the tragedies of ancient Greece, and was the better able to do so because the Aran peasants still lived closer to the Greeks than most other people in Europe did. When Lawrence tried his hand at something similar in his play, *The Widowing of Mrs Holroyd,* he already had greater difficulties: Nottinghamshire miners' speech did not lend itself to poetry in prose as Irish did, and life in a mining village was less primitive, even though still exposed to elemental disasters. Sean O'Casey, who also imitated Synge, in the final scene at least of *Juno and the Paycock* (1924), used Dublin Irish, and was deprived of the confrontation with the elements through his city-setting: his play also is less tragic than Synge's.

It is argued that the War was on such a scale that individual tragedies could no longer be given such serious attention as before: against millions of deaths a single death acted on a stage seemed trivial or inflated. Certainly, apart from Eliot's

Murder in the Cathedral and O'Neill's *Mourning Becomes Electra,* there have been very few modern plays related to tragedy in its classical form. It is also said that the industrial proletariat affords no subjects for tragedy of that kind: the life of a factory-worker, however much it may cause grief, is never ambitious enough to engage attention as Lear, Phèdre, or Oedipus do. It is also true, however, as Brecht saw, that twentieth-century people seem disinclined to accept tragedy. When there are Olympiads for paraplegics, and deaf children are taught to appreciate music through vibrations, and funerals are celebrated for the most part with a complete absence of pomp and panoply, the emphasis lies so much on making the best of such life as there is, that tragic gestures are out of place. If Oedipus were to put his eyes out today, Creon would probably call an ambulance.

Yet tragedy is not ruled out because of these changed conditions and attitudes. It hangs over the fourth quarter of the century like the threat of atomic warfare, and against that background the optimism of healers looks puny. It would look puny in any case, so long as death means bereavement and sorrow. In the same way, the elements still have final mastery in many parts of the world. Long droughts in thickly populated areas, floods covering thousands of square miles still occur, and their results have to be borne without regard to what social reform or international co-operation may be able to achieve at some far-off date.

Thus Synge's play – which Brecht both imitated and tried to improve upon – is not merely a work that belongs to an outmoded tradition. Portraying as it does the mastering of complete dereliction by a mother who loses not only her husband but all her sons at sea, it treats of one of the deepest concerns of both tragedy and life. Maurya, the mother, is a poor woman living in a fisherman's hut off the West Coast of Ireland. She has no intention of ridding a town of plague, as Oedipus has, or of winning a throne, or defending a just cause. She is fearful and acquiescent for the greater part of the time, and it is only at the end, when her son Bartley is brought home drowned, that she finds a dignity and courage that have nothing strained about them, and establish an unshakable peace in resignation: 'No man at all can be living for ever, and we must be satisfied.'

Despite his debt to Yeats, who suggested the Aran Islands to him, Synge was reacting against him. At a personal level, Maurya's final sentence was, to all appearances, a rejection of Yeats's call to arms in *Cathleen ni Houlihan,* where Yeats writes, speaking of the Irish heroes, 'They shall be alive for ever.' Synge's Maurya will have nothing to do with such talk. Synge himself was also, very probably, modelling his play on a well-known work of the time, the *Op Hoop van Zegen* by the dramatist Heijermans, a play about Dutch fishermen who lose their lives at sea. Heijermans had also introduced a certain political note: one of the fishermen sings the *Internationale,* and there is some suggestion that the owner of the fishing-vessels should have known they were not in a fit condition to sail, but was too interested in his profits to care.* But Synge rejected all such concern with possible reforms. He was not interested in improving the safety of the Aran fishermen, but in writing a play about death as the Islanders might have met it, and in making the language tell.

Brecht's *Die Gewehre der Frau Carrar* (Señora Carrar's Rifles), written in 1937, deliberately imitated Synge, transferring the scene from Ireland to Spain, and making the central character a woman who tries to remain neutral and pacifist during the Spanish Civil War. The setting is the same, a fisherman's cottage by the sea, and the conclusion is the same, the bringing in of a drowned son, accompanied by a group of keening women. The play ends with the mother's grief. But Brecht writes in the spirit of Vishnevsky's Communist *Optimistic Tragedy.* In the age of Communism, as Vishnevsky saw it, there is no room for portrayals of unavoidable disaster. Catastrophes are to be avoided or conquered, not acquiesced in, and so Brecht makes Señora Carrar conclude by taking up a gun and resolving to fight the Fascist enemy.

---

* The subject-matter owes something to Ibsen's *Pillars of Society,* but there are several parallels with *Riders to the Sea*: the mother, Kniertje, like Maurya, has already lost a husband and several sons at sea, and loses two more at the end of the play; she feels partly responsible for the death of one of them, and is comforted by two young women; one son is recognised by what he was wearing. Max Beerbohm thought (in *Around Theatres*), when he saw *Riders to the Sea,* that Synge must have seen the Heijermans play.

No one claims much for *Señora Carrar's Rifles* now, and Brecht himself included it in his first post-war collected edition only as a volume outside the series. It has no characters who sound like peasants, the language is literary rather than colloquial, there is no action, no rhythm, only a brief climax when the dead son is brought in, in a scene which parodies Synge closely. The conversion of Señora Carrar from pacifism to political action is caused only by the fact that her son is machine-gunned at sea by a Fascist patrol-boat: where she had seemed to be against all forms of warfare she is converted because it is brought home to her that someone dear to her can be killed in war, so that the political issue is over-shadowed by the purely individual determination to revenge.

The final passage of dialogue is over-simple both in its suggestions and in its motivations, as when the mother is persuaded that her son has been killed because of the cap he was wearing: 'It is shabby. A gentleman wouldn't wear a thing like that.' This is not the response of a woman stricken with grief. One has the impression that Brecht sides with the mother in this simple-minded attribution of class-motives to the Fascist soldiers and, when one of the fishermen protests that they would not fire at anyone merely because he was wearing a shabby cap, her answer – at this climactic moment – seems like a message:

Doch. Das sind keine Menschen. Das ist ein Aussatz, und das muß ausgebrannt werden wie ein Aussatz.

No. They are not men, they are a leprosy, and they must be burned out like a leprosy.

This is too similar to the ruthless and bloodthirsty conclusion at which Johanna Dark arrives, in *St Joan of the Stockyards*, to be discounted as merely one moment in the play. Just as Johanna denounces the clergy, moreover, Señora Carrar unaccountably asks the keening women, who are now engaged in prayer, to leave her, as she has other business in hand. The rejection of religious comfort, however imperative Brecht thought it, strikes an unnatural note in this particular woman. And her final actions are embarrassingly symbolical. She takes up the bloodstained sail in which her son's body has been brought to the hut, saying with a rhetorical flourish: 'A while ago I tore up a flag. *You* have brought me another.' With this she reveals the hiding-place of the rifles, which she has been refusing to hand over throughout the play until this moment, and, to the sound of distant gunfire starting up, seizes one of them herself. Her answer to the question whether she is now going to join the workers is 'Yes. For Juan.'

As Brecht himself said, this is a piece of Aristotelian or 'empathetic' drama,[2] though it is a melodramatic example, and it is doubtful whether, as he proposed, the disadvantages of this technique – they are really the faults of his own dramatic writing – can be cancelled out by 'showing the play together with a documentary film showing events in Spain, or with some propagandistic occasion'. The play advances purely personal and vengeful reasons for joining in the war against Franco; no weightier reasons are given and no amount of documentation of the political issues could have any relevance to it.

There is only internal evidence to show that Brecht's dissatisfaction with *Señora Carrar* led to the writing of *Mother Courage and her Children*, a few years later. The title is drawn from the seventeenth-century novel by Christoph von Grimmelshausen, *Trutz Simplex*, or as it is often known, *Die Landstörtzerin Courasche*, about a canteen-woman in the Thirty Years' War of 1618 to 1648, though the character in the play has little more than the name in common with her predecessor. The main outline, however, resembles both Synge's and Brecht's earlier plays about the mother who loses her children, while the moral reverses that of *Señora Carrar*, since it purports to show that capitalism leads inevitably to war, and that the loss of the children is neither an elemental catastrophe, as in Synge, nor a call to arms against Fascism, but rather an inevitable consequence of going to war at all. Brecht was always prone to be caught between preaching pacifism and proposing revolutionary violence.

How far the new moral was sustained by the play is a point to leave aside for the moment. *Mother Courage* is decidedly one of the best things Brecht wrote, and it is significant of it, as an example of 'epic' or 'narrative' theatre, that it is not the story or the political implications, not a connected theme, which remains most strongly in the memory, but a series of isolated moments. Mother Courage, a woman who makes a living at one remove from the war by selling food, drink, and equipment to the soldiers involved in it, is bereft of her grown-up children one after another. She flirts with a Dutch cook, takes a refugee army chaplain under her wing, but is abandoned even by these at the end, and is left to drag her covered wagon alone, while the war continues into grey infinity.

In the production of the Berliner Ensemble, personally directed by Brecht, and with the main part played by Helene Weigel, the visual power of the play was strong. Above all, the wagon containing sausages and brandy, boots and clothing, which Mother Courage and her children pull from place to place in the wake of first the Protestant, then the Catholic army, was a binding force, fascinating in its Wild West shape, and in its rumbling movement on the turntable which Brecht expected a theatre normally to have. Just as effective were the ragged quilted jackets and Hessian cloaks which draped the characters in an unsentimental, yet aesthetically 'right', shape. One remembers such occasions as that in which the plump Swisscheese (Schweizerkas) sits sunning himself on the step of his mother's wagon, though the text here gives no more than the line 'Not many more days now when you can sit in the sun in your shirt-sleeves.' The sun – or rather the floods and spots and battens, for Brecht made no attempt at naturalism and the light felt purely white and electric – beat down with an intense warmth, and in the long silence which followed the spoken line a sense of pleasure at it was curiously evoked. The dramatic irony in the words was soon, however, to become apparent, for within a few moments Swisscheese was hauled off to execution by an enemy patrol, and in recollection the warm sunlight was felt to have been merciless as well as warm. And in this simple effect of stage-lighting, apparently achieved in a typically Brechtian way by turning every available light full on, there was contained, moreover, an essential mood of the play as a whole.

This dual aspect of the beneficent yet ensnaring sunlight was a reflection of the duality running through every scene and in all the major themes. Despite the catastrophic ending, in which Mother Courage dragged her wagon round the stage to the accompaniment of a sardonic chorus from the wings, there were moments of affirmation as well. Equally prominent in memory as that final scene was the earlier one (Scene 5) in which a chaotic panorama of human motives was presented in the ruins

of a destroyed village: Mother Courage refusing to sell schnapps
on credit, the chaplain burrowing in the shell of a farmhouse
to save the trapped occupants, Mother Courage refusing to give
up her officers' shirts to make bandages, a soldier making off,
while she argued, with a whole bottle of liquor, unobserved –
and finally the dumb daughter Kattrin holding up a living baby
in her arms as the curtains closed: an instant of triumphant
compassion which could not abolish, and yet stood out against,
the greed, malice, and uncharitableness on every hand.

The impressiveness of the play was enhanced by the acting
and production of the Berliner Ensemble, as shown still in the
volume of photographs and comments called *Theaterarbeit*,
which contrasts the Ensemble versions of certain scenes with
those of other companies. In the Ensemble version of *Mother
Courage* the mother lolls back almost luxuriously against the
canvas flaps, one arm extended along the curved roof: she is
grinning to herself with some satisfaction. The sons are striding
out smartly, in step, the simple, kindhearted, thoroughly honest
Swisscheese showing rather more determination than his brother
Eilif, who has more of a swagger, and a slightly abashed smile.
Both are plainly soldiers already in wish and imagination; they
may have to pull their mother's cart for the time being, but
their minds are on the future, and if Swisscheese overdoes the
part, that is because Eilif will in fact prove the better fighter.
Eilif, meanwhile, already shows by his smile some awareness of
the absurdity of his future career, an absurdity which will become more pronounced as the play continues. Dumb Kattrin,
behind the brothers on the step, glances apprehensively to one
side, crouched a little over her mouth-organ. She too is playing
her part in the family business for the moment, but something
of the protest she is to make is already apparent in her bearing.
In this way the four parade round the stage, leaving the audience
to receive its first impressions of the characters it is to meet for
the rest of the evening: every detail of gesture and motion has
been thought out to lend emphasis to the purely verbal aspects
of the work.

A complete contrast to this was provided by the BBC Television production of 1959. Here, the general positioning was
almost identical, with roughly the same wagon, the women on
the step, and the young men at the head of the shaft. Mother

Courage, however, sat upright, chin slightly raised, eyes proudly and fondly cast down towards her sons, mouth cheerfully singing to the music of Kattrin, who was also smiling. The sons toiled manfully; Eilif with a slightly rueful smile, his eyes lifted to some distant horizon, Swisscheese with one shoulder determinedly thrust forward and a wistful good humour in his expression.

The actors showed here a general appreciation of their roles. Swisscheese had been seen as the kindly son, well-intentioned, and this characterization emerged in each action. Mother Courage was the woman who cheerfully endured the worst, the embodiment of eternal virtues, and again this single aspect dominated the actress's interpretation. There were thus no surprises, or rather no surprises for the unreflecting, and considerable surprises for spectators who looked for some inconsistency. Where Mother Courage and her sons are so well-disposed, it is not at all clear how, later in the play, they come to be so cynical on the one hand, or so blindly trustful on the other. Their continued endurance in war becomes incomprehensible: they are people with high ideals, tragically beaten down by an inscrutable, external fate, instead of human beings observed in the round, detesting war and desiring it, cynically decrying their own potential and yet surprisingly showing extreme heroism and devotion, each ignorant of his own most fundamental urges whether towards good or evil. Brecht's actors in themselves reveal a good part of his meaning. The grin of Mother Courage and her lolling body are indications of the enjoyment she has from her trading off the war, while the very fact that her expression is a grin and not a smile suggests the inner uncertainty that accompanies this mood. Swisscheese's pursed lips reveal the naivety with which he will join the Protestant armies, fully convinced that virtue will bring its own reward, while Kattrin's apprehensiveness is in itself a comment on these illusions. The acting establishes a sympathy with these characters as human beings, while at the same time it promotes a sense of the folly and on occasions the wickedness of their activities. This dual mood defines what is best in Brecht's later plays; it is part of the complexity which spectators of all persuasions have most been able to enjoy.

Equally impressive, in contrast to *Señora Carrar*, was the use of language. It is not at all the case that *Mother Courage* is 'written in the forceful, coarse language of its period';[3] Brecht had no taste for naturalistic historicism. He has, however, created a language which suggests both Bavarian speech – mainly by such devices as omitting 'e' ('*Sie hörn*'), abbreviating "*Sie*', writing 'nix' for 'nichts', rather than by attempting a dialect which to many Germans sounds coarse and comic – and an extremely modern economy and directness of diction. It is difficult to convey this achievement to English readers who have no German, since a part of this directness derives from English idiom transformed into German, where it looks less natural. When Mother Courage observes that 'Auf was ich aus bin, ist, mich und meine Kinder durchbringen mit meinem Wagen', it sounds very much as though Brecht were translating the loosely-bound phrase, 'What I'm out after is to get me and my children through with the wagon', but the syntax is much more shocking in the stricter context of German. (Brecht enjoyed this anglicisation often: in *Galileo* he takes an obvious pleasure in allowing a character to repeat the terse phrase 'Das ist ein Fakt', rather than the accepted German 'Das ist eine Tatsache', whose rhythm is more mellifluous and 'feminine'. At times, in *Galileo* even his idioms are translated from English, and are not consistent with German usage.) Again, the strictly German passages often have the ring of peasant earthiness and yet are unmistakably Brechtian, as in a passage like this:

DER FELDHAUPTMANN. Ich wett, dein Vater war ein Soldat.
EILIF. Ein großer, hör ich. Meine Mutter hat mich gewarnt deshalb. Da kann ich ein Lied.
DER FELDHAUPTMANN. Sings uns! [*Brüllend*]. Wirds bald mit dem Essen!

THE CAPTAIN. I bet your father was a soldier.
EILIF. A great one, they say. My mother warned me about it. I can sing a song about him.
THE CAPTAIN. Sing it to us [*Shouts*]. What about something to eat!

As Mennemeier says, this is 'apparently realistic dialogue which in fact works with subtle abbreviations and is "popular" only *idealiter*'.[4] And to quote him again, '*Mother Courage* shows very clearly that Brecht's drastic yet intimate popular style seeks to imitate less the reality than the "idea" of natural speech, and its typically alogical structure. The whole drama is, so far as popular usage is concerned, alienated.' Thus it is never possible to accept the characters on stage as figures from everyday or historical life: they are constantly bordering on reality in their speech and as constantly veering away from it.

The character of Mother Courage herself is one of the most attractive features. She is adept at turning every situation to her own advantage, conforming with and adapting herself to it in a way that recalls Schweyk and Galileo. She has the vitality of Puntila without his drunkenness or lapses into sobriety, and at the same time she contributes a laconic cynicism of her own, a cunning and ingenuity which are essential for her sheer existence. As a rule she knows exactly how far she can go and how far she can let others go. When the recruiting sergeant threatens to take away her son, she pulls a knife on him, but it is clear that she means the threat as a move in the game, which will not be countered: there is shrewdness in her attitude, not heroism. When the Dutch cook's embrace trickles round into bosom-fondling her rejection of it is determined, but there is a look of wry appraisal in her eye. And do what Brecht might, he could not rewrite the tragic scene, in which she loses her son Swisscheese, in such a way as to destroy all sympathy for her in her grief. Helene Weigel's playing of the part in this scene, consciously styled as it was, would in any case have prevented that. Her drooped jaw, mouth agape with head thrown back and eyes closed, shoulders shrugged and hands lying in the lap,[5] is a purely physical posture that can be adopted without trace of emotion – it is pure 'showing', and said to have been copied from a newsreel photograph – but it gripped the mind of the spectator firmly enough for sympathy to be inevitable.

Yet when the structure of the play as a whole is considered, it becomes apparent that these qualities do little to bind it together. In its total effect, it is oddly without impact, a series of moments and *coups de théâtre* without coherence.

The consequences of all these visually and verbally interesting scenes can be that audiences are actually misled about the words and actions which are meant to be the main thing in them. Take for instance the intention, clearly expressed by Brecht in a footnote to the play, that the audience should not merely see the commercial ('merkantil') nature of war, as the characters themselves do, but also take action, no doubt along Marxist lines. We would expect to find some exemplification of this point in the character of Mother Courage, and on the surface it does appear that we get it, for Mother Courage does say at the conclusion of one scene 'Curse the war', only to change her mind immediately in the next, when she happens to be more prosperous, and to add, 'they're not going to mess up my war for me'. But this does not really illustrate Brecht's point; if we look at the occasion on which she curses war, we see that she is not perceiving the commercial nature of war at all. She curses it because her daughter has been assaulted, which might have happened in peacetime, because her daughter has been dumb since a soldier stuffed something into her mouth, which might also have happened in peace, and because both her sons have disappeared, and one of them has been killed. (She never learns of the death of the other.) All this has nothing to do with commerce, so that we must look elsewhere for evidence in favour of Brecht's assertion. We shall probably imagine we have found it in the scenes which show Mother Courage losing her children because of her exaggerated concern with money – indeed Brecht introduces this concern in the case of all three of her children. On looking closer, though, this demonstration appears forced.

In the first scene of all, Mother Courage loses her son Eilif to the recruiting sergeant because she is persuaded to haggle over the sale of a belt-buckle while Eilif succumbs to the blandishments of the recruiter – when she looks round, her son is gone. The main point of the first scene seems to be contained in this demonstration that greed causes her misery. Yet, even if we agree that to haggle is to be too much concerned with money, it has to be conceded that anything else might have distracted Mother Courage at the crucial moment – she might have been involved in an argument or a brawl or in fending off an embrace, while Eilif was being dazzled with promises of glory, and in any case she could not be expected to tie a grown man to her apron-strings.

Similarly, the death of Kattrin, shot by soldiers for raising an alarm, is laid partly at Mother Courage's door, although she had no direct part in it. Brecht is careful to let us know that when Kattrin performs her heroic action, beating a drum to warn a beleaguered city of impending attack, her mother is in the city.

buying goods cheaply from people who are fleeing from danger. He is thus enabled to put the words into the mouth of another character, after Kattrin's death, 'If you hadn't gone into town to carve yourself a slice, this might not have happened.' But this is quite an unjust charge – Mother Courage had left Kattrin in the care of peasants, having no one else to leave her with, and by the nature of her job she must have left her many times in pursuit of business. It is absurd to suggest that the desire for money implicates Mother Courage in guilt of Kattrin's death, which might equally well have happened if Mother Courage herself had been present. She would have been as powerless as the rest of them against the muskets of the soldiers.

Yet the fact that Brecht introduces the same idea into the scene of the death of Mother Courage's other child suggests a consistent intention. Swisscheese, like Kattrin, is killed by soldiers, in his case because he refuses to reveal where the regimental cashbox is. Mother Courage could save him if she were to offer the whole bribe demanded by the soldiers immediately it is asked for, but she tries to haggle and thus loses him. This, at any rate, is the superficial impression made by the scene of Swisscheese's death. But if we look more closely we see that it is not so straightforward. In the first instance, Mother Courage does offer the whole of the bribe demanded, 200 guilders, believing that she is bound to be able to get the money back from the cash-box, which she thinks Swisscheese has hidden. Only when she learns through her intermediary Yvette that Swisscheese has thrown the box in the river does she offer less, 120 guilders to be precise. But this, we have to remember, is well over half the value of her wagon and all its contents at the time. Her whole livelihood is at stake, and the times are extremely hard. She may be excused for thinking that the captors of Swisscheese will accept less, since they will get nothing at all by shooting him out of hand. What is more, when she hears that they have rejected not only 120 but the 150 which Yvette offered without her authorisation, she immediately offers the whole 200; that is to say, she offers to make over every single item she possesses to save her son's life. As it turns out, she is too late, but we are never told why the soldiers executed their potentially valuable prisoner so promptly. They know that Yvette is on her way back to Mother Courage, with the chance that the ransom-money will be raised, but they shoot him out of hand. All this makes the case against Mother Courage rather weak, in fact our sympathy goes entirely to her in this situation. Yet, we have to ask, why did Brecht write the scene, why did he let Mother Courage say 'I think I've haggled too long', and why did he suggest that the other two deaths were partly due to the same cause unless he wanted to make some case against her, suggesting greed for money? And why did he make the case so implausible? In this last instance, he provides so much in defence of Mother Courage as to suggest he was unwilling to press the point home.

The idea that Brecht was, all the same, mainly intent on making a case is borne out by the way in which he makes Mother Courage react to the war, and to the prospect that it may end. Mother Courage is, after all, a shrewd, hard-headed business-woman. She says she got her name for driving a wagon-load of loaves out of Riga while it was under cannon-fire, so as to sell them before they went mouldy, and she shows she can make a hard bargain with the cook who wants a capon for his captain's dinner table. Yet, the moment there is peace she is horrified: 'Don't tell me peace has broken out, just when I've bought in new stock.' Peace horrifies her: she will lose all her money, and she puts on funeral black at the very thought of it. But this seems scarcely likely to be a risk. A gypsy-like trader who has to find room in her wagon for herself, a man, and her daughter, as well as for supplies to sell, is not going to have a slow turn-over: she will get through most of her stock in a week or two with any luck, whether there is peace or war, and the kind of goods she sells are equally saleable in either event. Even as it is, she is giving credit to the troops, who have not been paid: there is not much profit in her line of business. If she were a capitalist with large stocks of munitions on her hands, and no prospects of a war breaking out somewhere else very soon, she might well talk like this with a show of reason. (Though Krupps have managed in peace and war pretty well all the same.) As things are, we can only suppose that Brecht thought of her in some way as being a large-scale capitalist – though he knew she was not – and put into her mouth words appropriate to that circumstance.

And this is not necessarily a far-fetched notion. Brecht did, after all, explicitly say that the highwayman Macheath in *The*

Threepenny Opera was a representative of bourgeois capitalism, and his only ground for saying that seems to have been based on Proudhon's epigram, 'Property is theft.' Besides, it is only on the basis of some such association as this that Mother Courage can be said to see the purely commercial nature of war. Only by exaggerating her position, making her seem more concerned with matters belonging to high finance than she possibly can be, was Brecht able to suggest that he had done more than sketch a few scenes from the life of a remarkable, but historically insignificant woman. But when we come to look at his play and its pretensions, we surely must see that it scarcely gets beyond trivialities, so far as economic analysis is concerned. The policies of Richelieu, Mazarin, Gustavus Adolphus, the Emperor, are scarcely thought of, nor is there any trace of what Fisher calls the 'undiminished gusto' with which the soldiers on all sides carried on their trade to the end. There is no account of the unendurable injustice which first gave rise to the war, or of the high motives that inspired at least some of the rulers. So far as the causes of the war are concerned, what is heard is not much different from pub-talk about the self-evident iniquity of the bosses.

A more consistently presented issue here, as in *The Good Woman,* in *Galileo,* and in *The Caucasian Chalk Circle,* is the possibility and the desirability of virtue in a corrupt world. To this question Brecht gives, as always, an ambiguous answer.

The issue is stated where we would expect it to be stated, in the opening scene of the play. The first conversation, between the recruiting officer and his sergeant, is entirely concerned with the idea that virtues like loyalty, faith and honour, and morality in general, are associated with war, while peace is a time of lounging about, feeding off the fat of the land, and indulging oneself. It sounds an absurd argument, it is true, when the sergeant says, 'You can see there's been no war here for much too long. Where's your morality to come from, I ask you?' Or when he adds, 'It's only when there's a war that you get proper lists and registers, and your shoes properly packed and your corn in sacks, and man and beast properly counted and carried off – because people know if you don't have proper order you can't have a war!' But since this argument is placed in the mouth of an unsympathetic character we need not suppose

Brecht to be presenting it for our serious consideration, despite the apparently thematic role suggested by its position in the play. It is only when we find Mother Courage repeating the idea in the second scene that we begin to wonder whether we ought to be paying more attention. 'Wherever you get these big virtues', she says, 'it proves there's something rotten', and she goes on to demonstrate this by saying that if a general is stupid his soldiers have to be specially courageous in order to carry out his orders, and if he is lazy they have to be very cunning, and if he expects too much of them they have to show a quite remarkable degree of loyalty. This argument is as unconvincing as that of the recruiter, since soldiers need to be courageous whether their leaders are good or bad, and the same applies to the other virtues. In fact, Mother Courage runs into total self-contradiction when she concludes, 'They're all virtues that a proper country and a good king or a good general don't need. In a good country there's no need of virtue; they can all be quite ordinary, fair to middling, and cowards too for all I care.'

Since this happy state of affairs is only possible where there is a 'good country' (whatever that may be) and a 'good king' we may well wonder what Mother Courage is driving at when she talks of there being no need for virtue, since goodness is presumably a virtue in her eyes. And we may once again pass on, thinking that we are not supposed to pay any respect to the argument on this occasion either.

Yet Brecht reverts to it a third time in Scene 9, when the Dutch cook sings his song about the folly of wisdom, boldness, honesty, selflessness and Godfearingness. True, the cook has just shown a total lack of several of these virtues by suggesting to Mother Courage that she should live with him and abandon her dumb daughter, who would have to pull the heavy wagon alone in the depths of a bitter winter in a starving countryside. We may thus once again suppose that Brecht does not want us to take the argument seriously, though we may begin to wonder why he keeps repeating it, and repeating it in so unpersuasive a form. The cook sings of St Martin, who cut his cloak in half to help a man in poverty, with the result that they both froze to death – but this is not the necessary and only consequence of charitableness. Similarly, the wisdom of Solomon is repre-

sented as that of a man who curses the hour in which he was
born, which sounds more like despair than wisdom, though
wisdom may not exclude such a curse. And the death of Julius
Caesar is attributed not to any overweening ambition, or to the
envy of others, but quite simply to his boldness. There is too
much sweeping generalisation in all this to impress, and we
may well be left asking why Brecht continually thrusts such
matters forward for our attention.

The answer to this, if we look at the play as a whole, appears
to be that to some extent, though ambiguously, Brecht did take
these arguments seriously. The whole structure of the play (for
it has one, despite Brecht's theoretical disavowals of structure)
tends to, but does not in fact, bear out the kind of thing said by
the recruiter, the cook and Mother Courage herself.

Once again, returning to the final scene, we see that not only
is the need for virtue questioned, it is actually presented by
Mother Courage as a thing to be avoided. She warns two of
her children against the virtue to which they seem most inclined: Eilif is not to be too bold, and Kattrin not to be too kindhearted. Swisscheese she wants to be honest, but she is really
meaning to make sure he brings back the change when he goes
shopping – honesty is not truly her concern here. In the course
of the play we see how all her warnings are in vain – we see, or
seem to see, how each child dies precisely because of the virtues
about which he or she has been warned. (In a poem for children about the play ('Die Geschichte von der Mutter Courage')
Brecht is explicit: 'Her eldest child died because he was a hero,
the second because he was too good, the daughter had too good
a heart, when the bullet struck her!') And we might well conclude from this that Brecht meant us to see Mother Courage's
warnings ironically – that he meant to praise virtue by showing
up the true nature of those who decry it – were it not that here
once again, in most cases, the argument runs badly off the rails.
Eilif, for instance, is executed for a deed which, we are told,
would have been accounted an act of boldness in war; his misfortune is that, whereas a few months earlier he was honoured
for precisely the same thing, he happens now to have done it
in peace-time and is therefore condemned. Thus he seems to
be introduced into the play in order to exemplify the cook's
cynical song: here is boldness, and this is where it gets you.

Yet if we look at what Eilif has done, we see that it is not what soldiers are usually praised for. He is no Hector, or Spitfire pilot. In war-time, he plundered some peasants of their cattle, and, when they set upon him, 'cut them to pieces', as he says with relish – they being armed only with clubs whereas he had a sword. In peace-time, he has tried to burgle a peasant's cottage, and killed the man's wife. In neither case has he displayed more than a criminal low cunning, and since this is all we hear of Eilif's military activities, the case is different from that of a soldier who kills in the course of opposing tyranny. (It was an irony that Brecht wrote *Mother Courage* just when war, against Hitler, seemed more justifiable than any war had for a very long time.)

We turn then to Swisscheese, who becomes a regimental paymaster, entrusted with the custody of the regimental cash-box during a chaotic retreat. He dies, apparently, because he is too honest and loyal to betray to his captors what he has done with the box – with a little less honesty, Mother Courage might suggest, he could have got away with his life. Yet here again, though the case is very different from that of Eilif, Brecht does not provide a really satisfying contribution to the general argument. Swisscheese is certainly honest and loyal, but he is also presented as extremely simple-minded, so that the moral issue never comes clearly into view. He believes, for instance, that the sergeant who has entrusted the box to him must have the money it contains in order to pay the soldiers who are in flight from the enemy – 'if they don't get their pay they don't have to run away. They don't have to move a foot.' And he has a child's dream of the fatherly sergeant patting him on the back when he does turn up with the cash: 'Won't the sergeant be surprised? You have given me a pleasant disappointment, Swisscheese, he'll say. I give you the cash-box to look after, and you bring it back again.' Swisscheese would be incapable of such sophisticated imaginings. But apart from this, Brecht spoils his own case by making Swisscheese throw the cash-box in the river instead of hiding it. Why Swisscheese does this we are never told: it is a reported action which we never see, and about which we hear nothing from Swisscheese himself. But if he were loyal, he would presumably hide the box, as in fact he intends to do, rather than throw it away, and Brecht does not tell us why

Swisscheese behaves as he does – it may well be that fear overcomes his loyalty when he thinks he may be endangered, but in that case he has acted immorally, or with less than full virtue.

And having once thrown the box in the river, there is nothing Swisscheese can do. When the enemy tortures him and finally executes him, he cannot be persisting in loyalty, but only enduring helplessly without hope of escape. Thus the fact that he looks after the cash-box in the intention of restoring it to the regiment does not in itself lead to his death. He might have died in just the same way if he had kept the box to use the money for himself. And certainly no general conclusion follows about honesty being a bad policy. Yet the scene does have the superficial appearance of bearing ont Mother Courage's cynicism about virtue in the first scene.

The case of Kattrin is different again. Here the deed of charity which she performs not only occurs at a climactic moment in the play, it is also one which is indisputably good. In beating a drum to warn the inhabitants of Magdeburg of an impending attack, Kattrin is trying to save the lives of the children in the city, about whom she has just been told, and her refusal to give up when threatened with instant death is an act of genuine heroism, so moving as to make us forget for a while all previous argument. Kattrin has a definite purpose, and she knows what she will suffer if she goes through with it. Her horror of war and of all cruelty, which makes her groan at night in her sleep and perhaps has robbed her of the power of speech, finds its true outlet and fulfilment here, and, though she dies, we are glad for her and know she has acted rightly. Mother Courage may say, beforehand, that she 'suffers from pity' ('leidet am Mitleid'), but this Nietzschean comment is of small account in comparison with the prolonged and exciting enactment of her bravery and compassion. (All the same, the fact that the comment is made at all is significant.)

We may, then, be inclined to say that the whole sense of the play is a refutation of the cynical and confused arguments put forward earlier, and that at its climax it asserts (in contrast, say, to *Galileo*) the value of martyrdom in a good cause. Given the position of the scene of Kattrin's death within the whole, this is an attractive view, and one which helps to account for a good deal of the praise which has been accorded to the play. But while there is no occasion to scorn that praise, the scene can also have the effect of seeming to cap the arguments of the recruiter, the cook, and Mother Courage, invalid as these are. The two sons of Mother Courage have died 'because they were virtuous', and now her daughter does the same, because she suffers from pity. There is both the possibility of a complex view, and a more meretricious one which seems to gain support from the structure of the play.

The way Brecht swayed to one side of his deepest creative centre is shown by the attempts he makes, through the structure, at writing the systematic play which, with one part of himself, he wanted to write: three demonstrations of the power of economic forces, three of the sad or bad consequences of virtue. If one looks at the play in the context of the time at which it was written, it seems likely that another part of him did not want to write so systematically. He had seen, in *Señora Carrar*, what effect purely political concern could have on his playwriting, and it looks probable that *Mother Courage* was, in a sense, his self-correction, as well as, possibly, his alignment with Popular Front policy. He was not prepared to alter course to the extent of converging with Synge, but he was willing to allow passionate statement in a more disciplined form than he had managed in the Spanish Civil War play. So it is that the most stirring scene is the one in which Kattrin sits on the rooftop, beating her drum, not in a heroic gesture, as she has done in some productions, but as she did in the Ensemble performance by Angelika Hurwicz, with a grim, masterful determination to see that due warning of the attack on Magdeburg is given. She makes each drum-tap count.[6] This protest against the killing of children comes from an impulse in Brecht which had never, until this moment, found clean-cut dramatic expression in his plays. Formerly, irony had always intervened; now, it plays only a minor part, as in Mother Courage's one 'Nietzschean' remark.

It is true that Kattrin's protest can only provoke more fighting: probably no additional lives will be saved in the total sum, when the citizens of Magdeburg begin to defend themselves, and the death-roll will merely bear the names of different, not fewer people. But that is significant for Brecht's whole situation at the time he was writing the play. Politically, in the late 1930s a pacifist work was not needed so much as a call to arms against Nazi Germany. But in terms of dramatic art, which outlasts the needs of a particular occasion, the passion of Kattrin has its proper place, and the continuing pressure in Brecht to make manifest in the theatre his detestation of war at last bursts out in a controlled flow.

Against the effects of that pressure, the flawed structure of *Mother Courage* is of less account. The impelling power in the play is the sense of waste – not of tragedy, as Synge would have had it (though tragedy was right for him and for Maurya as he made her, and his play 'works') but of the life that is running out. As Raymond Williams says of Mother Courage, 'If she were not so strong and persistent, there would be no life at all; and at the same time, because she is strong and persistent, in a destructive society, she destroys the life that she has herself created. . . . It is by looking this action, this character, in the face, that we see what we are doing: the essential contradiction; the destructive acquiescence in the name of life; the persistent vitality in a continuing destruction.'[7] This is surely the sense of the ending: Brecht did not want a sense of tragedy; he was angry with the first-night audience who wept in traditional mood over the bereaved mother, and he included a sardonic chorus offstage, chanting a raucous injunction to her to look alive, as she humped the empty wagon round the stage in the final scene. The mood is akin to the mood in which he had Kattrin beat her drum – a ferocious insistence on the idiocy of the destruction, spoken by a Thersites in the wings, biting in its almost cynical desperation, which is only not cynical, in the last resort, because it is desperate.

But there is no cure offered. All that Brecht gives – as in all the maturer plays – is the intolerable awareness of how things are, not a Marxist or any other solution. He may have thought, it is true, that he had shown sufficient of the causes of war to justify him in maintaining he had written something other than a tragedy. If, on the other hand, we find his analysis too flimsy, we are left with an irremediable awareness of a tragic situation. The difference between this kind of tragic situation and those of earlier centuries is that, in Lawrence's phrase, it does not provide us with a cheap seat in the gods, but kicks us in the shins. That is the peculiarly twentieth-century quality of it, and a reason why it attracts audiences unattuned to its political philosophy.

'PUNTILA' AND 'THE GOOD WOMAN OF SETZUAN'

Squire Puntila and his Man Matti, written in 1940–1 on the basis of stories by the Finnish author Wuolijoki, is more of an 'epic' play in its structure than almost any other of Brecht's works, a possible exception being *Mother Courage.* There is no argument, no problem, but rather a loose sequence of scenes, and almost no plot; at one point all thought of 'dramatic' interest, in the traditional sense, is abandoned while four women sit by the roadside to exchange stories and reminiscences. That scene, which has its value, since the last story to be told has a sharp political point, is sheer 'narrative theatre' – and 'episch' means 'narrative' as much as anything else – it is theatre in the form of a short story or novel.

Not having the wartime background of *Mother Courage,* *Puntila* relies on comic incidents to sustain interest. Puntila himself bursts through wooden gates on to the stage in his Studebaker; he 'walks on the water', which is in fact aqua vitae; he piles all the chairs in the room in a heap to represent a mountain, which he climbs to survey the Finnish countryside. It is boisterous humour, unintellectual – there is no religious satire in the walking on the water, or any political point to any of Puntila's larking, but it establishes the relaxed mood of the whole work, and its prime aim of entertaining.

The sequence of events could never carry any heavy-weight message. Puntila is a Finnish landowner of no great wealth, having only 90 cows, and some forest-land of unknown extent, and he can hardly stand for capitalism generally; though he is an employer of labour, his relationships are rather feudal. His odd characteristic is that, when drunk, he is overflowing with good humour, amatoriness and generosity, while, when sober, he becomes calculating, business-like, and mainly interested in money. In this the play resembles others of Brecht's later works in which a character is divided between a good and a bad self,

as in *The Good Woman of Setzuan,* or two characters are contrasted, as in *The Caucasian Chalk Circle.* Clearly, Brecht was
personally interested in such dichotomies. In *Puntila,* they serve
the purpose of pointing out Puntila's inhumanity by means of
contrasts. Drunk, Puntila sees that his servant Matti[1] is a human
being, and thinks of marrying his daughter Eva to him. Sober,
he is interested only in seeing her married to the foppish attaché from the diplomatic service. Drunkenness is for him what
a mask is to the 'Good Woman', Shen Te, a means of adopting
a different personality.

The political message is correspondingly simple: Puntila owns
the land he surveys from the top of his mountain, and Matti
does not:

PUNTILA. Say that your heart leaps up when you see all that.
MATTI. My heart leaps up when I see your woods. Sir.

These final words say not much of political consequence. Few
people can have had their aesthetic enjoyment of the countryside much spoiled by knowing it was private property they
were looking at, and the economic points are less strongly made
in this play than in others. As a curtain-line, Matti's words lack
punch. So do the verses of his epilogue:

> Es hilft nichts und 's ist schade um die Zähren.
> 'S wird Zeit, daß deine Knechte dir den Rücken kehren.
> Den guten Herrn, den finden sie geschwind,
> Wenn sie erst ihre eignen Herren sind.

> It's no use, and never mind the tears.
> It's getting time your servants turned their backs on you.
> They'll quickly find a good master
> Once they've become their own masters.

This sounds like the anarchical view of society put forward in
the crowd-scene in *Galileo:* as though by getting rid of Puntila
each of his servants would become a law unto himself. It may
also be construed as meaning that the servants will 'quickly' find
a good master in a Communist State. If so, Brecht's naivety in
the political morals of his plays shows here as much as anywhere. He could not have thought, after any reflection, either
that a good leader was likely to be the result, quick or otherwise, of an expropriating revolution – he knew enough about

Stalin, when all is said – or that a tolerable society could result from every man following his own interests. Walter Benjamin, a close friend, relates that when he referred to conditions in Russia (in 1938) Brecht was highly sceptical, seeming to believe political prisoners were maltreated. To the question whether their friend Ernst Ottwald was in prison (colloquially, whether he was 'sitting') Brecht said, 'If he can still sit, he's sitting.' Ottwald was executed in 1943.[2]

Some attempt was made, in Michel de Saint-Denis' production at the Aldwych in 1965, to put fire into the play by changing the character of Matti. As the critic of *The Times* reported, Patrick Magee's performance transformed Matti 'from a contemptuously composed witness of the foibles of the rich to a figure smouldering with unexpressed anger'.[3] That certainly made a more revolutionary play of it. The trouble is, there is very little cause for smouldering anger. In the first place, Brecht chose this time to write about a rural community in a fairly undeveloped part of the world, rather than about industrial capitalism in its worst manifestations. Second, he made Puntila such a figure of rough fun that there was nothing to feel really angry about. That Puntila enjoys more wealth than anyone else in the neighbourhood is obvious. Yet the four girls he pretends to want to marry, using curtain-rings for engagement rings, hardly expect him to be serious and are not particularly aggrieved by his rejection. Though they work long hours for not much pay, they are not made to look oppressed, and they don't go short of alcohol. Puntila at the hiring fair makes apparent how degrading it is for a labourer to be sized up as though he were cattle, but that is not a point that an industrial proletariat equipped with trade unions will find very relevant.

The rest of the London press, apart from *The Times*, had scarcely a good word to say for *Puntila*; in the main it was abusive. Bernard Levin in the *Mail* called it 'merciless rubbish'. In the *Mirror*, Arthur Thirkell said that Brecht bored him more than any other playwright, 'though the acting almost made you forget the idiotic story'. The *Sun* said that if anything would prick the bubble of Brecht's reputation in Britain it would be the Aldwych *Puntila*, and even Gerard Fay in the *Guardian* wanted to know what Brecht had got against the human race, that even his workers and peasants were parodies of humanity.

He thought the Royal Shakespeare Company had been wrong to 'dredge this muddy piece of Brecht up out of the textbooks'. Only Penelope Gilliatt in the *Observer* had a good word to say for the play, but she seemed to disqualify herself by saying that it was 'nothing like as funny as the great Wooster chronicle' of P. G. Wodehouse. The only qualities Miss Gilliatt actually praised were 'jolliness', and 'the sort of obstreperous and noisy spirit that Brecht clamoured for'. Brecht could have wished for a better advocate.

In defence of *Puntila* it can be said that Brecht described it on the title-page as a 'Volksstück', that is, a popular play or perhaps even a peasant-play. The genre is scarcely known in the English-speaking world, or, for that matter in Germany – it is in Austria, rather, that it has had its chief representatives. One should imagine, then, a rather rough-hewn work, made in the spirit of peasant-carving, and yet with a particular kind of vigorous beauty. Brecht himself, in his 'Remarks on the Volksstück' observed that the language is popular ('volkstümlich', 'of the people'), and that at the same time it is poetic. There is a clue here to what he hoped to achieve, and to the reason why the political moral seems so inept.

From his early days, in *Baal* especially, Brecht had had a strong lyrical feeling for scenes of nature, which he expressed in his poetry more than in his plays. With time he began to feel that in the industrial world such a feeling had to be killed off. There was no time for luxuriating in beauty while the workers were living in poverty. Only towards 1945, though the plays concerned were written during the war itself, did an appreciation of natural scenes come into his dramatic work: Swisscheese enjoying the sun in *Mother Courage,* Grusha, in *The Caucasian Chalk Circle,* looking forward to the spring, hearing the icicles melt. In *Puntila,* where an expansive, genial mood is more in evidence than anywhere else, the enjoyment of the Finnish landscape is one of the main themes, and Brecht's appreciation of it breaks through the political significance he tries to attach to the whole.

The Zürich production of 1948 made a special point of the discrepancy between the action and the landscape against which it was played. The background of the stage was a screen of birch-bark, in front of which hung emblems of the sun, moon and clouds as stylised reminders of the beauty that is there to be enjoyed. This background screen was illuminated according to the time of day represented, and so had a certain naturalness. The acting area in the foreground, however, was fully lit all the while. As Brecht wrote: 'The atmosphere was thus established in the background, and separated from the rest of the production.' This separation had the effect of making the action on the forestage seem more harsh, more in the spirit of Puntila sober, while the background was a continual reminder of the beauty which existed despite Puntila's seeming appropriation of it to himself alone.

The clue to the best reading of *Puntila* is Brecht's expectation that not only Nature but all natural things would become available to all, once exploitation of men by men had vanished. The political aspect is secondary, in such dialogues as the one in which the Judge complains of the number of cases that come before him on account of people making love. Brecht, in an unusually unironical mood, said of this speech that it was to be 'treated as a poem, that is, with distinctiveness, "proffered on a golden platter"'. Though the speech would be the better for being spoken without any hint of precosity, it shows an enthusiastic appreciation of all that Brecht felt was denied (and yet, apparently, allowed) by so-called bourgeois society:

ADVOCATE. Finland's midsummer night is a marvellous institution!
JUDGE. Yes, causes me plenty of work. All the suits for alimony – they're one long hymn in praise of Finland's summer night. In court you realise what a delightful spot a birch-wood can be. They can't take a stroll by the river without going weak at the knees. There was one girl the other day who blamed it all on the hay because it smelt so strong. They oughtn't to go berry-picking, and milking the cows is just as bad. There ought to be barbed wire round every bush by the roadside. The men and the women go separately to the steambath, so as not to be led into temptation, and then they go in couples out over the meadows. It's no good, you just can't hold them in summer. They jump off their bikes and do it, they slink up into the hayloft and do it. They do it in the kitchen because it's indoors, and out in the open because the fresh air's so wonderful. They're always getting kids, part of the time because the summer's so short, the rest of the time because the winter's so long.

The mood produced by passages like that – by 'alienation', since the Judge's words are meant to have an effect opposite to what they say – is the mood in which the play is conceived. Puntila is a sort of Baal, at many removes, enjoying himself in his middle-aged and at the same time childishly innocent way by ignoring everybody's interests but his own. This is the first play since *Baal* to introduce any such enjoyment, whether of nature or of love, as a main theme, though *Galileo* also makes a good deal out of sensual pleasure.

How wrong a political interpretation can be is shown by two interpretations of the part of Puntila given by the same actor. 'Steckel', a spectator wrote, 'played Puntila in Zürich before playing him in Berlin. In Zürich he played him almost without a mask, and most spectators had the impression of a sympathetic character with a few bad moments in a state of sobriety, which looked rather like a hangover, so that even these bad moments seemed excusable. In Berlin, learning from his experience, he chose a disgustingly shaped bald head, and made himself up to look like a roué. This time, his charm when drunk looked dangerous, and his genial approaches became those of a crocodile.'[4] Such crudity of performance would run against the nature of Puntila's actions, which are for the most part not crocodile-like. The women he asks to marry him are well aware that he is not serious; they would be foolish not to be, and they bear him no grudge. His self-importance at the hiring fair, when he accuses another employer rather than himself of behaving like a capitalist, is either funny or nothing – to emphasise his blindness would spoil the simple joke.

At the climax, however – and there is a climax despite the 'non-Aristotelian' construction – the good humour drops its mask. Confronted by the Communist Surkkala, whom he has thoughtlessly hired and brought to the estate together with his large family, Puntila recognises his true enemy. Through drunk, he is, this time, benevolent only on the surface. His reasons for dismissing Surkkala are specious:

Staying's no good to Surkkala. Puntila's too small for him, he doesn't like it here. I can see how he feels. If I were in his skin, I'd feel the same way. For me the squire would simply be a capitalist and do you know what I'd do with him? I'd stick him in a salt-mine for him to learn what work means, the parasite! Isn't that right, Surkkala? You needn't think of my feelings.

– and he makes a deduction from the three months' wages he

offers Surkkala in lieu of notice. The protestation of the Surkkala family, that they want to stay on – their prospects of other
work are small – is ignored. In the showdown, the real interests
of employer and employee are shown to be in complete conflict, and Puntila is hard-headed enough to see that. The final
flick is given when Matti sees the impossibility of staying in
Puntila's employment after this revelation of the face beneath
the friendly mask. Thus in the final scenes a seriousness enters
the play that earlier scenes might not have led the audience to
expect. Properly staged, this could be telling. Over-acting of
either Puntila or Matti kills the insistent point Brecht is making,
that a rich man's humanity is certain to be suspect. Both Steckel
and Magee overplayed.

The laconic tone of *Puntila* at its best is in complete contrast
to the impassioned mood of parts of *The Good Woman of Setzuan*, though this is still not a straightforwardly passionate play.
The Good Woman recalls *Puntila* in the dual aspects of its principal character. In other ways it is more of a dialectical counterpart, a swing of the pendulum in the opposite direction. Where
Puntila is almost casual in its understatement, *The Good Woman*
presents the issue of poverty and riches, worker and master, in
an extreme form. On the other hand, the moral of *The Good
Woman* is much more indeterminate.

The theme of the compassionate reformer had occupied
Brecht before, in plays like *The Measures Taken*. In contrast
to *Puntila*, *Setzuan* is by no means 'epic' theatre: the plot is an
extremely complicated affair rather than a concatenation; in
addition, there is an intensity of argument, an exaggerated caricaturing of situations, which both recall the earliest plays and
make it difficult to preserve an attitude of detachment, although
devices of alienation are employed. The clarity of outline in
the propagandist plays has gone. Yet this lack of clarity adds
to the dramatic interest. Instead of a biased message, a dialectic
of opposing attitudes emerges, providing tension and involvement in the manner of the traditional theatre.

The 'argument' concerns three Chinese gods who come in
search of good men, as Jehovah once came to Sodom. They
find none except the prostitute Shen Te, and reward her with
money which she uses to set up a shop. At once, however, she
is besieged by beggars and needy friends, and her generosity
is so great that she is soon on the verge of ruin. Later, she falls

in love with an unemployed airman, Sun, a ruthlessly selfish man to whom she still shows complete devotion, and here again her goodness leads to disaster. In her dilemma, she sees no way out but to disguise herself as a male cousin, Shui Ta, who puts an end to the innumerable claims on her love by showing a hard insistence on principle. As Shui Ta, she helps both the poor and her lover, setting up a factory which provides work and wages; but in so doing, she foregoes almost all her charity, and her mental plight is even worse. At length, she is arrested as Shui Ta for the supposed murder of Shen Te. The gods enter the court to try the case, whereupon she reveals that she is herself Shen Te. At this, the gods are delighted, for there is still a good woman on earth, but Shen Te desperately protests that she is not merely the good woman: she cannot do without her cousin. The gods, however, are unconcerned. A sparing use of Shui Ta, they suggest, say once a month, is permissible, and with this they return to heaven in pink clouds of glory, leaving Shen Te writhing in her agonies of conscience. An epilogue (omitted in some translations) informs the audience that this is not a satisfactory conclusion, and urges them to think of a better one themselves.

There is a strong temptation to respond to these situations in traditional fashion, to see the play as exploring a literal interpretation of the commandment to love our neighbours, and showing the disasters attendant on such a course, as Ibsen did in *Brand* or Tolstoy in *The Light Shines in the Darkness*. On these terms, the play is tragic in that it shows the utter impossibility of human goodness. Alternatively, there is an interpretation in existentialist terms, demonstrating the absurdity of virtue but affirming it nevertheless as a human achievement poised over a void of meaninglessness, roughly as in Miller's *The Crucible* or Sartre's *The Flies*. There is something to be said for this, for Shen Te's extreme devotion, folly as it is, arouses a deep admiration. But Brecht's play is more complex, and yet a third possibility needs to be borne in mind. In a foreword (omitted in the later edition), Brecht once observed that 'the province Setzuan in this parable, which stood for all places where men are exploited by men, is such a place no longer'.[5] In other words, this is essentially a picture of a competitive society, its problems are those of capitalism and not of modern Communist

China, and with this an entirely new 'distancing' attitude is gained. If an audience receives the play in the spirit advocated by Brecht, it may well feel, in part at least, not admiration for Shen Te's quixotic charity, nor oppression at her tragedy, but amazement that such ideals could ever capture a human heart. 'I wouldn't have thought that. – That's not the way to do it. – That's most remarkable, scarcely believable. This has got to stop. – I am shattered by the suffering of this man, because there could be a way out for him.'[6] This is the attitude Brecht expected, and it may well lead us to consider more closely the discussion between Wang the water-carrier and the three gods, in which Wang proposes that the ideals set before men should be not love but benevolence, not justice but fairness, not honour but decency, in short that almost unattainable absolutes should be replaced by more human qualities. Indeed, there is a sense in which the play sets out to show that it is precisely Shen Te's devotion to an impossible ideal which transforms her into her ruthless counterpart: because she cannot love all men equally, she despairs and seeks to achieve her ends by cruelty. Love, in short, paradoxically gives rise to capitalism. A Confucian attachment to 'the mean' is more human-hearted. On these terms, the moral of the parable is not so much, as John Willett suggests, 'that in a competitive society goodness is often suicidal',[7] but rather that the competitive society is a concomitant of the quest for absolute goodness.

Yet whatever Brecht may have thought, this solution still leaves problems. It has been seen how, in his own life, the desire to do good led to the deliberate injunction to 'embrace the butcher', and Communism demands as much as capitalism that evil be done so that good may come. In fact a Communist critic sees the message of the play precisely in the need for determined action. Fantastically taking Shui Ta as his model, he declares that 'to be good, I must be cruel',[8] recalling that in every country Communism has been achieved only by means comparable in violence and oppression, though not in intention, to Shui Ta's. Benevolence, fairness, and decency do not provide the driving urge to 'change the world' (a phrase which recurs several times in the play); only the impossible standards, with all their dangers, spur men on.

Shen Te's love for Sun is not an impossible standard, but

rather an impossible emotion. It is sheer folly, and Brecht does
not allow us the flattering thought that it is divine 'foolishness',
to use St Paul's term, nevertheless. Equally, however, he cannot
mean to ask for detachment alone. We are shocked at Shen Te's
unreasoning devotion to her lover when he has already revealed
to her, in her guise of Shui Ta, his unscrupulous intention to
exploit her, and his total lack of any reciprocating love. We feel,
as Brecht intended, astonished indignation at this blindness of
hers. On the other hand, when she explains her motives later,
it is impossible to feel only detached:

> I saw him at night, puffing out his cheeks
>   in his sleep: they were evil.
> And in the morning I held his coat up to the
>   light: I could see the wall through it.
> When I saw his cunning laughter I was
>   afraid, but
> When I saw the holes in his shoes, I loved
>   him very much.

Only a complete inhumanity could find this absurd, want to
change it, or claim that there is another way out.

And so also in the final scene, there is a mingling of deep
sympathy and surprise. This is not at all the ending of *St Joan*,
where once again a rosy light shines down on a woman who is
being canonised for all the 'wrong' reasons. There, the one-
sided intention was obvious: in the eyes of Christians, Joan was
a saint; in her own eyes, enlightened by Communism, her Christian charity had been a subtle poison. Here, while the gods
sing the praises of the good woman, she herself is conscious of
her failure not by Communist but by charitable standards. We,
the spectators, meanwhile, see Shen Te's folly and find ourselves unable to give any other name to it. We reach out for
alternatives such as those suggested by Wang and find them
unsatisfying too. We reach out for traditional stand-bys: 'suffering purifies', 'courage grows with danger', 'good wins in the
end', and find these already stultified by the mouths of the gods.
There is no way out, universal charity reveals itself as the
nearly suicidal doctrine which we see it to have been in the life
of the modern saint, Simone Weil. But, with all this, Brecht
makes clear his thorough personal acquaintance and even his

sympathy with the dilemma of Shen Te. He sees the absurdity, but unlike the existentialists he does not affirm any need for commitment to the absurd. Rather, he looks for another way out, and it is this that gives the play its completely open ending, leaving decision this time entirely in the audience's hands. It is no longer the case that only those associations are permitted which the author had in mind; instead, a real freedom is accorded.

A real freedom, however, with one limitation. In the epilogue, the audience is asked to think whether it is a new Man that is needed, a new world, new gods or perhaps none at all. It is suggested, then, that the situation of the play is relevant to the religious problems of contemporary Europe, to which answers may be found either in a new religion or in atheism. Yet the three Chinese gods do not remotely correspond to any Christian doctrines of divinity. The notion of a God who requires men to be perfectly good but provides them with no assistance ignores completely the Christian belief in the Holy Spirit, and makes of Christianity a purely moralistic religion. Christians do not believe that man is called upon to be perfect by his own efforts, rather that all good acts proceed not from man but from God. This is a belief that has its difficulties, but in a portrayal of present-day religion it cannot simply be swept aside as Brecht does here. Our ancestors were not so naive as all that. What Brecht has written in this play is in fact an exploration of the moral position of the deist, and its unresolved conclusion, frank as it is, belongs rather to deism than the theistic religion of traditional Christianity.

Yet with all this, the really essential quality of the play is still untouched, for the operation of the alienation effect has unpredictable results. Picasso has explained his own policy in art in terms closely similar to Brecht's. 'My landscapes', he writes, 'are exactly like my nudes and my still-lifes; but with faces people see the nose is crooked, whereas nothing shocks them about a bridge. But I drew this "crooked nose" on purpose. I did what was necessary to force people to see a nose. Later on they saw – or they will see – that the nose isn't crooked at all. What I had to do was to stop them from going on seeing only "beautiful harmonies" or "exquisite colour".' Whether Brecht has in the end done the same for moral issues in this play as Picasso did for the nose is something that can only be discovered by arguing with the play, entering into its disputes, opposing it and at the same time being ready to admit defeat.

What does not emerge from all this is any indication that the solution need be Communist. When the audience is asked to find a solution of its own it has the whole range of political nostrums to choose from. Politically, the play does no more than state the basic problem underlying all politics: how to create a just society out of a crowd of largely unjust individuals. The answers proposed range from total subordination of the individual through democratic voting procedures to total anarchy, but, since the play offers no basis for choosing between these, it does no more than raise the issue. But that is, presumably, what Brecht meant when he called it a 'parable play'. The distribution of wealth is unequal both within the industrialised countries and in the global relation between them and the Third World. Whatever else it does, Brecht's play remains to point a moral, as, in its day, the parable of the Good Samaritan did.

LAST YEARS AND
'THE CAUCASIAN CHALK CIRCLE'

The climaxes of Brecht's career as a dramatist, as distinct from a man of the theatre, were in the late 1920s and between the years from 1937 and 1944, the periods of *The Threepenny Opera* and *Mahagonny*, and of the 'mellower' plays. The second climax had passed by the time he had to decide in which part of Germany he might best settle, and the work he did after 1945 was more concerned with producing his own plays and adapting and producing those of other dramatists than with creating new plays of his own.

The decision to return to the Soviet zone of Germany, as it then was, rather than to the American, British or French zone was partly, in Brecht's eyes, what Martin Esslin has called a choice of evils. He settled in East Berlin in 1949, having made a visit there a year earlier, and was to remain there, apart from trips abroad, until his death in 1956. His choice was made and, though the Democratic Republic was not the realisation of his ideal, he preferred it to the capitalism of the Federal Republic in the West. Here in the East, he must have hoped, a reasonable use would be made of the industrial revolution that had begun shortly before his birth.

Several events in the West could have persuaded him he had been right. It was already clear in 1949 that the U.S.A. and the U.S.S.R. were sharply divided, after their recent alliance, and the granting of economic aid to the West through the Marshall Plan, together with the call by Churchill, as early as 1950, for a European Army including a West German contingent, underlined the conflict, though there was no army of the Federal Republic until the year of Brecht's death. The revelation in 1951 that many former Nazis were still in high office in the West, the Waffen S.S. rally held in 1952, the release in 1953 of the armaments manufacturer Krupp, who had provided Hitler with most of his weapons, would all have been seen by Brecht as evidence that the old order was being restored by capitalists who, on a Marxist interpretation, were themselves involved in a historical process which must end in Nazism. The capitalists might destroy their own kind, but once the war was ended they must revert to type, and re-establish a regime like Hitler's. Against such a background of beliefs, though they proved to be mistaken, Brecht's appeals from East Germany to Western intellectuals to work for peace, which were interpreted as enticements to submit to Soviet demands, become understandable, however difficult it is to see how the resemblance between Stalin and Hitler came to be overlooked. Brecht believed in a vast, universal movement spreading over several centuries, the first victory of which had happened in the Soviet Union. It was satisfying that even a part of Germany was now following suit.

There were events that could have given him pause. He knew what had happened to writers in the Soviet Union who opposed the régime; but then his willingness for self-sacrifice in the cause of the Party could take extreme forms, as some of his 'didactic plays' show. There were signs, even before he decided for East Germany, that totalitarian ideas were in force there too. As early as 1947 there were reports of young political suspects, of liberal views, being sent to imprisonment. In 1948 the 'Kasernierte Volkspolizei', or People's Police, a paramilitary organisation with policing powers, partly under former Nazi officers, had been set up, and in the same year liberal students' leaders in East Berlin and several other towns were arrested. The 'Freie Deutsche Jugend', meanwhile, looked remarkably like the former Hitler Youth in its uniform, its banner-carrying, its mass parades, and the support it had from government sources in outvying rival youth organisations. There was no one in the West, not even Senator McCarthy, to rival the ferocious political judge, 'Red Hilde' Benjamin, who in 1949 became Vice-President of the High Court and passed severe sentences on political offenders. But it could still be held that it was too early to allow freedom of expression, when so many of the population had been fighting in the Nazi cause only four or five years earlier.

The intense dissatisfaction of many East Germans must have been known to Brecht. It was partly due to economic causes: unlike the U.S.A., the U.S.S.R. demanded reparations from the former enemy country, despite its being ruled by Communists, and recovery from the war was slower than in the West. Dissatisfaction was partly also political, and gave rise to such vast numbers of emigrants to the West that in 1952 the Democratic Republic sealed off its frontier with the Federal Republic. Hundreds still risked death by crossing the barbed-wire fences or swimming rivers and canals under fire from East German guards. Indeed, Brecht had not returned without some forebodings. As early as April 1949 he was attempting (on the grounds of his wife's being Austrian) to obtain an Austrian passport, and his grounds for doing so showed how much he mistrusted the East German regime. In saying that he needed such a foreign nationality in order to gain access to as many German-speaking stages as possible, he conceded in effect that an East German passport could not be relied on for getting out of the country even for so innocuous a purpose. When he did at length become Austrian he kept the fact secret for over a year, after which it was discovered through an indiscretion. Like Galileo, Brecht was securing a means of going on writing what he thought.

The need for compromise was perhaps greater than he imagined. Having been Austrian since 1950 he was under no absolute compulsion to make the political – not aesthetic – concessions required of him in March 1951 in connection with *Lucullus*.[1] He may well have felt that in these early days a show of compliance would be beneficial, as in fact it was, for in the autumn of the same year he was awarded a 'National Prize, First Class'. Yet he was more than discontented, politically, if the authoritative report is to be believed, that in July 1952 he was considering exile in China.[2] Judging by this, there must have been times when he despaired of Communism in East Germany. Yet again, he seems to have felt a very strong impulse to say exactly what the regime might be expected to require of him. In 1953, when Stalin died, he published as fulsome a eulogy as any:

The oppressed people of five continents, those who have already liberated themselves and all who are fighting for world peace, must have felt their hearts miss a beat, when they heard that Stalin was dead. He was the embodiment of their hope. But the intellectual and material weapons he produced are at hand, and so is the doctrine with which to produce new ones.[3]

We still do not know under what tension Brecht had to live at this time, whether he was cajoled or threatened, blackmailed or tricked. The moral quality of his compliance, as one of the few writers in East Germany who were actually free to walk out, must remain obscure for the present at least, as must his real attitude towards Stalin, on which there has been some controversy.[4] The point to be observed is that he concurred with official rulings and attitudes on all crucial matters. Within three years of Stalin's death, after the Soviet denunciations of Stalin's 'personality cult', Brecht was talking just as readily of the need for Stalinism to be liquidated.[5] At no point did he make any personal contribution to the formulation of Party policy.

The testing time came on 16 and 17 June 1953, when tens of thousands of East Berliners rose in revolt against the ruling Socialist Unity Party, to be followed by workers in Dresden, Chemnitz, Leipzig, and many other cities. For twenty-four hours there were mass-processions and demonstrations, Party officials and People's Police were attacked; for rather longer there were strikes throughout the Soviet Zone. Government buildings were stormed, the Red Flag over the Brandenburger Tor was hauled down, the Soviet Zonal Headquarters besieged. For a very short while it looked as though the population of the whole Zone were about to demand its rights, particularly free elections, better working conditions, and a reunited Germany.

Soviet tanks and People's Police had everything in Berlin under control by the evening of 17 June: even an armed rising would have stood no chance against the Red Army. Berlin was the first to experience the power which later crushed Budapest and Prague.

On the morning of 17 June, Brecht attended a meeting of theatre staff in the rehearsal building of the Berliner Ensemble, during which he wrote various letters, including one to Walter Ulbricht, First Secretary of the Socialist Unity Party, reading as follows:

History will pay respect to the revolutionary impatience of the Socialist Unity Party. The great dialogue with the masses on the speed with which Socialism is being built will lead to a review of, and a securing of Socialist achievements. I am impelled to express to you at this moment my solidarity with the Socialist Unity Party of Germany.[6]

Given the explosive situation, this was an obscure way of putting things, and it is not too surprising that Ulbricht, ignoring the mild criticism perhaps implied in the words 'revolutionary impatience', passed the letter to the Party newspaper for publication. In fact, even the reference to impatience failed to be heard, since *Neues Deutschland* published only the final, apparently unambiguous sentence of Brecht's letter.

Brecht properly complained of this treatment, although nothing in his letter amounted to an objection, and the main point of it is to affirm his solidarity with whatever the Party decided to do, though he was still ignorant of what that might be. His later explanations thus sound inadequate.

He may have genuinely thought, as he told Peter Suhrkamp, that the revolt was being stirred up by columns of West German pro-Nazis, and he may have thought that he had done justice to the workers when he wrote in the Party newspaper a few days later, on 23 June, that they had demonstrated in 'justifiable discontent' and should not be treated in the same way as the provocateurs. It is understandable, at a time so close to the Nazi past, that Brecht should have mistrusted any anti-Communist demonstrations whatsoever. Yet his mild protest contains no reference to the brutality with which Soviet military power had been used against working men, and he seems to have been, all the time, more concerned about solidarity than with making his own independent contribution. There is no public utterance of his on record in which he makes any protest at governmental iniquities in politics, though in a poem he suggests that a government which feels the people have forfeited its confidence might do well to elect another people. He also protested at bureaucratic interference in art.[7] He sympathised with the reformist views of Wolfgang Harich, who was sentenced a few months after Brecht's death to ten years in prison, and he certainly stated, late in life, that Communism had been 'only hinted at, never put into practice'.[8] On the whole, this self-preserving, chameleon attitude, which enabled him to pay lip-service to authority while quietly getting on with his own interests, remained predominant.

He also benefited, considerably, though he had not necessarily aimed at the benefit. Within six months he had been appointed to the Advisory Committee on the Arts of the Ministry of Culture. Shortly afterwards came the allocation to himself and the Ensemble, in March 1954, of the Schiffbauerdamm Theater in Berlin, so that at last he had a place of his own to work in. In December 1954 came the award of the International Stalin Peace Prize, to receive which he later travelled, already a sick man, to Moscow. Though he died in 1956, he was on the way to an influential position in the Communist world, and his adaptability no doubt prospered his chances.

In his own world of the theatre, a greater degree of nonconformity was possible. The opportunity for practical experimentation was too good to be missed, and two phrases used by Brecht at rehearsals suggest the mood in which he took it. 'I'm not trying to show that I'm in the right, but to find out whether.' This was humble language in contrast with the dogmatism of earlier days. And again, this time to an actor: 'To hell with the play, its your turn now.' Nothing Brecht had written was sacrosanct; if the occasion demanded it, whole speeches could be inserted, new characters invented, sometimes even whole scenes concocted to put right some defect that stage production had revealed. And in this 'dialectical' approach to the theatre, keeping his work constantly in a state of flux, lay Brecht's most important contribution to the post-war Communist world. Marxism is a philosophy of adaptation to circumstances and careful observation of reality; if these qualities have been obscured in recent times, that is because it has become, as Christianity once became, a rigid system of dogma. Brecht's virtue is that he broke up the rigidity and thereby restored the system to some of its former dynamic force.

He had not lost his sly humour, nor his passion for a new world, though he was more content to wait for it now. The scroll containing a portrait of a Chinese sage, which he had carried about all through his exile and still retained, gives a clue to his ideals, and it was not for nothing that he wrote, apparently during the war, scenes for a play on the life of Confucius. The 'human-hearted' philosopher, also an exile, with his this-worldly religion, his unassuming ways, his attempts at transforming the 'Great Society' of China, and his adaptational approach to most human problems, had a good deal in common with the later Brecht. A greater tolerance was noticeable in him than had been seen before; he sat easy to the world, despite the fact that he was still bent on changing it out of all recognition, and there are many tributes from technicians, workmen, actors, and actresses both to his sharply critical attitude and to his willingness to adapt every situation and every talent to the best end in sight. Moreover, Brecht's view of the function of the theatre had changed. It was no longer to be directly political, but rather, as he wrote in the *Little Organon* of 1948, a place in which the worker might 'enjoy his terrible and never-ending labours as entertainment, together with the terrors of his ceaseless transformation'.[9] In short, it was fundamentally a much more aesthetic philosophy with which Brecht had returned: 'the easiest form of existence is' – not in the proletarian state, apparently, or that only incidentally, but – 'in art'.[10] A contemplative attitude is thus yoked with the revolutionary one that Brecht still maintained.

The plays of the seven years in which Brecht experienced day-by-day life in a Communist State at first hand do not express the mellower philosophy, however much it may have been expressed in his daily life. His version of the *Antigone* of Sophocles (1947), based on the translation by Hölderlin, deliberately avoids the tragic, and by destroying all possible sympathy for King Creon turns him into a flatly rapacious caricature of Hitler. Something similar is done for *Coriolanus* (1952–3), where once again the traces of nobility, in the most unlikable of all Shakespeare's heroes, are erased to leave only the lineaments of the bloody warmonger. (Nevertheless, if Brecht's account of the hero-worshipping line normally taken by German producers is still correct,[11] his version has its uses.) Only in *The Days of the Commune* (1948–9), written in reply to the Norwegian Nordahl Grieg's play on the same topic, *The Defeat*, did Brecht create afresh, and the moral here remains ambiguous: whether the Parisian Communards of 1871 were mistaken in their tactics, is a problem that the play leaves unsolved, though one has the impression that Brecht may not have thought so. The remaining plays are all adaptations. *The Tutor* (1950), from the late eighteenth-century play by Reinhold Lenz, reinterprets the social criticism of the *Sturm und Drang* age; *The*

Trial of Joan of Arc (1952) (the third play involving this heroine) is almost a 'documentary', based on contemporary records
– taken from a radio-play by Anna Seghers, it is difficult to see
Brecht's hand in it at all. He also completed in 1954 the play
Turandot (which has scarcely any relation to earlier works by
Schiller and Puccini of the same name) after many attempts
dating back to 1930. It was never performed or published in
his lifetime, and is one of his weakest pieces. Undoubtedly the
best of all these post-war works is the version of Molière's *Don
Juan* (1952) already referred to – a lively satire on wealthy
epicureanism. Yet in the last work of all – to an unstated extent
the fruit of collaboration – Brecht appears to have succumbed
once more to the propagandistic strain. *Drums and Trumpets*
(1955), based on Farquhar's Restoration comedy *The Recruiting Officer,* is a tedious satire on a British colonial system which
ceased to exist in anything remotely like this form many decades
ago. The fact that it was written is a portent of what might
have become of Brecht's dramatic talent had he lived to old
age in the atmosphere of the Democratic Republic.

Yet the play with which, so to speak, he entered the Republic, *The Caucasian Chalk Circle,* would not have led anyone to
expect a hardening of attitude. Always susceptible to his environment, Brecht may later have readopted some of his former
propagandist ways under the influence of his surroundings after
1949. Certainly, this play written in 1944–5 is only superficially
related to the Communist moral it appears to inculcate. The
simple story of the young Georgian girl, Grusha, who saves the
infant child of a tyrannical governor during an insurrection,
seems to be sufficient in itself. The fact that, when the real
mother disputes possession of the child with her before the
'good, bad judge' Azdak, the verdict goes in her favour because
she alone has shown a true motherly nature, is politically irre-
levant. It does not follow from this, as the epilogue would suggest, that the Soviet authorities are entitled to deprive indus-
trious farming peasants of their land in order to hand it over to
others who will use it for growing vines. Either group might
make good use of the land, for all one knows, and the moral
claim which Grusha has, compared with the real mother, is not
represented in this purely economic and political issue. Besides, the prologue, in which this contemporary problem is out-

lined, is remarkable for the prim diction of the Soviet officials, the conventional picture it gives of shrewd, but good-hearted peasants, and the 'socialist realism' of its style and presentation. The play could exist without either the prologue or epilogue, and the lack of political relevance would not be noticeable.

The framework is in complete contrast with the non-naturalistic, many-faceted, lyrical, humorous, yet socially conscious elements of the 'play within the play'. The girl Grusha is not in the least conventionally drawn, though she too is shrewd and good-hearted. We do not sit back in uncomfortable or smug contentment telling ourselves that this is what sturdy peasants are really like, as we are invited to do in the prologue. She shows considerable courage in crossing a rickety bridge over a mountain chasm while being pursued by insurrectionist soldiers; she combines this with artfulness, a ready wit, blunt honesty, stubborn insistence, and an unshakable moral probity. When she is married for convenience sake to a dying man who will be at least a nominal father for the child she has saved, and when the man, a skrimshanker, rises from his 'deathbed' on hearing that the war is over, she continues to pay him a wifely respect, shows no resentment or self-pity. When, later, her lover Simon to whom she is betrothed returns from the war, she allows him to suspect her of infidelity rather than betray the child to its enemies. Courage, perseverance, motherliness, dutifulness, self-sacrifice she shows time and again. Yet because of her equanimity and lack of self-regard, these qualities have no false ring.

This is due in part to the deliberately non-naturalistic language Grusha speaks. Brecht makes no attempt to reproduce peasant speech faithfully: Grusha's is sprinkled with proverbs and dialect forms, but it also includes direct translations of English idiom; when she sings a lullaby to the child it is at once a song that vividly recalls ancient German folk-art and at the same time has a modern ring. Subtly and continuously through the language Brecht persuades us not quite to believe in Grusha, to accept her as a creation of art, and to look beyond her to a reality which in part we re-create ourselves. The formality of his presentation reaches its climax in the scene, concluding the first part of Grusha's adventures, where Simon returns and speaks with her across a river that separates them. The lovers address each other at first in an exchange of proverbs which is both humorous and characteristic of their peasant origins. It is also, however, quite impersonal, a drawing on common tradition, and it is only by reflection that the deep personal relationship between them is felt. In the climactic moment of the scene, in fact, neither speaks, and it is left to the narrator to reveal what each 'thought, but did not say'. Thus they confront each other in formal attitudes which are never realistically portrayed but are at the same time deeply moving, and it is by a similar estrangement that Brecht succeeds in making the outstanding human qualities of Grusha credible and acceptable.

The scenes of Grusha's escape, adventures, marriage, and rejection by Simon, forming about half the play, make a loosely-strung narrative in the fashion of 'epic' theatre. While there is a certain thread connecting them, however – they do not stand 'each for themselves', as Brecht suggested earlier that 'epic' scenes should do[12] – the interest is sustained not so much by the thin plot as by the detailed interactions of the characters and by the beauty of the portrayal. Since *Baal,* Brecht had scarcely made any use in his plays of the natural scene. In *The Caucasian Chalk Circle,* as in *Puntila* and *The Good Woman* and in his later poetry, the world of nature returns. The scene by the river itself, indicated on the stage merely by two ground-rows of reeds, evokes by its bareness, coupled with the lyrical song of the narrator preceding it, an awareness of loveliness. The icicles above Grusha's hut, as she waits in isolation for the winter to pass, become moving tokens of spring as they melt, and the musical notes of a xylophone offstage, recording the falling drops of water, add excitement by their rising intensity. There is time for contemplation and for exhilaration in these austerely presented moments; the spectator is not whirled along as he was by the action of earlier plays, and not encouraged to indulge in ecstatic Nature-worship, but rather to recognise with pleasure the delight that is to be had from Nature, off the stage. There is both detachment and attachment.

The settings also, in this part of the play, evoke an astringent delight. The descending white backcloth has already been mentioned. There is also the scene of Grusha's wedding, contrived to give a Brueghelesque harmony of brown, oatmeal, sepia, with an occasional splash of red: peasant colours in a peasant setting, crowded, earthy, vulgarly frank, but shaped into a frame of unity that is comic, sympathetic, and has a lop-sided symmetry of its own. There is the strange effect of the empty stage after the insurrection has passed by, with the voice of the narrator emerging from one side to comment on the silence and thereby, oddly enough, to intensify it. Meanwhile, from time to time, the prose speech breaks into verse such as that in which Grusha affirms her love at Simon's first departure:

> Simon Chachava, I will wait for you.
> Go in good heart to the battle, soldier,
> The bloody battle, the bitter battle
> From which not all come back:
> When you come back, I will be there.
> I will wait for you under the green elm
> I will wait for you under the bare elm
> I will wait till the last man comes back
> And longer.
> When you come back from the battle
> No boots will stand by the door
> The pillow by mine will be empty
> And my mouth unkissed.
> When you come back, when you come back
> You can say it is all as it was.

It comes as a shock to go on from this moving language and these scenes to the following series which forgets Grusha entirely in order to introduce the story of the judge Azdak. From Azdak's first speech, the spectator is hit by a forceful language which English can barely reproduce: 'Schnaub nicht, du bist kein Gaul. Und es hilft dir nicht bei der Polizei, wenn du läufst, wie ein Rotz im April. Steh, sag ich. . . . Setz dich nieder und futtre, da ist ein Stück Käse. Lang nichts gefressen? Warum bist du gerannt, du Arschloch?' The crudity of this, the rough vigour, the cynicism and humour and the underlying sympathy introduce the character of Azdak himself, which stands in strange contrast to Grusha's. Azdak is a thief, a time-server, a coward, who by a lucky accident is raised during the insurrection to a position of authority. As a judge he is corrupt, licentious, contemptuous of law and order, a lickspittle. His life is spent, unlike Grusha's, not in rebellious opposition to society's moral standards, but in careful adaptation to them, going along with the tide, and keeping an eye on the main chance. But such an account does less than justice to this unpredictable Brechtian rogue. In the first scene, finding that the poor man he thought he was sheltering is in fact the Grand Duke, fleeing from the insurrection, he still does not hand him over to the police, although whether from sheer contempt for the police, as he says, or contempt for the Duke, or from an inscrutable sympathy such as Ernst Busch implies when he plays him, is never clear. Promptly, he rushes into town to denounce himself, believing that the soldiery will welcome the news of his treachery — some strange conscientiousness is at work in him. Yet on discovering them to be indifferent to the rights and wrongs of the insurrection, he willingly allows them to clothe him in judicial robes, and goes off on his rampaging procession through the countryside, delivering sentences that completely reverse accepted standards of justice. He accepts bribes, but (though he keeps the money) only as an indication of the wealth of the litigants, which stands in his eyes in inverse proportion to their rights. He makes an award in favour of a poor woman who has been helped by a bandit, on the grounds that only a miracle could explain how a leg of pork came to fly through a poor woman's window: those who accuse the bandit of stealing the pork and throwing it through the window are condemned for godlessness and disbelief in miracles. When a buxom young woman accuses a farmhand of rape, he considers her luxurious gait and the shape of her buttocks and finds her guilty of assault and battery with a dangerous weapon, after which he goes off with her to 'examine the scene of the crime'. And when order is reestablished he falls over himself with dutiful promises that Grusha, whom he has not yet met, shall be beheaded as soon as she is found.

Azdak is a standing affront, and at the same time a standing reminder of the questionable values on which society is based. He has one principle, that the rights of the poor are disregarded and that this situation must be reversed. Apart from that, he proceeds *ad hoc*. If a buxom girl is likely to commit rape he offers her the opportunity. On the other hand, if he foresees danger in maintaining his one principle, he gives way immediately: 'I'm not doing anyone the favour of showing human greatness.' Yet all this is not mere self-gratification or concern for his own skin. There is nothing that can properly be called a self in Azdak, nothing consistent or foreseeable in his actions: he acts on impulse. He sets no store by his actions, any more than Grusha does by hers, and it is this that helps to make him the most fascinating character in the play, insulting and generous, preposterous and humble, ignorant and wise, blasphemous and pious. In his Villonesque song to the poor woman he addresses her as though she were the Virgin Mary and begs mercy for such damned creatures as himself – a strange translation from religious into human terms which still has an atmosphere of genuine devoutness. In the scene where he is buffeted in his false robes by the soldiery, the production of the Berliner Ensemble was deliberately styled to recall the buffeting before the crucifixion. And in the comment of the narrator there is a further suggestion of a wider scope: 'And so he broke the laws, as he broke bread, that it might feed them.' The suggestion need not be taken too far. A thin thread of symbolism suggesting Christ runs through Brecht's work, it is true, from Baal and Bargan onwards. The slightly Biblical language here, however, is not much more significant than the commiserating nod that Ernst Busch, playing the Dutch cook, gave to the crucifix by the wayside. Yet there is in Azdak, the scandal, the gnome, the cynical good-liver, something disturbing and provocative as well as attractive. He denies all the virtues, mocks at repentance and charity, ridicules courage, and, strangely enough, he gets our sympathy in the process. For he is plainly being himself to the top of his bent, lusting and helping the poor, crawling in abject fear and at the same time inviting the soldiers to recognise their own doglike obedience, answering every prompting with instinctive recklessness. If we give him our sympathy, as we cannot help doing, in a way, so long as he dominates the stage, he sets all Grusha's virtuousness at naught. This is Baal, returned to the scene in a new guise, and all Baal's fascination pours out from him.

In the final scene of all, the two sides are confronted with one another, the disruptive, ambiguous underminer and the calm, shrewd, motherly girl who would rather die than forego her humanity. Azdak is called to try the case in which the real mother of Grusha's 'child', the wife of the former governor of the province, claims possession of her son. By a fortunate turn of events, the same Grand Duke whose life Azdak saved earlier on has now returned to power, and thus Azdak's servile promise to the governor's wife no longer has any hold over him, if indeed he ever meant to keep it. Azdak proceeds, however, as usual, accepting bribes from the wealthier party, while abusing Simon and Grusha who have nothing to offer him, and it is this which brings on the first serious opposition he has had to encounter. Grusha declares that she has no respect for a judge such as he is, 'no more than I have for a thief and a murderer that does what he likes'. Her moral protest is a straightforward indictment cf his libertinism (which is no mere show), and none the worse for that; in fact she has all, or nearly all, our sympathy. Yet the end will have already been guessed. After the 'trial of the chalk circle' in which each woman is to pull at the child from different sides, and Grusha fails to pull for fear of hurting the boy, Azdak ceremonially declares that Grusha is the true mother since she alone has shown true motherly feelings.

This is not a sentimental ending awarding victory to justice against the run of the odds. Rather, it is the fusion of two conceptions of justice. Azdak's instinctive prompting on this occasion (he is, after all, in safety now, with the governor's wife in political disgrace) is to award Grusha the custody of the child. But this instinctive prompting is a part of his elemental originality, his closeness to the roots of his nature, and his complete detachment from them. His decision has gathered the weight and incontrovertibility of a natural phenomenon, and despite his mockery of the virtues here is one virtue in Grusha that he respects without thought of argument.

Thus the two sides come together. Like Nietzsche, Azdak demands opposition such as he gets from Grusha, and thrives on it. Like Nature itself, he is ambiguous and amoral and requires the rebelliousness of humanity to bring out his qualities to the full. Then, however, when he meets with opposition, he reveals an unexpected generosity (as Nietzsche never did). He is like Baal, it is true. But Baal was never opposed, lived his life in pure self-fulfilment, and died only to the tune of contempt from others. Azdak is Baal, and all that lies behind Baal, brought into relationship with human beings, and this relationship and conflict serve to make *The Caucasian Chalk Circle* far greater in scope than its predecessor. The virtue of Grusha is both convincingly stated and confronted with Azdak's zest, the amoralism of Azdak is made to look both repugnant and curiously attractive, and yet in the final moments a fusion of Grusha's human demands and Azdak's inhuman unpredictability brings about a sense of at least temporary fulfilment. As the narrator has it, the period of Azdak's life as a judge could be looked back upon as 'a brief Golden Age almost of justice'. It was not *the* Golden Age, and it was not a time of complete justice. Both Azdak and Grusha have been too 'estranged' for us to be able to accept them as models or heroes. But while steering clear of absolutes Brecht creates here an ending which is satisfying on a purely human plane. Despite the riotous exaggeration of a great part of the play, from which he never recants for an instant, the conclusion is moderately and accurately stated.

But it is not a political conclusion, or only the vestige of one. The epilogue, with its moral that tractors should go to those who can drive them well, is unexceptionable, but says little politically beyond the barest statement of principle, and clearly involves an inequality and a control of distribution that one would have thought inimical to Brecht. As Aristotle says, and for once Brecht would have been in agreement, 'If one man is outstandingly superior in flute-playing, but far inferior in birth or good looks . . . even then, I say, the good player should get the best instrument.'[13] But this is only the beginning of an argument which does not by any means inevitably lead to a Communist solution, and might even lead to an anti-Communist one. (Who, for instance, should be provided with tractors in a country where white settlers happen to be the most mechanically-minded citizens?) Brecht had been welcomed back to East Germany, but the question remained, what influence his work could have, from a political point of view.

Initially, it had very little. To this day, Brecht's political influence in the world at large probably consists more in the general idea that his plays convey a Marxist message, rather than in the actual conveying of one. Yet the growth of his reputation in Germany, East and West, though it has been almost equal on both sides of the Iron Curtain, has not corresponded to any political developments in the two states.

The way in which Brecht increased in official estimation in East Germany has already been mentioned, though he was still not entirely *persona grata*. The 'Brecht Archives' clearly contain a great deal of unpublished material which the custodians, Brecht's relatives and friends, have been circumspect in making available even to *bona fide* researchers, perhaps out of anxiety that too many of his views might prove unpalatable in governmental circles, once they became public property. Brecht's death, from coronary thrombosis, on 14 August 1956, came too soon for him to see for himself more than the beginnings of his international fame, though he had prepared the Ensemble for its London engagement that year, and must have seen the governmental recognition this implied.

Since that time, he has become far and away the most popular dramatist in the Federal Republic, after Shakespeare, and has remained so for many years. A count of his plays listed in *Die Welt* on 24 April 1971 shows that there were, at 75 theatres and opera-houses, 11 productions of Shakespeare that week, and 10 by Brecht, the nearest rivals being Schiller with 6 and Goethe with 3 productions, while Chekhov, Molière and Shaw had 2 each. A similar estimate results from analysing the figures for West German productions in 1965.[14] Yet, although the Social Democrats have gained power in the West in recent years, they are far from being the Marxist party they once were, and Brecht's long-lasting popularity cannot be attributed to a Leftward trend in the Federal Republic.

A similar picture emerges from the East, so far as popularity is concerned. In the eight and a half years before May Day 1973, the numbers of performances of Brecht's plays in all theatres of the German Democratic Republic, apart from that of the Berliner Ensemble, were:

> *Señora Carrar* : 457
> *Herr Puntila* : 376
> *The Caucasian Chalk Circle* : 299
> *The Threepenny Opera* : 243
> *The Good Woman of Setzuan* : 182
> *The Mother* : 155

while between 60 and 120 each were given of *Happy End, Galileo, Arturo Ui, Mother Courage, Drums and Trumpets,*

Days of the Commune, Mahagonny, Don Juan, The Condemnation of Lucullus and *Schweyk*, and less than 30 each of *Fear and Misery of the Third Reich, Edward II, Simone Machard,* and *The Trial of Jeanne d'Arc*. In all, about 2,600 performances were given at 47 theatres.

Performances by the Berliner Ensemble, for a longer period than eight and a half years in some cases, numbered (by 1 May 1973) –

> *The Threepenny Opera* : 575 since 1960
> *Arturo Ui* : 522 since 1959
> *Schweyk* : 409 since 1962
> *Coriolanus* : 226 since 1964

while less than 70 each had been given of *Galileo* (since 1964); *St Joan of the Stockyards* (since 1968); *Señora Carrar* (since 1971); *In the Cities' Jungle* (since 1971) and *Turandot* (since 10 February 1973).[15]

The great majority of these had been performed before the National Brecht Week held, in celebration of the 75th anniversary of his birth, in February 1973 throughout the Democratic Republic under the auspices of the Ministry for Culture. By that time he had become almost wholly respectable: the organisers were able, after all, to quote words of his from the time of his first settling in the Republic:

> When I came back
> My hair was not yet grey
> I was glad
> The toils of the mountains lie behind us
> Before us lie the toils of the plains.

It was over sixteen years since the Hungarian uprising had been quelled, nearly twelve since the Berlin Wall had closed all prospect of escape to the West, four since East German tanks descended on Czechoslovakia, and Brecht had seen nothing of these events. The country was much more prosperous, and the official claim that the population was more contented than ever before contained a degree of truth.

The question, so far as Brecht's plays were concerned, was whether they did enough to arouse genuine and fruitful criticism, whether they did not induce too easy an assumption of the Party truths which the government was eager to have accepted. It is noticeable that by far the most frequently performed work, apart from the performances by the Ensemble, was a work of the crudest propaganda, which Brecht seems scarcely to have recognised, not including it in the main series of his *Versuche*. The Theatre in the Democratic Republic has become one of the most subsidised in Europe, with lavish expenditure on buildings and décor and costumes.[16] Its task certainly includes the inculcation of acquiescence in Communist Party methods and plans, for, though criticism is allowed, criticism of the main trend is not. What harm to the Establishment could the most frequently performed works do? *Arturo Ui, Schweyk, Señora Carrar* and *The Mother* are about the evils of the past, *Coriolanus* clearly denounces only the Fascist warmonger, and the milder plays remaining, *Puntila*, the *Chalk Circle*, and *The Good Woman*, have nothing in them to promote an independent spirit except the incalculable Azdak. More may come of that distant descendant of Baal than could ever have seemed foreseeable in the 1920s. But by and large Brecht's work stands in danger of being swallowed up in the state's machinery for the inculcation of official precepts. It is outside Communist countries that his work still has a chance of being effective politically, as he intended it should be. It takes its place there as part of a theatre that is revolutionary in dozens of senses, and it is time now to see it within that wider frame of reference.

10

CONCLUSION

Since 1789, and more markedly since 1848, theatre has taken on a meaning it never had before – a very small portion of theatre, that is. All discussion inevitably excludes what millions of theatregoers are really interested in: *Chu Chin Chow, The Mousetrap, The Student Prince,* a fact which is worth recalling when the matter in hand is the effect of Brecht's work in the political field. But within the small area of serious theatre, it is possible to agree very much with Robert Brustein, who sees almost all its major figures in the last hundred years or so as participants in a 'Theatre of Revolt'. 'Revolt', Brustein writes, 'is the energy which drives the modern theatre',[1] and though the word applies less, say, to Chekhov than to some others, it is relevant to Wagner, Ibsen, Strindberg, Shaw, Artaud, Genet, and many more.

A question about Brecht's work that presents itself at once is, then, whether his particular methods – above all his epic theatre and alienation – are more or less effective, convincing, stimulating to revolt, than others', and a first, very sweeping answer might be that the effect depends on the audiences themselves. Auber's opera *La Muette de Portici,* which Peter Demetz calls 'a truly "culinary" work', so inflamed its Brussels audience in 1830 that it sparked off one of the most successful revolutions in modern Europe (Beaumarchais' *Figaro,* on the other hand, which might have been expected to have had more effect in 1784, led politically only to the author's imprisonment.) Audiences of the first half of the nineteenth century were in any case more easily roused. As an observer in 1859 wrote, 'modern audiences are less easily worked up to a demonstration than they were at the beginning of the present century',[2] and this was due partly to the fact that variety theatres and music halls drew off the more boisterous elements, partly that eating and drinking during performances ceased, partly that self-conscious respectability had become more widespread. With the advent of cinema and television as competitors with the theatre, audiences changed completely or were reduced to tiny groups: cinema audiences ceased even to applaud at the end, and even less of a broadly shared, common experience can be felt by the T.V. watcher. Brecht on television is in no better position than the political commentator, one more voice among hundreds.

The special value of Brecht's methods may be compared with Ibsen's. By the standards of epic theatre, Ibsen's naturalism could not have aroused the intense political discussions or created the great effect on theatre that it had. It is true that Ibsen by his own account had no interest in supporting the suffragettes of his day, or of supporting any other of the particular social or political programmes connected with his name. But audiences saw *A Doll's House* and demanded rights for women, they saw *Rosmersholm* and derived a justification for free love, they saw *Ghosts* and agreed for or against euthanasia. Naturalism had no inhibiting effects there. Official attitudes could be equally arbitrary about the effect of plays. Hauptmann's naturalistic work, *The Weavers*, though a politically neutral account of a workers' revolt in 1845, was for several years prevented by Prussian censorship from being performed, on the grounds that the mere treatment of such a theme was tantamount to revolutionary incitement. Shaw, following in Ibsen's wake, but with his own style of comedy, brilliant dialogue, and tomfoolery, brought political discussion into thousands of places where theatre was normally never thought of.

It is not the method or the style, then, that we need most to consider. Creating political awareness is at least as much a job for public relations officers as for dramatists. The distinctive mark of Brecht's theatre is that he sought to make a particular effect on particular audiences. Ibsen would speak, in private, of a general world revolution, but nothing definitely suggesting that appeared in any of his plays except *An Enemy of the People*. Shaw would propound all manner of nostrums in the course of his life, but his purpose was to enliven rather than achieve through his theatre any specific political programme, and his appeal was to middle-class audiences. Brecht, on the other hand, as Günther Anders remarks, 'says what he has to say to particular people, in particular situations, to reach a particular end for particular reasons'.[3] No other dramatist of revolt has done quite that.

Robert Brustein goes on to say that modern theatre, 'in its negative critique of existing conventions and institutions . . . rarely offers any substitute ideas or ideals'.[4] That could not be said of Brecht without qualification. The fact of poverty in the modern world – which is not a major concern of Ibsen, Chekhov, Strindberg, O'Neill, Pirandello, or indeed any of the major dramatists of the last two centuries, with the exception of Hauptmann, Synge, Büchner – is always with him, and is not simply a matter for a negative critique. The army of English beggars in *The Threepenny Opera,* the Russian poor in *The Mother,* the Spanish peasants in *Señora Carrar,* the American slum-dwellers in *In the Cities' Jungle* and *St Joan of the Stockyards,* the Finnish women in *Puntila,* and the German workers in *Fear and Misery*: wherever he went Brecht was drawn to make dramatic images of working people, and neither O'Casey nor Gorki nor Hauptmann nor Lorca so persistently or for so long maintained that sharp focus of interest. Brecht's people were not always so vividly realised: old Hilse in Hauptmann's *The Weavers* is more credible, in realistic terms, than Frau Luckerniddle in *St Joan of the Stockyards* – to take an extreme example – and generally speaking Brecht was seldom at home in drawing working-class characters. Like Shaw, portraying Todger Fairmile in terms of a music-hall sketch of a working man, Brecht's different upbringing inclined him towards caricature and gratuitous comedy. Yet he was also capable of presenting working-class characters with the panache and verve of Mother Courage, or the solid humanity of Grusha.

Humanity, not shown when Brecht felt it to be mere self-indulgence, is also the distinguishing feature when one compares his work with the plays of Artaud, Genet, and Beckett, and even more in comparison with Ionesco, his chief rival as a world-dramatist in the 1960s. The arguments brought by Ionesco against Brecht[5] take on a different aspect when one recalls Brecht's actually achieved characters. Ionesco sees Brecht, along with many other dramatists and critics, as an ideologist, a man with a committed theatre, and therefore one which 'leads directly to the concentration camp'.[6] (This was not said explicitly of Brecht in particular, though for a time he was Ionesco's chief

target.) Though a committed theatre may imply such dangerous consequences, the existence of characters like Mother Courage and of Grusha demonstrates how remote those consequences
are from almost everything Brecht wrote: the sole exception
would seem to be the one-sided trial and ruthless condemnation
of the warmonger Lucullus, which is troublingly close in spirit
to the Soviet treason-trials of the 1930s.

Again, in comparison with Ionesco, to say nothing of Artaud
and Genet, Brecht stands for a certain rationality in theatre. He
was capable of writing 'absurd theatre', as *The Elephant Child*
shows, and he was also capable of providing some questionable
models of rationality. Yet there is no doubt at all that Galileo's
demonstration that dropped pebbles do not fly upward was
characteristic of the kind of point Brecht wanted to inculcate.
He did not regard 'total reality', in Ionesco's phrase, as essentially absurd, but rather as a condition in which the full potentiality of man for good could be realised. That essentially
though not exclusively Marxist belief is the most distinctive
thing about Brecht as a humanist playwright.

There is some truth, all the same, in maintaining that, like
almost all modern dramatists of revolt, Brecht does not, in
Brustein's phrase 'offer any substitute ideas or ideals'. Clearly,
he intends a transformation of the world, in which poverty and
exploitation no longer exist, but there is no more clarity about
it than that. The glimpses include the provision of legs of pork
for poor old women – to put it in the simple form proposed by
Azdak – but perhaps also a certain general arbitrary satisfying
of impulses: the crowd in Galileo is anarchic, when it cele-
brates its release from antiquated astronomy, and Brecht seldom
offers any picture of what life would actually be like in a world
where the expropriators had been expropriated. The nearest he
comes to it is the prologue to *The Caucasian Chalk Circle*,
where the bland, jolly relation between commissars and peasants makes so un-Brechtian an impression and belongs rather
to the spirit of a propaganda magazine. At the vital moment,
when the ideal has to be formulated, Brecht is as much in
difficulties as all other dramatists of revolt.

This may be explained by saying that, as a Marxist, and therefore in a certain unusual sense a neo-Hegelian, Brecht had as
little possibility of conceiving a future just society as had
Ionesco, a neo-Hegelian in a much more familiar sense. The

curious similarity between them is that both are dialectical thinkers, who believe in a constant flux and reflux as the characteristic of continuing life, but who look to a position outside the flux, outside the dialectical polarities, as the ultimate goal either of themselves or of mankind, or as the place from which the final, irreducible statement will have to be made. For Brecht, the polarities are in the relation between employer and worker, exploiter and exploited, but these are not ultimately real in the way that Silesian weavers were real to Hauptmann, or the Irish fisherwomen to Synge. They are warring elements, phenomena in a world that has not yet achieved the classless society, but just on that very account not to be taken entirely seriously – except on a few occasions. One can understand Brecht's flippant caricatures of working-class men and women, as well as his off-handed way of illustrating an argument with inadequate material, as deriving from an occasional, temporary yet fundamental unconcern with the affairs of the present age in comparison with those of the age which Marxist politics is to bring about. His concern with poverty is real enough, but it is coupled, paradoxically, with a more deeply-held conviction that the millennium will put an end to such injustice. The pity felt for the poor of today must not obstruct the programme for abolishing poverty soon, and this stifling of pity can lead, in Brecht's case, to absurd exaggeration in portraying workers.

The similarity, though by no means identity with Ionesco's position is that Ionesco sees all human activity as absurd, without logical justification, and endeavours to bring home to his audiences a realisation of this, just as Brecht, by different means, seeks to bring home the self-contradictoriness of the capitalist economic system. Ionesco's audiences, if they react as he predicts, will realise with increasing intensity the isolation of man, the breakdown of language, and ultimately the total reality which is complete spontaneity, unpredictability, gratuitousness. But they will also, in Richard Coe's words, experience moments when the terror of absurdity reaches its highest pitch of intensity:

for only then do we realise that, between the total and the sham reality, there is, in the last analysis, no effective contrast. Both are gratuitous, both are void, both are meaningless; the choice is never between wholly true and false, real and unreal, but merely between an intolerable recognition of the absurd, and an equally intolerable refusal to admit it.[7]

It sometimes appears that what Brecht sees as the state of society beyond the present one is similarly intolerable in both ways: the present egoistic society is to be condemned, yet the release, if the crowd in *Galileo* or the alienated comment of the judge in *Puntila,* or Azdak's chamaeleon adaptations offer a fair means of judging, would be equally egoistic, and no easier to respect or commend: a kind of free-for-all in which everyone would truly be provided for 'according to his needs', though not in the sense Marx intended. Brecht's ideas of people's needs are more robust, more gross, and more lively than is allowed for in more orthodox Marxist writings, especially where sexual needs are concerned. As a result, his utopia – so far as we see it at all – often looks like a reassertion of individuality in the highest degree, and without social restraints.

Where Brecht parts company with Ionesco is in his very liveliness, in his greater expectation of satisfaction: he is a kind of Nietzsche, in this respect, to Ionesco's life-denying Schopenhauer. The exuberance in *Rhinoceros* is something that Ionesco's Bérenger regards with envy, yet distrust. The exuberance of Galileo, Puntila, Azdak, though it is not presented as ideal, being still part of a capitalist world, is enjoyed by Brecht's audiences, and meant to be enjoyed. Though they have no justification in terms of a perfect society, and though Shen Te in her most agonised moments would condemn them, they are 'affirmed', to use a Nietzschean expression: not approved, not presented without the awareness of their opposites, but welcomed and asserted as part of the total complex of polarities.

The energy which Brecht derives from his revolt is greeted with enthusiasm not only because of the vitality of the plays at their best, but because of his equally lively concern with making theatre in every possible sense. Despite his long absence during exile from work in actual theatres, Brecht is always conscious of himself as a theatrical craftsman. He has not only the audience in mind but the stage as well: he is not spinning plots or recounting events that could take place in some real world outside the theatre; he is imagining, as he writes, an actor on a stage, and the extraordinary flow of his theatrical invention comes from that. In the whole history of theatre there can scarcely have been an innovator in so many fields as Brecht. True, masks had been used before, and so had many other devices, yet the variety of media, tricks, implements, gadgets, styles of decor, methods of acting and rehearsing he requires testify to a great theatrical imagination. There are the stilts, the padded chests, the masks in *Edward II*, the mountain of chairs in *Puntila*, the wagon in *Mother Courage*, the announcements on the blackboard about the whirlwind in *Mahagonny*, the carefree swinging of the backcloth in *The Caucasian Chalk Circle*, all of them objects conceived for a purpose. Ibsen is equally prolific in inventing naturalistic properties which add meaning to his plays. But he does not have also Brecht's gift for making scenes that are visually striking in themselves, apart from the words that go with them. There are few scenes in Ibsen (the avalanche in *Brand* would be an exception) that remain in one's mind not for what is said in them so much as for how they look, as do the scenes where Kattrin sits high on the roof, or Galileo carries a boy on a chair round the room to demonstrate the Copernican theory, or Hitler makes desperate attempts at goose-stepping towards all points of the compass, or Johanna Dark lies like a martyr on the ground while the Salvation Army banners mockingly bow over her, or Peachum's healthy beggars transmogrify themselves into figures that ought to, but don't, arouse extreme pity, or the loading down of the human Pope with robe after robe of divine authority. These, like the scene where Shakespeare's Richard II and Bolingbroke literally hold the crown between them, are only a few of the scores of occasions when Brecht shows himself as a man constantly thinking in terms of theatre.

Add to these the use of the half-curtain, of transparencies, exposed lighting, music as comment, documentary film reinforcing or contradicting events on stage, of addresses to the audience, the inculcation of critical attitudes in actors, and still only a small proportion of Brecht's devices have been mentioned. It does not matter that some of them may have come from Meyerhold or Piscator or the *commedia dell'arte*: the fact is that no other dramatist of any age has ever incorporated so many of them within his own work.

And yet, politically, it is almost a commonplace to say, that work is without notable effect on the political scene, and without any notable political vision. In European countries and in the U.S.A., theatre has not such a following as would make any remarkable political effect likely: Brecht has to compete now with hundreds of alternative forms of dramatic entertainment, very little of which is political. The dream of creating political change in the West through performances in theatres is remote, now. It belonged essentially to a time when Agitprop and similar organisations still promised to make theatre an everyday experience for working men, in or just outside their own factories. These were the particular people for whom, as Günther Anders says, Brecht was writing, but the efforts at reaching them in the same way today look pitifully meagre. On the other hand, the chances of political effectiveness are perhaps greater today in the Third World, in the 'market theatre' of Nigeria for example,[8] or in many countries where the simplicity of staging Brecht's plays makes them attractive and easy to perform, and where there is a strong desire to have his themes discussed. In contrast with the more sophisticated theatre of the absurd, and theatre of cruelty, the apparent straightforwardness and greater humanity of Brecht should be at an advantage in places where revolution is still imminent.

This appeal to unsophisticated audiences raises the question of the intellectual quality of Brecht's work in more acute form. It is extremely difficult to imagine a performance of *The Exception and the Rule* or *The Mother* having any political effect on a factory audience in West Germany today. Most of the later plays, though more frequently performed in West German theatres, do not carry such an obvious message that audiences are incapable of leaving the theatre unscathed. Yet one reason for Brecht's success with Western intellectuals has been the compliment he pays the audience of believing it capable of thinking for itself, and this reputation can do with some scrutiny. As Peter Brook says, 'For Brecht . . . there was no fourth wall between actors and audience – the actor's unique aim was to create a precise response in an audience for whom he had total respect. It was out of respect for the audience that Brecht introduced the idea of alienation. . .'[9] That attitude is inherent in the Marxist view of human capacity, the view that it is the environment, not the heredity of a man that makes him what he is, and that an 'open-ended' environment must therefore give him the chance to use those natural talents he possesses equally with all other men. It is not only a Marxist view, and the appeal of Brecht to many who would not call themselves Marxists is partly, at least, a result of this human regard for all men.

On the other hand, the distrust of theatre-audiences which not only Brecht had is shown when Mr Brook goes on, a little later, to say that in his own production of *Lear*, when Gloucester was blinded, 'we brought the house lights up before the last savage action was completed – so as to make the audience take stock of the scene before being engulfed in automatic applause'.[10] The expectation of an automatic response was not unjustifiable, though it suggests a respect for the audience that fell short of being total. Similarly the idea of 'making' the audience take stock of the details of the blinding suggests a misgiving about the capacity of the audience to feel that horror, which again is not consistent with respect. Mr Brook goes on to say, with regret, that his method was ineffective: both Gloucester, the sufferer, and the nauseating concentration-camp doctor in another play 'always left the stage to similar rounds of applause'.[11] But by that very remark he shows a comprehension of the audience's reactions that might well be questioned: he appears to suppose that the applause did not distinguish between the actor and the part he was playing.

It is true that people do fail to make such a distinction. Stratford Johns, the actor of Inspector Barlow in a television series about the police, is often reported in the press as having surprised people who expected him in ordinary life to show the same tough, harsh personality as the character he portrayed. Stendhal relates the story of a man who shot Othello to prevent him killing Desdemona. Until the present age, it has only been thought necessary to draw special attention to the difference between actor and part where very unsophisticated audiences were concerned.

If, however, the audience is really respected, in the sense that it is "allowed" to think and feel without controls imposed by the producer – and it seems as though the producer can have little influence anyway – then the creation of what Mr Brook

calls a 'precise response' is an impossible dream. As Raymond
Williams says, 'The spectator . . . is the one element the dramatist cannot control, in any form.'[12] Audiences, like political
voters, will go their own ways, despite press, stage and television, which is not to say that none of the 'media' can influence
those ways to a degree.

The reasons for Brecht's success surely lie partly in his constant and necessary injunctions to audiences to think individually, to reflect on their own ways of thinking and feeling, but
also partly in the fact that some spectators simply adopted
unthinkingly Brecht's own ways, or had already come to think
on Marxist lines so close to his as to render dissent unlikely.

The unthinking acceptance of the arguments of the chorus in
The Measures Taken, even by distinguished critics and scholars,
is as much a demonstration of the desperate need for individual
independence as any 'bourgeois' self-indulgences ever were. Despite himself, Brecht here abandoned that 'complex seeing'
which he enjoined on others. To quote Raymond Williams
again on this play: 'the chorus, instead of allowing the action
to be seen in its many aspects, in the end merely satisfies the
decision to execute: the critical-objective element is then
counter-seeing rather than complex seeing: a limited anti-
romantic action rather than a whole new form'.

Complex seeing is, on the other hand, very closely defined
in Professor Williams's account of *The Good Woman of Setzuan,* and his version of the play is worth close attention. The
special feature here is that Shen Te, the good woman, and
Shui Ta, the ruthless exploiter who is really herself wearing a
different mask, are both essentially the same person.

It is not fixed goodness against fixed badness – a cops-and-robbers
morality – but goodness and badness in the act of being produced in
the turns of an action, as coexistent possibilities. This is genuinely
complex seeing, and it is deeply integrated with the dramatic form.
No resolution is imposed; the tension persists, as it must, and the play
ends with a formal invitation to consider it. The evasive responses,
covering or weakening the tension, are expressed by other characters,
so that we can see their inadequacy while the fact of Shen Te and
Shui Ta is still evident.[13]

The complexity of this interpretation goes some way to explaining Brecht's success with spectators who are unwilling to yield to him on all points. One may urge against it certain other points. It is true, for instance, that there is no straight-forward 'cops-and-robbers' morality in *The Good Woman* – yet is not the choice presented to Shen Te equally black-and-white? She seems to have only the possibility of giving away all she possesses or of grinding the poor with the needless harshness displayed by Shui Ta. Drama of a kind is generated by such a clash of extreme opposites, but it is much less subtle than, say, the opposition between Antigone and Creon, or even between such a resolute pair as Chimène and Don Rodrigue in Corneille's *Le Cid,* not to speak of the complex checks and balances of modern industrialism. The many complexities inherent in Prince Hal's dismissal of Falstaff – the formerly priggish Prince who is obliged, now, to govern, and the roistering knight who has given more pleasure to us with his wicked ways than ever the Prince did, but who could only be a menace, close to the throne – nothing so close to life is touched on, and the two faces of Shen Te are adequately represented by the fixed masks she adopts. The complexity of Brecht's seeing is still, by these standards, a relatively simple one.

The truly valuable thing in Brecht's dramatic work, I submit, is not his extraordinarily wide range of theatrical invention and innovation, nor the cogency of his political message – though both of these may yet be more effective outside Europe and North America than we are inclined to suppose – but in something that needs a special effort of imagination in anyone who has not lived through the troubled times that Brecht him-self experienced. Even men now in their seventies, as Brecht would have been if he had lived so long, are unlikely to have had experiences close enough to his own to accomplish easily this act of understanding. Brecht was born into a Germany that seemed at the height of its powers. As a boy he would have heard on every side enthusiastic comment on the politi-cal strength of Germany, its military might, demonstrated in the Franco-Prussian War, its colonial expansion, the achieve-ments of it men of science, the inheritance of Goethe, Kant, Beethoven, Schopenhauer, Wagner, and perhaps Nietzsche. In his earlier days, at school, he was inclined to believe all this without reservations: it is typical of his passionate nature –

masked, afterwards, but never completely obscured – that as a schoolboy he wrote exhortations to his classmates to join him as volunteer aircraft spotters, or that, even in 1915, he wrote a poem in celebration of the Kaiser's birthday.

Before leaving school, Brecht had seen further than this, and almost incurred expulsion for his essay mocking Horace's praise of heroic death for the fatherland. Yet when the war was over, and with it the Armageddon which some of his contemporaries supposed would lead to a New Jerusalem, the detachment he had acquired through contact with the satire of Wedekind and others allowed him no such easy confidence. He wanted to believe in 'the big, white, broad bed', as both his first marriage and the conclusion of *Drums in the Night* testify, but the defeat of the Spartacists still sounded in his ears, as it does at the end of that play, and he was still looking for a more than personal solution.

The agony of doing that – though Brecht did not allow himself such language, and preferred the crew-cut hair-style, leather jacket, and fast car which seemed to disown agony – was common to every German of the 1920s who thought and felt. Brecht, being a dramatist before anything else, gave vent to his thoughts and feelings in ways that now look not only shocking, but even repulsive, if one forgets that they were experiments in imaginative art, not personal statements or political policies. The relish with which Mortimer, in Brecht's *Edward II*, seems to envisage a bloody consummation, is a projection into drama of a possibility which Brecht foresaw, but which he did not necessarily endorse with his whole self, however the play may end. The same may be said of *The Measures Taken*: Brecht was not here a politician, advocating such measures as the killing of the errant comrade, but an artist trying out in concrete, dramatic form the possibility that such actions might be essential.

As the threat of a Nazi takeover increased, such extreme action could have looked more and more inevitable. Being a dramatist, not a politician, Brecht was not concerned with the possible consequences of a play seeming to recommend the political execution of the more moderate socialists from whom resistance to the Nazis might have been expected. He may not have been aware of the weakening of the common opposition that such works must have produced. His whole nature was, as his masking laconic utterances reveal, so passionate that he could have no patience with compromises, deals, the bargaining and yielding that characterise parliamentary democracy and sometimes bring it into bad repute. Besides, the German political scene in the early 1930s was rapidly becoming so 'polarised' that a choice for moderation could seem a betrayal of the real opposition. By 1930, it must have seemed to Brecht, nothing but totalitarian opposition to the Nazi threat could suffice. It was a decision not too far distant from the decision many parliamentary democrats took in 1939, in deciding to accept military discipline for the duration. Brecht's misfortune was that he had no chance of voting the leader out of power, once the war was over.

These are political, not dramatic considerations. But the two interact. Once committed to Stalin against Hitler, Brecht was also committed, for a time, to the kind of drama which Stalin, if he had taken any interest in it, might have approved. The brusque illogicalities of the propagandist plays do no credit to Brecht as an artist, but they witness to the desperation with which he saw the Nazi cause sweep the country. The fact that the only opposition tightly-knit enough (as he saw it) to offer a real resistance was also itself guilty of evil at least equal to anything that Nazism achieved in the whole of its existence could not, in the early 1930s, take full possession of his conscience. And even when it began to force itself on him – when he began to realise what had happened to Soviet artists under Stalin's repression, and when personal friends were arrested, and in one case executed by Soviet authorities, his vision of a future in which men would not exploit men did not seem to be invalidated.

The plays of the late 1930s and early 1940s show how much Brecht was inwardly compelled to withdraw from Stalinism. What he wrote about Stalin in 1953 is another matter. He had his theatrical livelihood to think of, and like Galileo, he saw where the best chance of continuing to speak some or all of his mind really lay. But *Mother Courage, Galileo,* and *The Caucasian Chalk Circle* show, sufficiently, where it did lie. Neither Grusha nor Azdak would stand a chance of surviving in any really totalitarian regime, nor would Mother Courage, however much Brecht may try to condemn her for her acquiescence in another corrupt system. The contrast between Azdak and the prim Soviet officials who introduce the play in which he appears is evidence enough of the independence which Brecht, intuitively and not necessarily consciously, still managed to keep alive in the most difficult circumstances.

Without having lived under a totalitarian regime it is difficult to imagine how insidious, how unapparent, its methods are. A failure to give the Nazi greeting on entering a shop could have serious consequences, at the least a brutal beating, in the period 1933–45. Things were not so bad as that in the early years of the German Democratic Republic, but the fact that Brecht was implicitly under pressure cannot be in dispute. All the more reason, then, to see his conduct in 1953 as a desperate, Galilean attempt at preserving some freedom of speech and possibly even of action. Brecht was, one suspects, not a man of great physical courage. His courage of the mind, in going on asserting the necessity for each man to decide for himself, is all the more remarkable: it could have led to torments that for him would have been completely unbearable.

His best answer was Schweyk, and it is still the best answer for many who live today under a regime that will not brook real opposition in the slightest degree. Schweyk runs the risk of unspeakable pain, if his light-hearted opposition ever encounters more than stupid obedience to orders from the higher-ups. In Brecht's play the risk is never allowed to incur its probable consequences, any more than it is in Hašek's original version. That is as it should be, in a play or novel – to pursue grimly every possibility of retribution would be to destroy the possibility of even imagining opposition. But ultimately, we have to recognise that the forces opposing Brecht, on both sides of the political coin, were so powerful that only a Schweykian, satirical compromise was really effective, or rather useful as a means of still keeping one's head up. It is condescending, and almost, though not quite, pointless, for people living in a parliamentary democracy where dissent does not inevitably involve retribution from the State, to reprove the kind of adaptive tactics which Schweyk uses: it took more than Schweyk to defeat Hitler, and may take more still to modify the totalitarian régimes of today. yet among Brecht's plays are some which will always remain as a potential challenge, even if only by virtue of appearing to require personal decisions. At their best, they do more than that. Mother Courage, Azdak, and even Baal, have a resilience and an individuality inimical to any societal regime, and if one wants to point to what matters most, politically, in Brecht's achievement as a dramatist, one could do worse, in the present state of the world, than point to them, all three.

EPILOGUE
BRECHT AND POLITICAL THEATRE
IN AMERICA AND BRITAIN

Against the background of German political theatre, Brecht is impressive, as he is by comparison with all German drama. In English terms, he comes from outer space. There was no political theatre in England before 1890, and very little until the 1960s. The new growth coincided with, but was not solely due to, the first visit of the Berliner Ensemble to London in 1956.

Plays in English with a political interest have existed since the 1890s. The whole of the Irish theatre movement was political, and O'Casey's plays about the troubles, *Juno and the Paycock, Shadow of a Gunman,* were nearest of all to Brecht's *Drums in the Night.* It was only in *A Star Turns Red,* it is true, that O'Casey wrote anything that could be called a Marxist work, and it is not remarkable for subtlety or insight.

Shaw's politics are more masked than Brecht's, and more uncommitted: Brecht would never have written such an apparent defence of capitalism as there is in *Major Barbara.* Closest to Brecht is *Mrs Warren's Profession,* where the guns are suddenly revealed at the end, and the condemnation of international brothels is seen to be as much a condemnation of international financiers. But though Shaw is concerned with class-distinctions, and makes satirical use of them in *You Never Can Tell* and *Pygmalion,* the greater part of his work in the theatre is about anything disputatious that comes to mind, including himself. Though Shaw is dialectical, and a Socialist, he is not really close to Brecht, nor has Brecht, on the other hand, Shaw's disarming wit or gift for merriment.

John Galsworthy had more direct effect on reform than any other dramatist. His play *Justice,* written as part of his campaign against the current practice of sentencing all convicts to an initial three months' solitary confinement, was immediately successful both in the theatre and in real life. Winston Churchill,

then Home Secretary, wrote to Galsworthy after long correspondence to say that, partly as a result of seeing the play, he
had decided to have the period of solitary confinement reduced
to one month. No other play, except perhaps Jeremy Sand-
ford's television play *Cathy Come Home,* which resulted in
some alleviation of housing conditions for homeless couples, has
been so obviously a cause of alterations in legal procedures. But
these were purely reformist works, like Galsworthy's *Strife,* not
comparable to the activist German works of that time, and
quite unlike Brecht, who aimed at much greater changes.
Lawrence's naturalistic plays about miners had almost no hearing until the 1960s.

During the 1920s the idea of a People's Theatre was circu-
lating. Yeats had spoken of one; Lawrence treated the theme
in the preface to his play *Touch and Go,* and the name was
taken up by both J. T. Grein in 1923 and Nancy Price in 1930,[1]
but it never acquired any party-political meaning, and the West
End theatres showed nothing, apart from Shaw, that could bear
comparison with the new German drama. C. K. Munro wrote
Progress (1924) and *The Rumour* (1922), showing how war
could be brought about by the vested interests of capitalists
behind the scenes. Ralph Fox in 1922 wrote *Captain Youth,* 'a
romantic comedy for all socialist children'.[2] At a different level
T. S. Eliot's *Sweeney Agonistes,* in accord with the vogue which
was leading Stravinsky and Milhaud to jazz, used popular
speech-rhythms for poetry, but Eliot had no remotely political
interest at that time. He gave only a hint that the murder of
Becket in *Murder in the Cathedral* was relevant to the political situation in the 1930s. For fifteen years after the War, there
was scarcely a hint of political theatre in England.

The impetus for political plays in the 1930s came partly direct from Germany, partly via America, which had a much
livelier and more experimental theatre than England.[3] In the
U.S.A., the profusion of political plays, mostly Marxist, was
greater even than in Germany. The Workers' Theater founded
in 1926, which developed into the New Playwrights' Theater,
was largely inspired by the new stagecraft of Meyerhold and
others in Russia, though German Expressionism and both German and Russian agitprop had some influence. By European
standards, the sheer number of Marxist plays and sketches, by
such writers as Michael Gold, John Lawson, John Dos Passos

and E. J. Basshe, which appeared in the late 1920s, was aston-
ishingly large, though any influence of Brecht, then still a dramatist in the process of making his name, is out of the question
at that time. Some of the methods of American dramatists may
look Brechtian, but are thought much more likely to have been
inspired by the Russian theatre.[4]

The Wall Street crash of 1929, though it brought an end to
the New Playwrights, saw an even greater development of proletarian theatre groups of the Trade Union Unity League, whose
origins went back to the Workers' Laboratory Theater, founded
in 1926. Like the German-speaking 'Prolet-Bühne', W.L.T. presented plays with factory employees as actors, and, like Brecht
in the same period, did everything possible to promote a confrontation of class against class. This was in accordance with
Stalinist directives to which presumably Brecht also paid some
heed. By 1932 as many as fifty-three proletarian troupes
throughout the U.S.A. were able to send delegates to a national
conference in New York, and for much of the period 1929 to
1935 the dominant message in the plays of these troupes
was that of the Communist Party.

In such a profusion, the contribution of Brecht was scarcely
heard. *Lindbergh's Flight*, a version of the *Baden-Baden Cantata*, was performed in 1931 in Philadelphia, *He Who Said Yes*,
in New York, off Broadway, in 1933, but without success. By
the time *The Mother* was presented in 1935 the climate of
opinion had changed to its disadvantage.

During the early 1930s many who were not necessarily
Marxists or members of the Communist Party had been attracted to the proletarian theatre: Elia Kazan and Orson Welles
were two actors and producers who were later to make great
names for themselves (Welles's later film, *Citizen Kane*, used
'epic' methods) while the dramatists included both Clifford
Odets, the great figure of American proletarian drama in the
whole period and Archibald MacLeish, who used agitprop
methods in his Broadway venture, *Panic*, in 1935, with Marxist
support. Maxwell Anderson's *Winterset*, of the same year, re-
sembled German documentary theatre in its treatment of a
cause célèbre, the trial for murder of the two anarchists, Sacco
and Vanzetti. With these writers, only one of whom, Odets,
was temporarily a member of the Communist Party, a leaven-

ing of more liberal opinion was mixed into the American political theatre, and increased in strength through the operations of Theater Union, Theater Guild, and Group Theater, all of which promoted plays from a fairly wide spectrum.

In August 1935 the Comintern representatives in Moscow announced the formation of the Popular Front, embracing all liberal and Left-wing opponents of Fascism, and reversing the exclusive policy of earlier years. The old revolutionary idea of class warfare was shelved, and even the word 'communism' was now used guardedly. Purely agitprop and proletarian drama almost ceased, and in their place came a new appeal, through such organisations as New Theater League, to middle-class opinion. Singing the Internationale at the end of performances was no longer appropriate, even though the Communist Left still predominated in political theatre up till the bewildering, discrediting Soviet–German pact of 1939.

These changes were unfortunate for Brecht, for though *Señora Carrar's Rifles* was welcome enough during the Spanish Civil War, many plays on which were sponsored by the New Theater League, the performance of *The Mother* in November 1935 was another failure. It had come at exactly the wrong moment, three months late in fact, and its appeal for revolution, as Goldstein says, 'ignored the new leftish politics of accommodation with the bourgeoisie'.[5] Into the bargain, the production was, on the whole, so devoid of Brechtian methods, and was in such contradiction to the cool, distancing style he required, that Brecht himself, who saw the production, offered to director and cast a simple condemnation: 'Das ist Scheisse.' (He was angered, later, by the rewriting of part of *The Mother* in Paul Peters' and George Sklar's *Stevedore*).[6] Public criticism, though in part favourable, and in any case not able to appreciate Brecht's real intentions, tended to regard the production as insufferably patronising. The class of audience at which the proletarian theatre now aimed felt itself too sophisticated to appreciate such over-simplification, and *The Mother* even became the subject of Left-wing parody.[7]

It was not, therefore, until after Brecht himself emigrated to the U.S.A. that his dramatic work made any notable impact there, and even that impact was delayed. In the late 1930s, it is true, the Federal Theater initiated by Harry Hopkins as a means of nationally subsidising unemployed actors and theatre technicians performed many hundreds of plays of a social and political nature. These, as Hallie Flanagan wrote in her magazine, *Federal Theater*, were intended to play a part in 'the attack on injustice, poverty and despair, so graphically described by President Roosevelt in his Second Inaugural'. Topics included New Deal projects, soil conservation, farm relief, public housing. But the plays were intended to support Roosevelt, not to denounce him as a tool of capitalism, and in any case Federal Theater's subsidised programmes were very largely concerned with presenting the classics of world drama, despite the leftish reputation it acquired, which finally destroyed it in 1939. The *Living Newspaper* series 'edited' by Arthur Arent, another project under Hallie Flanagan's aegis, presented documentary plays of topical interest. Joseph Losey, a participator in *Living Newspaper* better known today as a film-director, has since mentioned that he met Brecht in 1935, when they were both visiting Moscow, but without being aware of his reputation. *Living Newspaper*, he confesses, was 'Brechtian theatre without my knowing it'.[8] But this is no more than a recognition of similarities which political-social theatres were likely to have in any case.

By 1941, when Brecht arrived in Hollywood, he was still comparatively unknown in America, and by 1945, only some scenes from *Fear and Misery of the Third Reich* had actually been performed. Brecht got to know Chaplin, whom he had always admired, and was helped greatly by Charles Laughton in the rewriting of *Galileo*, which was not performed, however, until 1947, shortly before he left for Europe. In 1942 and 1943 he wrote with Lion Feuchtwanger *The Visions of Simone Machard*, based on a novel of Feuchtwanger's, and between 1941 and 1944 he wrote *Schweyk; The Caucasian Chalk Circle* completes the list of plays written in the U.S.A., but was also not performed during his stay there. In September 1947 he was cited before the House Committee on Un-American Activities,[9] and, though not detained, immediately left for Switzerland.

Success in the U.S.A. was still a long way off. Both the production of *Galileo* in California, and the slightly later one in New York had poor notices, despite the fact that, for the first time, Brecht had taken a personal part in the production of one of his plays in America. The climate of opinion had changed:

since the Stalin–Hitler pact Communism had ceased to be remotely popular, and within a few years the inquisitorial methods of Senator McCarthy, whose rise to power began in 1952 and whose powerful influence lasted until the end of 1954 (though he did not die until 1957) made even remote association with Marxism a dangerous matter.

In the late forties there were performances in college theatres from coast to coast, often inspired by Eric Bentley. In March 1954, a production of *The Threepenny Opera* by Marc Blitzstein at the Theatre de Lys, Greenwich Village, was Brecht's first notable success, running to two thousand performances, though the distinguished critic Francis Fergusson saw in this only a fashionable performance providing a new *frisson* for well-to-do audiences.[10] A performance in San Francisco of *Mother Courage* in 1956 was reckoned by some to represent the real breakthrough.[11]

After the publication in 1959 and 1960 of the books by John Willett and Martin Esslin, both of which provoked great discussion, the change began. Brecht was by this time established in Europe, with notable productions of his own – and several by other producers – in France, Italy, England and other countries. The revolutionary mood of the 1960s was in his favour.

Recognition by the commercial stage had still not come about. Before 1959, no reference to Brecht performances in the U.S.A. were made in the *New York Times*. From that year to the present day several have been reviewed in that paper each year, and the series of translations begun in 1961 by Eric Bentley, as well as the Collected Works begun by John Willett, meant that texts were available for many less noticed productions at smaller theatres and on student stages. In the 1960s Brecht made his mark across the continent, with an outstanding production of *The Caucasian Chalk Circle* at Minneapolis in 1965, and another at the Lincoln Center in 1966; *Galileo* was acclaimed for the performance by Tony van Bridge at Boston the same year, and Minneapolis scored another success with *Arturo Ui* in 1968.

It would seem difficult to maintain that Brecht had had an overwhelming impact on American drama. No survey of his role in the period since 1959 has appeared, but the impression created by reports is of a multifarious theatre in the U.S.A.

which is as much concerned with sexual liberation, the drug-subculture, the theatre of cruelty (Artaud was the rage in 1968), and racial discrimination, as with the Brechtian classics, and which uses an equally great variety of means, from the 'happening' to the breaking of all barriers with the audience, from stroboscopes to quadraphonic sound and from nudity to mass-spectacle. Despite Brecht's great popularity on the Left, he is now one new force among many.

Yet even on the Left, a questioning voice has recently been raised. Lee Baxandall, who has little use for the commercial Americanisation of Brecht, yet finds that the many college groups, municipal repertory acting groups, and even New Left theatre companies who have principally performed Brecht have done so in an undesirably emotional manner. Though he holds that 'Brecht has done more for socialism in the United States in this generation' (he is writing of 1971) 'than did Stalin and Russia', he also affirms that many thousands of younger radicals are 'sceptical of any American production of a Brecht play',[12] which they suspect will display a 'hand-to-shoulder immediacy, eyeball-to-eyeball relevance, in place of a structured invitation to the imaginative cognition of reality'.[13] Baxandall himself also expresses anxiety lest the typical American inheritors of Brecht should not only be college-focused and white, but well-educated and wealthy. He does not make it sound as though, by the 1970s, the impact of Brecht had been anything like as great as that of the prewar Federal Theater Project.

Nor have the numerous performances led to any such influence on American playwrights as Brecht had in England during the 1960s. The situation is now reversed: where the 1930s saw a politically neutral or conservative British theatre, commitment on Brechtian lines is now paramount, and it is American theatre that has ceased to have so many Marxist-proletarian features.

Arthur Miller has been more influenced by Ibsen than by Brecht, Tennessee Williams treats of social ills more in terms of sex than of politics, and Edward Albee belongs rather to the Theatre of the Absurd. Though many similarities can be traced between Brecht's work and that of Thornton Wilder, there is no positive evidence of direct influence.[14] Playwrights with a closer affinity to Brecht are in any case – like Wilder – of an older generation. Maxwell Anderson's *Joan of Lorraine,* for instance, (first performed in 1946), includes a rehearsal-scene in which Joan play-acts what she will later do 'in reality', and the coronation of the Dauphin is similarly 'alienated', though Anderson does not use the term. There is a similar quasi-Brechtian note in the opening words of the producer to the cast:

My notion is that the more you kid the play and the actors and everybody concerned the better it is for all of us. If there's anything or anybody that won't stand kidding, now's the time to find it out. So I razz everyone in sight, including myself.

The essential difference, though, and a characteristic one for American drama, is in the next few lines, when the same producer goes on to say that, starting cold in this distancing way, they will find 'that holy fire'll begin to play around one actor – and then another – ' and so on. The point, for Anderson, of presenting a play through a rehearsal of the same play, is to awaken that latent holy fire; just as the doubts of the actress about her ability to play Joan are reflected in the 'real' Joan's own doubts, so the outcome is the faith which both actress and character gain through their doubts.

There is, in short, an emotional quality in Anderson's work here, as in his other plays, for which Brecht would have had no use, and that emotional quality is general in American drama. It is surely related to the strong American stress on the individual rather than on society. The nearest parallel to a play by Brecht from the theatre of Clifford Odets, for example, is *Till the Day I Die*, corresponding to *Fear and Misery of the Third Reich*. But where Brecht provides a series of scenes about a variety of characters who have no links with one another across the scenes, and allows no appeal from the stage to the audience's emotions, Odets concentrates on the fate of a single Communist, who is tortured by the Gestapo, mistaken by his comrades for a stool-pigeon, and finally shoots himself. The emotional effect of Odets's repeated scenes of torture, which Brecht uses more sparingly, is to create a strong sympathy and indignation. It is true that Odets tends to pull out all the stops: a powerful sentimentality obtrudes in many scenes, and the language can become rhetorical. Even in the final moment, as the hero leaves the room with the gun with which he will shoot himself, the literary flourish prevents the play from having its desired effect today:

ERNST. . . . Brothers will live in the soviets of the world! Yes, a world of security and freedom is waiting for all mankind! (*Looks at them both deeply. Walks to door of room L.*) Do your work, Comrades. (*Exits*)

TILLY. (*for a moment stands still. Then starts for room. Carl stops her.*) Carl, stop him, stop him. (*Carl holds her back.*)

CARL. Let him die . . .

TILLY. Carl . . . (*shot heard within.*)

CARL. Let him live . . .

The slow curtain which follows this would have been as inimical to Brecht as the language itself. Yet Odets in his day had a powerful effect on his audiences, even when, in a play like *Waiting for Lefty*, he came closer to Brecht's structure. *Waiting for Lefty*, the most celebrated of all the proletarian plays of the 1930s, shows a strike committee on stage, and goes on by a series of flashbacks to show how each member of the committee came, through some incident in his life, an injustice, a deprivation, to declare himself for the Communist cause. In the final scene, when it is learned that the man they have been waiting for has been found shot dead, the meeting breaks into impassioned demands for an immediate strike, and this led, at the first performance, to a tumultuous reception. It was more than an appeal to strike. To quote Harold Clurman, a friend of Odets, 'Our youth had found its voice. It was a call to join the good fight for a greater measure of life in a world free of economic fear, falsehood, and craven servitude to stupidity and greed.'[15] Yet to quote Clurman again, on a different occasion, 'the whole quality of the American playwright [it is not clear whether only Odets is meant] is active, impulsive and rather lusty',[16] and a similar thought was expressed by the prominent proletarian dramatist Mike Gold, when he asked, about Brecht's *The Mother*, 'does it belong in a pioneer theatre that set out to explore the virgin continent of American life?'[17] Such language would be out of fashion today, yet the impression remains, that an emotional tone is inherent in the American tradition from O'Neill onwards, though its roots go at least as far back as Lincoln, and Jeffesron's language in the Declaration of Independence. It is not questionable on that account, though the emotion may, as sometimes in Odets, become excessive. So long a tradition, coupled with individualism, makes it doubtful whether Brecht's laconic tone can make itself felt. On the other hand, it is in the U.S.A. that the International Brecht Society has now established its headquarters.[18]

The contrast between English and American theatre, where Brecht is concerned, could hardly have been greater. There was not only no agitprop in the late 1920s or early 1930s, there was nothing at all that could be called political in the American and German sense. The Group Theatre, which called itself a private club to avoid censorship, performed Auden's *Dance of Death* in 1933, but though this ended with the appearance of Karl Marx it was not even superficially a Communist play. Auden's boyishness, coupled with a mystical vagueness, kept the play from having any appeal beyond what were thought of as sophisticated circles. *The Dog Beneath the Skin*, written with Christopher Isherwood and performed by the Group Theatre in 1935, had Marxist leanings but still contained many private allusions and obscurities which prevented it from reaching a wider public, while *The Ascent of F.6* was more inward-looking than political. *On the Frontier*, published in 1938, is about Fascism and war, but again makes no popular appeal. Politically, Auden and Isherwood's plays had no effect, and were never seriously meant to have any.[19] Auden, who has been called the first Brechtian in England, has since explicitly denied any possibility of having been influenced by Brecht at that time, though he acknowledged a general debt to German drama, especially to the Expressionists and Ernst Toller. (The statement by Martin Esslin that the early plays of Auden and Isherwood are indebted to the early Brecht is invalidated by this.[20])

Two other poets of the 1930s wrote political plays: Stephen Spender's *Trial of a Judge* is about Nazis and Communists, and the futility of liberalism under the threat of totalitarianism; Cecil Day Lewis's *Noah and the Waters* interprets the Deluge as the masses of England who will some day rise and prepare for a better world – a symbolism which could have been borrowed from Mayakovsky's *Mystery-Bouffe*.

Meanwhile, as in Germany, but on a much smaller scale, there were movements toward a purely political theatre. The

Left Theatre put on Montagu Slater's plays, *New Way Wins*, about Welsh miners, and *Easter 1916*, about the Irish rising. A Theatre Guild was formed in association with Victor Gollancz's Left Book Club, with branches all over the country. And in London, behind Euston station, there was the 'Unity Theatre,' where not only plays by O'Casey, Odets, Afinogenov and Stephen Spender were produced, but perhaps the first English performance of a play by Brecht was given, *Señora Carrar's Rifles*. The Unity Theatre also staged a large number of 'agit-prop' sketches after the German manner, topical scenes in the style of *The Living Newspaper*, and had a success at Christmas 1938 with a satirical pantomime, *Babes in the Wood*, including songs directed against the Fascist Oswald Mosley. The revue *Where's that Bomb?*, by Herbert Hodge and another London taxi-driver, also achieved a reputation. But the number of people who saw these productions was limited by the tiny premises where they were performed.[21]

Otherwise, there was no representation of working-class men and women, or of themes seriously touching their lives, apart from the adaptation (1934) of Walter Greenwood's novel *Love on the Dole*, made by Greenwood with Ronald Gow, chiefly known till then as a writer of plays for schoolboys, and Emlyn Williams's *The Corn is Green* (1938), about a young man from a Welsh mining village. Like Stanley Houghton's *Hindle Wakes* (1914) and Harold Brighouse's many plays about Lancashire people – though these had more local pride – there was no question in them of presenting any grievances.

The theatre during the Second World War was not an occasion for either political or patriotic display: the cinema, rather than the theatre, was the medium for keeping up morale, though a number of West End companies went on tour, and local repertory companies performed at 'Garrison Theatres'. Politically, the only play of significance in the whole period from 1939 to 1945 was J. B. Priestley's *They Came to a City*, a utopian fantasy of a socialist future. Priestley's strength was in warm-hearted comedies of Yorkshire life, whether in the form of novels or plays. Thanks to the performance of this play in 1943, however, he achieved fame as a socialist dramatist and his *An Inspector Calls*, also socialist in tendency, was selected for a first performance in Moscow, in the summer of 1945. It was to have a very great success shortly afterwards in Germany.

Thus, until 1956, political theatre in England was still an extremely small part of the spectrum, even considering only the more serious theatre, mainly represented, so far as newer names are concerned, by Ronald Duncan, Christopher Fry, Terence Rattigan, John Whiting. In that year, which also saw the first performance of John Osborne's naturalistic *Look Back in Anger,* the Berliner Ensemble visited the Palace Theatre, London, with productions of *Mother Courage, The Caucasian Chalk Circle* and *Drums and Trumpets* (a free adaptation of Farquhar's *The Recruiting Officer.*) In addition, the English Stage Company was established at the Royal Court Theatre, with the explicit intention of persuading reputable novelists and poets to write for the theatre. The actual achievement, as Irving Wardle says, 'was to release a body of unforeseen new talent that flooded the theatre like a pent-up natural force'.[22]

Of the dramatists who were thus given their chance, those chiefly interested in politics rather than in theatre of the absurd or other schools were Arnold Wesker, Brendan Behan, and John Arden. More opportunities were provided by Joan Littlewood in the Theatre Workshop which she set up in 1956 (after earlier starts) in the East End of London, where the production of *Oh, What a Lovely War!* had some Brechtian qualities, though no Marxist message, and Wesker's brief-lived Centre 42, which was launched in 1960 with the object of making arts of various kinds available to working-class audiences.

Wesker is essentially naturalistic, rather than Brechtian. He differs fundamentally from Brecht in his view of art, not as a means towards achieving revolution, but as involving 'a pursuit for sanity, self-respect, understanding and reassurance'.[23] Thus although Wesker ranks himself with the extreme Left, and is only really concerned with 'the bus driver, the housewife, the miner and the Teddy Boy',[24] no real connections with Brecht exist, and even the closest scrutiny of his technique can ascribe no more than a general indirect influence, due to the Brechtian atmosphere of much avant-garde theatre.[25]

Very few English dramatists were strongly influenced by Brecht, though the marked difference between Osborne's *The Entertainer* and the earlier *Look Back in Anger,* as he admitted, was due to the insight into the limitations of realism he derived from Brecht. Osborne's *Luther* bore a strong family resemblance to *Galileo.* Yet Brechtian methods were not used for any Marxist end; it has been noticed in fact that there is, rather, a nostalgia in some of Osborne's work for 'the era of Edwardian settlement and complacency which in other contexts would be looked back on with the fiercest anger'.[26] The conclusion of *Luther*, where Luther is left mildly hoping for a better future, has none of Brecht's earlier definiteness – only *The Good Woman of Setzuan* is as vague. It is difficult to feel that Osborne did more in this respect than latch on to a fashionable trend that coincided with his own first success in a much more traditional vein. As Weise says, the use of 'epic' techniques by Osborne is rather 'an experimental episode in his creative life, conditioned by fashion'.[27]

Whether Robert Bolt used a narrator, in *A Man for All Seasons*, because of Brecht, or because he had been a radio scriptwriter, is open to question. The same is true of Peter Shaffer's *Royal Hunt of the Sun*, said to have been influenced both by Brecht and Artaud. Brechtian influence is claimed, too, on other plays by Robert Bolt, Brendan Behan, Christopher Logue, John Whiting, and is clear in James Saunders' *Hans Kohlhaas*, first performed in 1972.

By common consent, the English dramatist most influenced by Brecht has been John Arden, Brecht's 'leading British disciple', in the words of the *Times Literary Supplement*.[28] Arden himself, while demurring at so constricting a definition of his position, admitted that he belonged 'in the same dramatic tradition as Brecht',[29] and this is clear from many parallel features in his work. To some degree, Arden takes over actual devices of Brecht's: he prescribes in *Left-Handed Liberty* that the houselights may be left on as the play begins, and elsewhere uses back-projections, masks, and songs in a way not dissimilar to Brecht's. In *Happy Haven* a character addresses the public in the way that characters frequently do in Brecht's work, and in *Workhouse Donkey* there is a narrator who comments on the action but is also a character within the action. While these, taken individually, might have been derived from many sources, in combination they suggest quite a strong Brechtian influence, even direct imitation by Arden. Similarly, passages from *Armstrong's Last Goodnight* directly imitate Brecht's linguistic devices. When Lindsay proposes for the Border country a democracy on the Swiss model, and McGlass retorts: 'It is ridiculous and unpractical. England wad never

consent to it – why, it wad mean peace!' the echo of the irony
in Mother Courage's 'Don't tell me peace has broken out' is
unmistakeable.

Similarly, Arden's choice of historical or exotic settings, though
not very unusual in English theatre, may have been influenced
by Brecht, and it is even possible that the climax of *Serjeant
Musgrave's Dance* is based on Brecht's preference for re-
enacting a past event in the present moment. The whole
point of Musgrave's campaign is to bring home to English
people of his day their share of guilt in the killing of colonial people, and his means of doing so, forcing them to see in
the present situation a reflection of the past, has a decidedly
Brechtian ring, despite the fact that the plot is based on an
American film.

Naturally, Arden makes plays of his own, with a lot that has
no relation to Brecht, yet there is no other English dramatist in
whom so many similar features can be observed, and the influence has not always been beneficial. It would be unfair to
attribute to Brecht any shortcomings in Arden's work, though
the willingness of critics to encourage Arden's new talent has
led to its being over-esteemed, and the glamour of Brecht's
name has allowed even his own shortcomings to go largely un-
noticed. Thus one of Brecht's chief weaknesses is his proneness
to take some historical situation and allow it to be epitomised
in one or two characters, who then are obliged to stand for
great historical forces rather than individuals. In *The Measures
Taken,* the killing of the erring comrade is given no justification in terms of the actual situation, though the general case
for strict party discipline might have been argued on more
abstract lines, as a historical necessity. In *Mother Courage,* the
fact that there is a war and that the canteen-woman indirectly
makes a profit out of it is presented as though the economic
causes of the war were being shown, rather than the attitude
of one not very influential or representative woman. Galileo
greatly overrates the importance of his own recantation for the
history of science, supposing that, because he has recanted, no
further independent progress in science will be possible. Similarly Arden devises, in *Serjeant Musgrave,* a situation that might
abstractly, be thought instructive. The responsibility of English-
men for what happens in other parts of the world, in their name,

is to be taught by giving them a dose of their own medicine:
that is what Musgrave intends. The actual plot, however, is far
from making any such point. If the play persuades audiences
at all it is because Arden keeps dark what Musgrave's mission is
about until the dramatic moment when the skeleton is hoisted,
and the Gatling gun is turned on the crowd. Given time to reflect, it is obvious that Musgrave was so unrealistic in his planning that the very project was not worth considering. He could
never in seriousness have thought that by bringing four soldiers
and a gun to a Northern mining town, and threatening to shoot
five inhabitants for every one of the five killed by his detachment abroad, he could influence any of his audience to re-
nounce either colonies or war. To say that Arden meant that
to be clear is merely to say that he states the obvious. The play
does not begin to treat the question of war in a way that could
be fruitful.

Arden himself is unrealistic in the portrayal of characters and
situations. It is impossible to feel with John Russell Taylor,
when he says that 'in all Arden's plays, the characters we meet
are first and foremost just people: not concepts cast into a
vaguely human mould, with built-in labels saying "good" or
"bad". . .'.[30] In fact Taylor himself concedes that in *Musgrave*
'the Parson and the Mayor come perhaps closer to hostile caricatures than any other of his characters'[31] but that is not enough:
the Parson and the Mayor are Toytown puppets of extreme
political stupidity, as is the Trade Union Leader, Walsh. They
make it easier for Arden's play to seem momentarily credible:
if it were not for the Mayor, it would never occur to anyone to
hold a recruiting meeting, of all things, in a town full of dissi-
dent strikers, or to suppose that Musgrave's help could be useful
in breaking the strike, if he were able to persuade the ring-
leaders to enlist. Arden is thinking here, as Brecht did in *The
Measures Taken,* in very general terms. Granted that there
may have been something generally useful for Victorian employers in the fact that there existed an army which trouble-
makers might join, it is unlikely that any one employer could
think to get rid of his difficulties by asking the army to recruit a
few particular individuals. The circumstances do not fit English
nineteenth-century history, nor does Walsh's attempt at stealing
the Gatling gun look at all probable. English Trade Unionists
were and are too peaceable for such escapades – and if they

had not been, it would have taken an innocent to suppose that one gun would be of any use. Transferring the story from the Wild West film, where social circumstances were different, may have misled Arden here. But he has his own way with all circumstances of the plot: Sparky dies instantly on being accidentally stabbed in the stomach; the landlady who hears his cry is easily persuaded by Musgrave to do nothing about it; wherever attention to realism would impede the progress of the play to the point Arden wants to reach, he ignores or brushes over the difficulty. Yet in the preface he speaks of having written a realistic work.[32]

The language of the characters is unusual. At its best, it is memorable, as in Annie's lines to Musgrave:

> The North Wind in a pair of millstones
> Was your father and your mother.
> They got you in a cold grinding.
> God help us all if they get you a brother.

More often, it is puzzling, to the point that it seems not to be English. This is not a matter of poetic suggestiveness or ambiguity, though on some occasions, it is true, the obscurity is at least partly due to the thought. Musgrave's explanation of his mission is a case in point: the phrasing is strange, but the intention is fairly clear: 'We're each one guilty of particular blood. We've come to this town to work that guilt back to where it began.' 'Work that guilt back' suggests 'trace it back' and 'push it back', which could be a proper ambiguity. The difficulty is in seeing how the guilt for killings in a colony could have begun with English miners who are represented both as exploited themselves, and hostile to the military. But that is a difficulty about the whole play: it has not been thought out.

Other features of Arden's language are puzzling for a different reason. There seems to be no point, for instance, in altering English usage in the sentence: 'Now let's see if I can't turn some good cards on to my side for a difference.' or, in referring to the same card game: 'We throw the red Queen over.' Arden is supposed to have written in North country speech in this play, which certainly does contain Northern dialect words. But no dialect uses English as Arden does here:

'There's two ways to solve this colliery';

'You needn't reckon on to get any more here';

'I'll sing for me drinking, missus';

'Because we're there to serve our duty';

'Show 'em all the best equipment, glamourise 'em, man . . .';

'You seem a piece stronger than the rest of 'em' [the idiom would be right in German];

'I didn't want to pay for him [Billy Hicks, the man killed in the colony] – what had I to care for a colonial war?'

The awryness of this language corresponds to an awryness in the structure of the play and the thinking behind it. The reality of language is disregarded as everyday reality is.

It remains true that *Serjeant Musgrave's Dance* has more theatrical inventiveness than any other English play of the post-war period, and that much of this is original, with no relationship to Brecht. The use of symbol – the red of the soldiers' tunics, and of love, the black in Musgrave's nickname, and of death, the white of the snow, the dance of Musgrave's skeleton and the dance led by the bargee as though in retort to it – is un-Brechtian but theatrically striking. So is the use of traditional ballads and ballad-forms, while the refusal to give to economic motives the weight Brecht gives them allows Arden to make a suggestive web of emotions. He is more concerned with the passions than Brecht is, and the impression *Musgrave* leaves behind has more kinship with poetic drama in a Romantic vein than with party-political analyses.

Apart from Arden, it is hard to trace definite and far-reaching influences from Brecht on English dramatists generally. Yet it came to be widely accepted that his presence in English theatre was almost universal. As Alan Brien said in the *Sunday Telegraph* in 1966, 'If Britain were a Marxist State, perhaps with Kenneth Tynan as Minister for Culture, I do not believe that audiences could have been more relentlessly exposed to the works of Bertolt Brecht over the last ten years. He is rapidly replacing Shakespeare as the theatrical totem to be hoisted to the mast-head of any company wishing to advertise its "seriousness".' The last sentence at all events was true, if not unblemished, and is borne out by the satirical *Bluff Your Way in the*

Theatre,[33] which advised its readers during the 1960s that for cocktail party purposes Brecht alone deserved a four-star rating.

The fact is, that Brecht's own works, and their effect on English theatrical production, were more important than the influence of Brecht on individual dramatists. Until 1956, Brecht was scarcely known in England, despite his fame in Germany. By that year, only *Fear and Misery of the Third Reich* had appeared in print (1948), under the title *The Private Life of the Master Race,* though many more English translations had been published in the U.S.A.[34] Scarcely any articles on him or even references to his work had appeared in England, though *Mother Courage* had been produced in 1955 by Joan Littlewood, and two other productions had preceded the visit of the Ensemble by a few months.

The Littlewood production in particular had been severely criticised, by Kenneth Tynan.[35] The production of the same play by the Ensemble did not meet with great enthusiasm from the London theatre critics generally, apart from Mr Tynan himself. Others, suspicious of 'intellectual spoofery', critical of Brecht's condescension towards his audience, praised the acting but complained of slow-moving pace and boredom. The beauty of the settings was undisputed. But Brecht's work had not established itself with the press critics yet, even in the terms of his own productions, though there was still a barrier of language to reckon with. Nor did it succeed better in the English production that autumn of *The Good Woman,* at the Royal Court. Though Dame Peggy Ashcroft was praised for her playing of Shen Te, the play itself was thought dull. It may be, it is true, that the suppression of the Hungarian rising by Soviet forces that November contributed to a general anti-Communist mood.

The support for Brecht at the B.B.C. from Martin Esslin, at the Old Vic from Kenneth Tynan, and at the *Times Literary Supplement* from John Willett, meant, however, that Brecht continued to get a hearing, even though for several years the style of productions was still in an English tradition. The first really Brecht-like production, and therefore the first perform-ance in English which gave an idea of his own style in the the-atre, was the Royal Shakespeare Company's version of *The Caucasian Chalk Circle* in 1962, which was universally admired, with very few reservations. The fact that this was the least obviously Marxist of all Brecht's plays may have helped in the success, for by this time the Berlin Wall had been built, and in West Germany at all events Brecht's plays were temporarily out of favour. (The non-political way in which some of his work was regarded in England can be gauged from the fact that in 1961 *Galileo* was performed by undergraduates of the Conservative Association in the university church at Cambridge.) The production of *Baal* at the Phoenix, London, in 1963, was, however, unsuccessful, and for some time, until the second visit of the Ensemble, in 1965, most productions were seriously unsatisfactory – Esslin goes so far as to say 'the final summing-up of Brecht himself in England must be: if he is only seen without his words being heard, he is successful; if his texts [in translation] are understood, he is a total failure'.[36] That severe judgement does not reflect the view of the theatregoing public after 1965. The press was still hostile in some respects,[37] but the theatre-managers were convinced, and audiences were forthcoming. The breakthrough had been made.

During the 1960s, Brechtian techniques became increasingly popular. It became the custom to dispense with front tabs, and to show most of the lighting equipment in full view of the audience; for a time it was common to hang placards announcing the contents of the next scene. At Stratford-upon-Avon the covered wagon of Mother Courage became a symbol of Brechtian intentions: a version of it was seen in *Henry V*, in *Coriolanus*, and even in *As You Like It*. During the same period it was usual to provide Stratford theatregoers with programmes containing historical facts about the figures Shakespeare wrote about, as though the plays were documentary and relevant to the times in which they were supposed to take place, or to the politics of the present day. None of this was political to the extent that Brecht's rewriting of *Coriolanus* had been; in fact, when German producers of the Brechtian school attempted to produce Shakespeare's play at the National Theatre, giving it a modern political slant, the Old Vic actors dissented strongly.[38] At the Royal Shakespeare Company Theatre, politics were kept to non-Shakespearean productions such as Peter Brook's extemporised play about the war in Vietnam, *US*.

The effect of Brecht on Shakespearean performances could be bracing. One of the best R.S.C. productions was that of

Henry V in the mid-1960s, which gave the wagon to Fluellen for his library of tomes on the conduct of war, and brought him to life not as a comic, but as a seriously-thought-out scholar-in-arms. Ian Holm's Henry was a far cry from Olivier's, made just as the Second World War was ending, and in a Crispin Crispian spirit. When it came to the killing of the French prisoners, a Brechtian insight led to the King setting an example by cutting the throat of the first one himself. But this was presented more as an acceptance of a bloody necessity than as a condemnation. What was most Brecht-like about it and the whole production was its astringency, the sharp invitation to consider the full meaning. The long, cool look was penetrating.

In many ways, though, Brecht's influence was rather in the direction of debunking. He had inclined that way himself: his observations on the tragic heroes in the *Little Organon* were generally hostile,[39] and inaccurate – he misremembers *Oedipus* entirely – and his 'practice-plays for actors', rewriting famous scenes in Shakespeare so as to remind the performers of the dubious economic role of the characters they were playing, were insensitive to the full significance of such scenes. One cannot blame his influence entirely for the reversal of attitudes towards Shakespearean heroes, which had already begun with T. S. Eliot and D. H. Lawrence. The politicising in the new attitudes is certainly related to his views.

It would be extremely unfair to Brecht, for instance, to saddle him with the views on Hamlet expressed by Charles Marowitz, Peter Brook's assistant director in the R.S.C., *King Lear*, author of a 'collage version' of *Hamlet*, and producer of numerous West End productions. Hamlet, for Marowitz, is an aristocrat-playboy and a 'slob', who kills Claudius in a mindless state of panic. Horatio, at the moment of Hamlet's death, is 'desperately trying to contain a snigger' – and in one R.S.C. production this interpretation of him was given in performance. As the most obnoxious Yes-man in the Shakespearean canon, Horatio is for Marowitz a career-opportunist who realises at the last moment he has been backing the wrong horse. Ophelia is a hipster, who 'quite rightly shrugs off moralistic advice from a libertine', the libertine being her brother, who has 'done his share of whoring'. The ghost is a rasping, vengeful old codger, Polonius is a fool, while Claudius 'from all we see is an efficient monarch and a tactful politician'. (He has tact enough to keep murder secret.) The point of the play turns out to be simple enough: Hamlet is like those intellectuals who fume about the war in Vietnam, or the Greek dictatorship, but do nothing to end them.

This version of the play began as a practice-play, a 'clever exercise', apparently on the Brechtian model.[40] It is far harsher in its judgements on characters than any comment by Brecht, and though it has toured widely and had considerable success, by Marowitz's account, he also records a number of dissenting and outraged criticisms. Unlike Brecht's practice-pieces it was not meant to enhance appreciation of the original, and the point of mentioning it is that it originated as part of the 'Theatre of Cruelty' season at the LAMDA Theatre directed by Marowitz and Peter Brook.

Mr Brook was and remains the most strikingly original and successful producer in English theatre of the last fifteen years. His venture into 'Theatre of Cruelty', which is related to Artaud rather than to Brecht, does not exclude a profound admiration for Brecht, in fact Brook has regarded it as a challenge to all theatres in the world 'to saturate themselves in Brecht's work, to study the Ensemble and see all those facets of society that have found no place in their shut-off stages'.[41] Brook's productions have tended, however, along with many of the R.S.C. versions of Shakespeare, to interpret 'alienation' as though it meant not 'making strange' – which was at least part of Brecht's meaning – but 'making alien', 'arousing dislike or distrust' – which Brecht sometimes made it mean, in practice. A simple form of this was in the R.S.C. *Coriolanus*, when, to make sure that the audience was aware of the military man's weakness, he was shown sitting on the floor, pounding it between his knees with his fists, in a display of tantrums. Such condescension towards the audience was precisely what London and New York critics had complained of in Brecht from the outset.

The 'alienation' adopted by Peter Brook could affect not one character but the whole play. In his production of *King Lear*, a surprising number of reversals were effected, comparable to Marowitz's in *Hamlet* even though not expressed in such vituperative terms. Brook relates that at a lecture he gave the hypocritical protestation of love for Lear by Goneril to a woman from the audience who had never read or seen *King Lear;* she found it very difficult to read without eloquence and charm, even when told that it was supposed to be a speech of a wicked woman.[42] Whether or not as a consequence, he presented Goneril and Regan in his R.S.C. production as women of 'style and breeding, . . . ease and social aplomb', to quote his account of Goneril, and gave an initial impression that they were reasonably loyal daughters, prepared to give Lear some comfort in his old age. He also found Edmund, though 'clearly a villain', 'in the early scenes . . . by far the most attractive character we meet'.[43] The sincerity of Cordelia and loyalty of Kent in the early scenes apparently did not strike him: on the contrary, 'not only do we sympathize with Goneril and Regan for falling in love with him, but we tend to side with them in finding Edmund so admirably wicked . . .'[44]

On this reversal of traditional expectations, Brook introduced into his production a scene in which Lear caroused with his knights so noisily, ending like Coriolanus in a fit of tantrums and overturning a massive table with dozens of metal tankards on it, that Goneril was shocked beyond endurance and sent him packing to Regan. Similarly, at Regan's castle, Kent's rough treatment of Oswald was made to seem vindictive and bullying, while Lear was presented without majesty as a crusty, flat-voiced, grizzled, hectoring old spitfire. The pattern of the play could not, of course, be denied, and the production was not unmoving. Paul Scofield as Lear drew unexpected depth of feeling from the underplaying. But not surprisingly, Brook felt able to say in his book that, on the whole, 'we are compelled to face a play which refuses all moralising' (Edmund's deathbed repentance was cut out in performance), a play which is 'a vast, complex, coherent plan designed to study the power and the emptiness of nothing – the positive and negative aspects latent in the zero'.[45] Brecht would not have come to such a neo-Buddhist conclusion. Brook is closer, too, to Brecht's treatment of Marlowe's *Edward II*, which Brecht certainly turned into Theatre of Cruelty, than to Brecht's later adaptations of Shakespeare. Yet it cannot be said that in interpreting 'alienation in this sense, Brook was clearly wrong in his understanding of the theory. Brecht's approach both to Shakespeare and Sophocles, both in his adaptations and in his comments and practice-pieces, is capable of equal crudity and sensationalism. The chief difference between Brook and Brecht is that Brecht alienates in order to achieve a better world, whereas Brook's belief in one must be related to an inward realisation.

During the 1960s and early 1970s Brechtian techniques spread through all branches of theatre. There was alienation: Hamlet, in Jonathan Miller's production, 'was made to look a fool: the King was bored with the obviousness of the whole mousetrap scene, and called for lights to stop himself yawning rather than from fear of the play; Hamlet playing hide-and-seek after killing Polonius ran straight into astonished soldiers who could not fathom his childish behaviour. There was staging: in John Mortimer's unassuming play, *A Voyage Round My Father,* played with no thought but affording pleasure, the entire presentation, décor, lighting, narration, was Brechtian. Sean Kenny's set for the musical *Oliver!* has been praised for its Brechtian qualities.[46] The extremely popular play *Godspell,* which ran for a time in the crypt of St Paul's Cathedral, extended alienation of a sort to Jesus, who appeared as a clown; the explanation given by the author in a television interview was that the clown is the holiest of men. In the same play the remission of sins was presented literally as a whitewashing of Jesus, dressed in shorts and football stockings, with a paintbrush held by John the Baptist. The equally popular *Jesus Christ Superstar,* in its London production in 1973, presented the flagellation on a transparent floor marked with squares like a chessboard or bingo-card: as each blow fell, a new number lit up in one of the squares coloured red, until all thirty-nine had been given, and there was, so to speak, a full house.

In much of this, Brecht keyed in with developments of the times, rather than inspired them. He spoke in favour of both detachment and callousness, at certain times in his life, always in the ultimate aim of changing society, never in the cynical or merely all-embracing way of some English productions. The special emphasis on cruelty came not from him but from Artaud, whose purpose, once again, was not sadistic in the ordinary sense of the world, but rather more in the sense of the Marquis de Sade himself – that is, Artaud believed in the necessity of cruelty, which was in any case, as he saw it, not something purely physical, for the fullest realisation of human nature. Brecht had come close to this in *Baal,* and in *In the Cities' Jungle,* as well as in *Edward II*. In so far as these plays are influenced by Nietzsche, and very little that was written in German at that time was not influenced by him, Brecht's ideas are linked with Artaud's in a common ancestry, which extends, through Nietzsche, to de Sade himself. The cruel streak in Johanna Dark, in *St Joan of the Stockyards,* or in the agitators in *The Measures Taken,* has a philosophical background, for what that is worth.

There is thus a confluence of streams in a play with which Peter Brook achieved one of his most noted successes, Peter Weiss's *Persecution and Assassination of Jean-Paul Marat.* Weiss's play is, technically, a *tour de force,* in which many levels of interpretation are played off against each other, and in which both the tradition of Artaud and that of Brecht are usually thought to meet.[47] Presented by the inmates of the mental asylum of Charenton, under the direction of the Marquis de Sade, its main plot is concerned with the assassination of Marat, during the French Revolution, by Charlotte Corday. Its purport has less to do with the plot than with its presentation, for Weiss has not merely a narrator, who stands outside the whole affair, he also has de Sade on stage, rehearsing his own play in which Marat is only one character – though a character who is able to speak out of the play-within-a play to de Sade himself; at the same time there is a stage audience that is clearly meant to reflect Marxist expectations of the reactions of 'bourgeois' members of the real audience in the stalls. In addition to this Chinese-box complexity, there is a parallelism between the literal lunacy of the actors and the lunacy of the Reign of Terror which they enact, and a further parallelism between the Reign of Terror and the Nazi past, which Weiss certainly meant his German audiences to notice. The difficulty with so much alienation is that, whereas in Brecht as a rule a clearly opposite meaning is to be read into the apparent meaning of scenes and actions, in Weiss the meanings reflect one another infinitely, as in a pair of facing mirrors.

The problem of interpretation is considerable. Martin Esslin sees the essential quality of the play as 'a savage metaphor of the human condition itself'.[48] Susan Sontag comments that 'Insanity becomes the privileged, most authentic metaphor for passion; or, what's the same thing in this case, the logical ter-

minus of any strong emotion.'[49]   Of the two arguments Miss
Sontag's is the least tenable. Many strong emotions are unlikely
to end in madness, and there is no logical requirement that they
should. On the other hand, Mr Esslin's view of the play, while
it may correspond to Weiss's when he spoke of 'this madhouse
of a world',[50] says nothing of how the play comes to be such a
metaphor. The restriction of the play to a lunatic asylum has
the consequence that only two possibilities of changing the
human condition are presented. It is a question of choosing
either Marat's course of bloody revolution, on which the grisly
sport of the revolutionary lunatics is sufficient comment, or de
Sade's remedy, which is to have done with the mechanical
cruelty of the guillotine and replace it with a full-blooded acceptance of personal and individual cruelty, in fulfilment of the
whole of human nature. Understandably, such a play must have
appealed to Mr Brook, who felt compelled, in the case of *King
Lear*, to 'face a play which refuses all moralizing'.[51] The lack
of purpose in *Marat/Sade* accords well with that view of things.
Yet despite the great theatrical success of *Marat/Sade*, in
Brook's production, it has only extremes, logical and intellectual,
to offer. Brecht's later plays are strikingly more humane, more
balanced and considerate, even when in some other compari-
sons they have features that look grotesquely distorted.

The fact to be faced in England is, that Brecht's work came
onto the English stage as into a vacuum. There was almost no
history of political theatre in England, and what there was had
no prospect of political success. The Communist Party of Great
Britain was tiny, and though Marxism was still faintly fashionable, the tendency with almost all theatre-people was to take
over Brecht's techniques and theories while ignoring their roots
in Marxist philosophy. The alternative to Marxism, in terms of
comprehensive philosophies on the European model, 'Weltanschauungen', was some form of vitalism, whether derived from
Bergson, Nietzsche or some other source, and it so happened that
a powerful dramatic tradition in this vein descended through
Strindberg and Pirandello to the French theatre, to Artaud and
Genet. This converged on Brechtian theatre, and where the
adoption of his methods meant anything, where it was not
middle-brow or purely commercial, it tended to be in the form
of some assertion of life in the face of absurdity, something in

the spirit of the bargee's dance in *Serjeant Musgrave*, with its perpetual refrain of 'Michael Finnegan, begin again'. Only two 'Weltanschauungen' are really conceivable: acceptance of perpetual recurrence, or a revolutionary demand to change everything totally. Serious English theatre has, in recent years, tended to align itself with recurrence – accepting it with laughter, perhaps, but not looking for any fundamental change. Peter Weiss did the same, until his conversion to Marxism, but his plays since then have shown a decline.

Brecht, meanwhile, stands out, over against many of his imitators, as a dramatist who at his best still prized some human qualities without ironic withdrawal. The preference sometimes has to be sought for, and is not always there, but it remains as the distinctive mark of his spirit, in what he himself called dark times. We remember him at his best for the intensity of his probing into moral and social problems, the wise adaptability of his willingness to utilise every condition and limitation of the theatre so as to reflect on the conditions and limitations of living, the purification of his compassion from self-flattering benevolence to matter-of-fact cognizance of human needs, and his abundant vitality. If his Communism is less memorable, that is largely because it was, despite its professed aims, one of the main contributory causes of Brecht's adopting the hard mask, as well as of rigidities and forced contrivances in his drama. We can be certain, all the same, that the whole of him, masked and unmasked, will dominate in world-theatre for years to come.

REFERENCES

Full names and titles are given in the bibliography. *Versuche* and *Stücke,* both published by Suhrkamp, began in 1930 and 1955, respectively.

Chapter 1 (pp. 1–15)

1. Steiner, pp. 253–304.
2. Jakubietz and Koch, pp. 47–109.
3. Marx, p. xxx.
4. Dyos and Wolff, vol. 1, pp. 213–24, etc.
5. Knilli and Münchow, pp. 106–40.
6. Rowell, p. 405.
7. Knilli and Münchow, p. 100.
8. Marx, p. xxxi.
9. Marx, Chapter XXXII.
10. Marx, p. 789.
11. Ryder, Chapter 1 ('German Socialism Before 1914'), and Morgan, Chapter 2 ('The Lassallean Party and the International, 1864 to 1865').
12. See J. P. Nettl.
13. Lenin in Raddatz, vol. 1, p. 231.
14. Braun, p. 159.
15. Braun, p. 163.
16. Braun (in *Art and Revolution*, q.v.), p. 63.
17. Hoffmann and Hoffmann-Ostwald, vol. 1, pp. 88–9.
18. See Pfützner, also Kändler.
19. Hoffmann and Hoffmann-Ostwald, vol. 2, p. 16. Sung (but with innocuous words) by Ernst Busch in 'Lieder der Arbeiterklasse 1917–1933' on *Pläne* disc S77101, published by Pläne G.m.b.H., Dortmund, Humboldtstrasse 12.

Chapter 2 (pp. 16–41)

1. The early one-act plays, not treated here, are named in the Chronological List.
2. Esslin, p. 247.
3. Johst, p. 6.
4. Brecht, 'Bei Durchsicht meiner ersten Stücke.'
5. Ryder, p. 156.
6. Brecht, 'Bei Durchsicht meiner ersten Stücke.'

7. See Schumacher, pp. 64–5.
8. Schumacher, p. 65.
9. See p. 56 below.
10. *Stücke* III, 135.
11. *Stücke* III, 146 ('Notes on the Threepenny Opera').
12. Tr. D. I. Vesey and Eric Bentley.
13. But see Ewen, and Völker.

Chapter 3 (pp. 42–66)

1. Waley, pp. 230–235.
2. Mann, pp. 602-5.
3. Fischer, p. 618.
4. Esslin, p. 140.
5. Sokel in Demetz, p. 133.
6. Demetz, p. 10.
7. Esslin, p. 259.
8. Quoted in Esslin, p. 148.
9. Esslin, p. 41.
10. Esslin, pp. 49–50.
11. Esslin, p. 149.
12. Cp. Goethe's *Faust*, line 1112, 'Two souls there dwell, alas, within my breast.'
13. See p. 185 below.
14. *Theaterarbeit*, pp. 150–2.

Chapter 4 (pp. 67–89)

1. *Versuche*, 11, p. 97.
2. Willett, in *Adam and Encore*.
3. Redgrave, pp. 30–6.
4. *Versuche*, 12, p. 127.
5. *Versuche*, 11, p. 109. 'Übungsstücke für Schauspieler'.
6. Contrast photographs in *Theaterarbeit*, pp. 342–3.
7. *Versuche*, 11, p. 102.
8. *Versuche*, 11, p. 103.
9. *Stücke* III, pp. 266–7.
10. *Theaterarbeit*, p. 244.
11. *Versuche*, 12, p. 121.
12. See Knopf, pp. 21–7.
13. Quoted in Knopf, p. 25. (Ges. Werke in 20 Bänden, Werkausgabe, vol. 15, p. 264)
14. Compare John Donne's line about man's future state: 'Death thou shalt die.'
15. Quoted in Tucker, p. 114.
16. Stern and Herald, p. 106.
17. Carl Niessen, pp. 28–9.
18. Innes, pp. 185–7.

19. Piscator, quoted by Innes, p. 29.
20. Innes, p. 31.
21. Innes, p. 29.
22. *Stücke* v, 118.
23. *Stücke* v, 118.
24. *Stücke* III, 266.
25. *Stücke* III, 275.
26. Aristotle, *Poetics,* XI, ed.cit., p. 45.
27. *Stücke* v, 178.
28. *Versuche,* 9, p. 81.
29. House, pp. 102 and 109–10.
30. Quoted in House, p. 109.
31. *Stücke* v, 172.
32. *Stücke* v, 176–7.
33. *Versuche,* 12, pp. 109–10.
34. *Versuche,* 12, p. 122.
35. *Versuche,* 12, p. 119.
36. *Versuche,* 12, p. 137.
37. *Versuche,* 12, p. 111.
38. *Versuche,* 12, p. 140.
39. Marx and Engels, vol. II, p. 79.

Chapter 5 (pp. 90–108)

1. See Allen, *passim.*
2. See Thyssen.
3. Orwell, vol. 2, p. 40.
4. See p. 139 below.
5. Plays in other languages dealing with or directly alluding to Nazism, and written 1933–45, include W. H. Auden, *On The Frontier;* Charlotte Haldane, *The Crooked Sapling;* Stephen Spender, *Trial of a Judge;* Jean Anouilh, *Antigone;* Jean-Paul Sartre, *Morts sans Sépulture* and *Les Mouches;* S. N. Behrman, *Rain from Heaven;* Elmer Rice, *Judgment Day;* Kazan and Smith, *Dimitroff;* Elvin Abeles, *One of the Bravest;* Clifford Odets, *Till the Day I Die;* Lilian Hellman, *The Watch on the Rhine.*
6. Esslin, p. 176.
7. Esslin, p. 176.
8. Esslin, p. 176.
9. *Stücke* IX, 365.
10. *Stücke* IX, 369–71.
11. *Stücke* IX, 370.
12. Bullock, p. 247.
13. See Tobias, *passim.*
14. Bullock, pp. 284–307.
15. Bullock, pp. 326–8.
16. See Ryder, *Twentieth-Century Germany.*
17. Demetz, p. 11.

18. *Stücke* IX, 372–3.
19. *Stücke* IX, 368.
20. *Versuche*, 12, p. 121.
21. Ewen, p. 374.

Chapter 6 (pp. 109–116)

1. *Stücke* VII, 147.
2. *Stücke* VIII, 210.
3. *Sunday Times*, 19 June 1960.
4. *Stücke* VIII, 186–7.
5. For the historical background, see the account by Colin Ronan in the school edition of D. I. Vesey's translation, Methuen 1967, pp. xi–xx.
6. Tr. D. I. Vesey.

Chapter 7 (pp. 117–136)

1. D. H. Lawrence, Letter of 22 January 1925.
2. *Stücke* VII, 60.
3. Esslin, p. 264.
4. Mennemeier, p. 400.
5. Photo in *Theaterarbeit*, p. 265.
6. *Theaterarbeit*, p. 323.
7. Williams, p. 286.

Chapter 8 (pp. 137–148)

1. 'Knecht' suggests more of ג slave than 'servant' ('Diener').
2. Benjamin, p. 116(n.). Cp. p. 92 above. But see also Benjamin, p. 117.
3. *The Times*, 16 July 1965. Other daily papers on the same day, Sunday papers 18 July.
4. *Theaterarbeit*, p. 22.
5. *Versuche*, 12, p. 6.
6. *Schriften zum Theater*, p. 63 f.
7. Willett, p. 82.
8. *Sinn und Form 2*, p. 212.

Chapter 9 (pp. 149–166)

1. See p. 108 above.
2. Völker, p. 143.
3. *Gesammelte Werke*, Leinenausgabe, VIII, 881.
4. John Willett, *T.L.S.* See also Arendt, pp. 207–49.
5. *Ges. Werke loc. cit.*
6. Völker, p. 146.
7. Ewen, p. 455.
8. *Stücke* VIII, 199.
9. *Versuche*, 12, p. 140.

10. *loc. cit.*
11. See *Stücke* xi, 388–9.
12. See p. 72 above.
13. Aristotle, *The Politics*, Book III, chapter 12, ed. cit., p. 128.
14. See *Theater 1966*, annual special issue of the periodical *Theater heute*.
15. Hecht, pp. 319–25.
16. See Funke, and *Theater in der Zeitenwende*.

Chapter 10 (pp. 167–181)

1. Brustein, p. 415.
2. Quoted in Gascoigne, *World Theatre*, p. 258.
3. Quoted in Schoeps, p. 290.
4. Brustein, p. 415.
5. See Coe, pp. 38–40, 145, etc.
6. Coe, p. 103.
7. Coe, pp. 78–9.
8. See Gassner and Quinn, p. 8.
9. Brook, p. 81.
10. Brook, p. 82.
11. Brook, p. 83.
12. Williams, p. 278.
13. Williams, p. 283.

Chapter 11 (pp. 182–207)

1. Nicoll, p. 72.
2. Nicoll, p. 225.
3. Goldstein, *passim*.
4. Goldstein, p. 18.
5. Goldstein, p. 220.
6. For contrasted passages from Brecht's play and Peters' and Sklar's, see Gascoigne, *Twentieth Century Drama*, pp. 125–6.
7. Goldstein, p. 207–8.
8. Losey in *Les Cahiers du Cinéma*, p. 27.
9. For part of the transcript of the hearing, see Ewen, pp. 497–509, and Demetz, pp. 30–42.
10. Kern, pp. 157–65.
11. Himelstein, pp. 178–89.
12. Baxandall, p. 165.
13. Baxandall, p. 164.
14. Wixson, pp. 112–24.
15. Quoted in Goldstein, p. 54.
16. Odets, p. 9.
17. Quoted in Goldstein, p. 222.
18. See p. 217 below.
19. Lehmann, pp. 65–74.
20. Esslin, p. ix, and Hahnloser-Ingold, pp. 84–8.

21. Lehmann, pp. 136–8.
22. Irving Wardle in Gassner and Quinn, p. 248.
23. Quoted by Weise, p. 81.
24. Weise, p. 82.
25. Weise, pp. 78–110.
26. Taylor, p. 49.
27. Weise, p. 137.
28. *T.L.S.*, 30 June 1961, p. 400.
29. Quoted in Weise, p. 145.
30. Taylor, p. 73.
31. Taylor, p. 81.
32. See also Wellwarth, pp. 269–70.
33. By Michael R. Turner.
34. See Weise, p. 215.
35. Tynan, p. 229.
36. Esslin, *Brief Chronicles*, pp. 96 and 92.
37. See London newspapers 10–13 August 1965.
38. See Irving Wardle in *The Times*, 7 May 1971.
39. See Brecht, *Little Organon*, para. 33.
40. Marowitz, p. 41.
41. Brook, p. 95.
42. Brook, p. 16.
43. Brook, p. 102.
44. Brook, p. 103.
45. Brook, p. 105.
46. Esslin, *Brief Chronicles*, p. 87.
47. Milfull, pp. 61 seqq.
48. Esslin *Theatre of the Absurd*, p. 423.
49. Sontag, p. 165.
50. Weiss in *Theater heute*, October 1965.
51. Brook, p. 105.

CHRONOLOGY OF
BRECHT'S LIFE AND TIMES

1898
10 February. Eugen Berthold
Brecht born in Augsburg. His
father worked in a papermill,
later rose to be a director.
1914
Brecht, at 16, expressed patriotic
enthusiasm for war.
1918
October. After brief university
study, Brecht served as orderly
in military hospital, Augsburg.
Wrote *Baal*.
1922
Drums in the Night performed.
Several other plays performed in
next few years. Married Marianne
Zoff (Divorced 1927).
1926
'I am eight foot deep in *Capital*.'
1928
Threepenny Opera performed,
with great success.
1929
Married Helene Weigel. First
propagandist works written.

1933–47
Exile in Denmark, Finland and
U.S.A. Major works written
1937–44: *Mother Courage,
Galileo, Puntila, The Good
Woman, The Caucasian Chalk
Circle*.
1947
Return to Europe

1871–1918
Wilhelmine Empire. Repression
of Left-wing, but great growth of
Marxist socialism from 1900.

1914
Beginning of First World War.

1918
11 November. End of the war.
Socialist and Communist uprisings
during the winter.

1918–24
Period of severe privation and
inflation, strikes and revolutionary
attempts.

1925-1929
Economic recovery, terminated by
the 'Wall Street crash'.

1929-32
Increasing unemployment, growth
of Nazi Party, conflict with
Communists. Parliamentary
parties helpless against extremists.
1933–45
Period of Nazi rule, ending in
Second World War, 1939–1945.

1949
Foundation of 'Berliner Ensemble'.
Brecht devotes time to producing,
though some plays were also
written.

1951
Revision of *Lucullus* required by
State.
1953
Message of loyalty to head of
State at time of uprisings.

1954
Schiffbauerdamm Theatre became
home of 'Berliner Ensemble'.
1955
Brecht received prize in Moscow.
1956
Died 14 August, of coronary
thrombosis.
1956
August-September. First visit of
'Berliner Ensemble' to London.

1965
Second visit of 'Berliner Ensemble'
to London.

1949
Two German states founded, the
Federal Republic and the
Democratic Republic. More
liberal policy, briefly, in G.D.R.
after Stalin's death (1953).

1953
Uprisings in Democratic
Republic against regime and
U.S.S.R. Period of economic
recovery followed; G.D.R. became
the most prosperous Communist
country outside U.S.S.R.

1956
November. Hungarian uprising
suppressed by U.S.S.R.

1961
Democratic Republic sealed off
from West by Berlin Wall.

1973
'Brecht Week' celebrated in
Democratic Republic.

A CHRONOLOGICAL LIST OF
BRECHT'S PLAYS, AND TRANSLATIONS

The latest and fullest German editions are the Gesammelte Werke (Werkausgabe) in 20 vols., limp-covers, and the *Gesammelte Werke* (Leinenausgabe) in 8 vols. on India paper. Before these there were the *Stücke* and the *Versuche*, (see p. 209) neither of which were comprehensive. For fuller details see the *Bertolt-Brecht-Bibliographie* by K.-D. Petersen, Bad Homburg v.d. H., 1968 (intended to aid academic study, and not aiming at completeness), the bibliography by Walter Nubel in *Sinn und Form*, 'Zweites Sonderheft Bertolt Brecht', Berlin, 1957, and the bibliographical material in the books on Brecht by John Willett and Martin Esslin, both 1959. The first volume of a six-volume *Bibliographie Bertolt Brecht* was published in 1975 by Aufbau Verlag, Berlin and Weimar. There are also numerous variants for many of the plays, published in separate volumes by Suhrkamp.

The present state of textual confusion caused by so many editions is one major concern of the Brecht Society, whose chairman is Professor John B. Fuegi, Dept. of Comparative Literature, University of Wisconsin-Milwaukee, Wisconsin 53201, U.S.A.

Several 'collected' editions of the plays in English translation have appeared, though none is complete. They are referred to by initials in the following list:

Bertolt Brecht. *Plays*. vol. 1. Methuen, London, 1960 (P.).
Seven Plays by Bertolt Brecht. Grove Press, New York, 1961 (S.P.).
Bertolt Brecht. *Collected Plays*. vol. 1, ed. John Willett and Ralph Manheim. Methuen, London, 1970 (C.P.).
Bertolt Brecht. *Collected Plays*. vol. 1 and vol. 5. Pantheon Books, New York (C.P.P.).
Bertolt Brecht. The Grove Press Edition. Everyman Black Cat series. Grove Press, New York, 1964 etc. (G.P.E.).

The plays are arranged below in chronological order of writing. The first date after the title, in brackets, is that of the first performance in German, the second is that of the first German edition or date of writing.

Die Kleinbürgerhochzeit (*A Respectable Wedding*) (Frankfurt, 1926) written 1919, tr. in C.P. and C.P.P. by Jean Benedetti. One-act.
Der Bettler oder der tote Hund (*The Beggar or The Dead Dog*) written 1919, tr. in C.P. and C.P.P. by Michael Hamburger. One-act.

Er treibt einen Teufel aus (*Driving out a Devil*) written 1919, tr. in C.P. and C.P.P. by Richard Grunberger. One-act.

Lux in Tenebris, written 1919, tr. in C.P. and C.P.P. by Eva Geisel and Ernst Borneman. One-act.

Der Fischzug (*The Catch*) probably written in 1919, tr. in C.P. and C.P.P. by Eric Bentley. One-act.

Baal (Leipzig, 1923), Potsdam, 1922, tr. in C.P. and C.P.P. by Peter Tegel, also by Eric Bentley, Grove Press, 1964.

Trommeln in der Nacht (*Drums in the Night*) (Munich, 1922) Munich, 1923, tr. in C.P. and C.P.P. by John Willett, and in G.P.E. by Frank Jones (volume entitled *Jungle of Cities*).

Im Dickicht der Städte (*In the Jungle of Cities*) (Munich, 1923), Berlin 1927, tr. as *In the Jungle of Cities* by Gerhard Nellhaus in C.P. and in C.P.P., and by Anselm Hollo in G.P.E.; as *In the Swamp* by Eric Bentley, in S.P.

Das Leben Eduards II von England (*The Life of Edward II of England;* after Marlowe) (Munich, 1924), Potsdam, 1924, tr. by Jean Benedetti in C.P. and in C.P.P.; also in G.P.E.

Mann ist Mann (*A Man's a Man*) (Darmstadt, 1926), Berlin, 1927, tr. by Eric Bentley in S.P. and in G.P.E.

Das Elefantenkalb (*The Elephant Calf*) (Darmstadt, 1926?), Berlin, 1927, tr. by Eric Bentley in G.P.E. (volume entitled *The Jewish Wife*).

Die Dreigroschenoper (*The Threepenny Opera;* after Gay) (Berlin, 1928), Vienna, 1929, tr. Eric Bentley and D. I. Vesey in P. and in G.P.E.

Aufstieg und Fall der Stadt Mahagonny (*Rise and Fall of the Town of Mahagonny*) (Leipzig, 1930), Vienna, 1929.

Der Ozeanflug, originally *Der Flug der Lindberghs* (*The Flight over the Ocean*) (Baden-Baden, 1929), Berlin, 1930, tr. by G. Antheil, Universal-Edition, Vienna, 1930.

Das Badener Lehrstück vom Einverständnis (*The Baden-Baden Cantata of Acquiescence*) (Baden-Baden, 1929), Berlin, 1930, tr. by Gerhard Nellhaus in *Harvard Advocate*, cxxxiv, 4 (Feb. 1951).

Die heilige Johanna der Schlachthöfe (*St. Joan of the Stockyards*) (Hamburg 1959), Berlin 1932, tr. by Frank Jones, Indiana University Press, Bloomington 1969.

Der Jasager/Der Neinsager (*He Who Said Yes/He Who Said No*) (*Der Jasager* only, Berlin, 1930), Berlin 1930, tr. by Gerhard Nellhaus in *Accent* (Urbana, Illinois) vii, 2, Autumn 1946.

Die Maßnahme (*The Measures Taken*) (Berlin, 1930). Berlin, 1931, tr. by Eric Bentley in G.P.E. (volume entitled *The Jewish Wife*).

Die Ausnahme und die Regel (*The Exception and the Rule*) (Paris, 1947), Moscow, 1937, tr. by Eric Bentley in G.P.E. (volume entitled *The Jewish Wife*).

Die Mutter (*The Mother*; after Gorki's novel) (Berlin, 1932), Berlin, 1933, tr. by Lee Baxandall in G.P.E.

Die Horatier und die Kuriatier (*The Horatians and the Curiatians*) (Halle/Wittenberg, 1958), London, 1938, tr. by H. R. Hays in *Accent* (Urbana, Illinois), viii, 1, Autumn 1947.

Die Rundköpfe und die Spitzköpfe (*Round Heads and Pointed Heads*) (Copenhagen, 1936), London, 1938, tr. by N. Goold-Verschoyle in G.P.E. (volume entitled *Jungle of Cities*).

Die sieben Todsünden, also called *Anna-Anna* (*The Seven Deadly Sins*) (Paris, 1933), German text and tr. on sleeve of American recording, Columbia KL 5175, also on Phillips recording B 07186 L.

Furcht und Elend des dritten Reiches (*Fear and Misery of the Third Reich*) (Paris, 1938), Moscow, 1941, tr. publ. by Mezhdunarodnaya Kniga, Moscow, 1942; as *The Private Life of the Master Race* by Eric Bentley, New York, 1944 and London, 1948; three scenes tr. by Eric Bentley in G.P.E. (volume entitled *The Jewish Wife*).

Die Gewehre der Frau Carrar (*Señora Carrar's Rifles*) (Paris, 1937), London, 1937, tr. by K. Wallis in *Theatre Workshop* II, New York, 1938.

Mutter Courage und ihre Kinder (*Mother Courage and her Children*) (Zürich, 1941), Frankfurt a.M. 1949, tr. by Eric Bentley, Methuen, London, 1962, Grove Press, New York, 1963, also in C.P.P. vol. 5, and G.P.E.

Dansen, written 1939.

Was kostet das Eisen, written, 1939 (Stockholm, 1939).

Leben des Galilei (*The Life of Galileo*) (Zürich, 1943), Berlin 1955, tr. by Brecht and Charles Laughton, ed. Eric Bentley, in S.P.1 and G.P.E., by D. I. Vesey in P.; also in C.P.P. vol. 5. Also separately, by D. I. Vesey, Methuen, 1960. The latter translation also in a school edition, with introduction by Ronald Gray and Colin Ronan, Methuen, 1963.

Das Verhör des Lukullus (*The Trial of Lucullus*) (Berne radio, 1940), Moscow, 1940, tr. by H. R. Hays in P.1, also in C.P.P. vol. 5.

Die Verurteilung des Lukullus (*The Condemnation of Lucullus*) (Berlin, 1951), Berlin and Zürich, 1951.

Der gute Mensch von Sezuan (*The Good Woman of Setzuan*) (Zürich, 1943), Berlin, 1953, tr. by Eric Bentley (revised), Grove Press, New York, 1965, also in G.P.E.; as *The Good Person of Szechwan* by John Willett, Methuen, 1962.

Herr Puntila und sein Knecht Matti (*Squire Puntila and his Man Matti;* after stories by Wuolijoki) (Zürich, 1948), Munich, 1948.

Der aufhaltsame Aufstieg des Arturo Ui (*The Resistible Rise of Arturo Ui*) (Stuttgart, 1958), Berlin, 1957.

Die Gesichte der Simone Machard (*The Visions of Simone Machard*) (Frankfurt, 1957), Potsdam, 1956, tr. by Carl Richard Mueller in G.P.E., by Arnold Hinchliffe, London (1961?).

Schweyk im zweiten Weltkrieg (*Schweik in the Second World War;* after stories by Hašek) (Erfurt, 1958), Frankfurt, 1957.

Der kaukasische Kreidekreis (*The Caucasian Chalk Circle*) (Berlin, 1954), Potsdam, 1949, tr. by Eric Bentley in S.P. and G.P.E. (revised); tr. by Eric Bentley (revised), ed. Michael Marland, London and Glasgow (Blackie), 1967; tr. by James and Tania Stern with W. H. Auden in P.

Die Antigone des Sophokles (*The Antigone of Sophocles;* after Hölderlin's translation) (Chur, 1948), Berlin, 1949 (in *Antigonemodell 48*).

Die Tage der Commune (*The Days of the Commune*) (Karl-Marx-Stadt, 1956), Berlin, 1957.

Der Hofmeister (*The Tutor*; after Lenz) (Berlin, 1950), Berlin 1951.

Coriolan (*Coriolanus*; after Shakespeare) Frankfurt, 1959.

Der Prozeß der Jeanne d'Arc zu Rouen 1431 (*The Trial Jeanne d'Arc at Rouen in 1431*; after Seghers) (Berlin, 1952), Frankfurt, 1959.

Don Juan (*Don Juan*; after Molière) (Rostock, 1952), Frankfurt a.M., 1959.

Pauken und Trompeten (*Trumpets and Drums*; after Farquhar) (Berlin, 1955), Frankfurt, 1959, tr. by Rose and Martin Kastner, Toronto, printed at Trinity College [Toronto] for the Trinity College Dramatic Society, 1963.

Turandot oder der Kongreß der Weiwäscher (*Turandot, or the Congress of Whitewashers*) (Berlin, 1973).

SELECT BIBLIOGRAPHY

Allen, W. S. *The Nazi Seizure of Power. The Experience of a Single German Town, 1930–1935*, London, 1966.

Arendt, Hannah. 'Bertolt Brecht 1898–1956', in *Men in Dark Times*, London, 1970.

Aristotle, *Aristotle's Theory of Poetry and Fine Art with a critical text and translation of the Poetics*, S. H. Butcher (tr.). Fourth edition, Doverbooks, New York, 1951.

The Politics, tr. T. A. Sinclair, Penguin, Harmondsworth, 1962.

Art and Revolution, Soviet Art and Design since 1917. Arts Council of Great Britain catalogue of the exhibition at the Hayward Gallery, London, 1971 (Illustrations).

Baxandall, Lee. 'The Americanization of Bert Brecht' in *Brecht Heute: Brecht Today*. Jahrgang I, 1971.

Benjamin, Walter. *On Understanding Brecht*, London, 1973.

Braun, Edward. *Meyerhold on Theatre*, Methuen, London, 1969. (Illustrations).

Brook, Peter. *The Empty Space*, Penguin, Harmondsworth, 1972.

Brustein, Robert. *The Theatre of Revolt*, London, 1965.

Bullock, Alan. *Hitler, A Study in Tyranny*. Completely revised edn., Penguin, Harmondsworth, 1962.

Coe, Richard N. *Ionesco, A Study of his Plays*, London, 1971.

Demetz, Peter (ed.). *Brecht. A Collection of Critical Essays*, Englewood Cliffs, N.J., 1962.

Dyos, H. J. and M. Wolff (eds.). *The Victorian City*, 2 vols., London, 1973.

Esslin, Martin. *Brecht: a Choice of Evils*, London, 1959.

The Theatre of the Absurd. Revised and enlarged edn., Penguin, Harmondsworth, 1968.

Brief Chronicles. Essays in the Modern Theatre, London, 1970.

Ewen, Frederic. *Bertolt Brecht, His Life, His Art and His Times*, London, 1970 (U.S.A., 1967)

Fischer, Ruth. *Stalin and German Communism*, Cambridge, Mass., 1948.

Funke, Christoph. (ed.), *Theater-Bilanz. Eine Bilddokumentation über die Bühnen der Deutschen Demokratischen Republik*, Berlin, 1971 (Illustrations).

Gascoigne, Bamber. *Twentieth Century Drama*, London, 1962.

World Theatre, An Illustrated History, London, 1968.

Gassner, John, and Edward Quinn (eds.). *The Reader's Encyclopaedia of World Drama*, London, 1970.

Goldstein, M. *The Political Stage, American Drama and Theatre of the Great Depression,* Oxford, 1974.

Grimm, Reinhold. 'Brecht, Ionesco und das moderne Theater', in *German Life and Letters,* vol. XIII, April 1960.

Hahnloser-Ingold, Margrit. *Das englische Theater und Bert Brecht,* Bern, 1970.

Hecht, Werner. (ed.), *Brecht 73. Brecht-Woche der DDR,* Berlin, 1973.

Himelstein, Morgan Y. 'The Pioneers of Bertolt Brecht in America' in *Modern Drama,* vol. 9, 1966.

Hoffmann, Ludwig, and Daniel Hoffmann-Ostwald. *Deutsches Arbeitertheater 1910–1933,* Rogner und Bernhard Verlag, 2 vols., München, 1973. (Illustrations, extracts from plays and revues.)

House, Humphry. *Aristotle's Poetics,* London, 1956.

Innes, C. D. *Erwin Piscator's Political Theatre,* Cambridge, 1972.

Jakubietz, M., and H. Koch. *Marx-Engels-Lenin, Uber Kunst und Literatur. Aus ihren Schriften,* Reclam, Leipzig, n.d., pp. 47–109.

Johst, Hanns. *Der Einsame,* München, 1925.

Kändler, Klaus. *Drama und Klassenkampf. Beziehungen zwischen Epochenproblematik und dramatischen Konflikt in der sozialistischen Dramatik der Weimarer Republik,* Aufbau Verlag, Berlin and Weimar, 1970.

Kern, Edith. 'Brecht's Popular Theatre and its American Popularity' in *Modern Drama,* vol. 1, 1958.

Knilli, Friedrich, and Münchow, U. *Frühes deutsches Arbeitertheater 1847–1918,* Carl Hanser, München, 1970. (Illustrations. Extracts from plays.)

Knopf, Jan. *Bertolt Brecht. Ein kritischer Forschungsbericht,* Frankfurt a.M. 1974.

Lehmann, John. *New Writing in Europe,* Penguin, Harmondsworth, 1940.

Les Cahiers du Cinéma, no. 114, Dec. 1966 (special number on Brecht). See also *Screen: The Journal of the Society for Education in Film and Television,* vol. 15. no. 2. Special Number: 'Brecht and a Revolutionary Cinema', (Summer 1974).

Mann, Golo. *The History of Germany since 1789,* Penguin, Harmondsworth, 1974.

Marowitz, Charles. *The Marowitz Hamlet,* London, 1968.

Marx, Karl. *Capital: A Critical Analysis of Capitalist Production.* tr. Samuel Moore and Edward Aveling, ed. Frederick Engels. Photographic reprint of first edition, ed. Dona Torr, London, 1938.

Marx, Karl, and Friedrich Engels. *Selected Works,* Moscow, 1958. *Complete Works,* London, 1975. (Vols. 1, 2 and 3 published. To be in 50 volumes).

Mennemeier, Franz N. 'Brecht: "Mutter Courage und ihre Kinder"', in *Das deutsche Drama,* ed. Benno von Wiese, Düsseldorf, 1958, II, 401–14.

Milfull, John. 'From Kafka to Brecht: Peter Weiss's Development owards

Marxism'. *German Life and Letters*, New Series, vol. xx. no. 1. October 1966.

Morgan, Roger. *The German Social Democrats and the First International 1864–72*, Cambridge, 1965.

Nettl, J. P. *Rosa Luxemburg*, 2 vols., London, 1966.

Nicoll, Allardyce. *English Drama 1900–1930*, Cambridge, 1973.

Niessen, Carl. *Max Reinhardt und seine Bühnenbildner*, Köln, 1958 (Institut für Theaterwissenschaft: Reinhardt exhibition. Illustrations).

Odets, Clifford. *Three Plays*, London, 1936.

Orwell, George. *Collected Essays*, 4 vols., Penguin, Harmondsworth, 1970.

Pfützner, Klaus. *Ensembles und Aufführungen des sozialistischen Berufstheaters in Berlin 1929–1933*, Henschelverlag, Berlin, 1966 ('Schriften zur Theaterwissenschaft', Band 4).

Piscator, Erwin. *Das politische Theater*, Berlin, 1929.

Raddatz, Fritz J. (ed.), *Marxismus und Literatur, Eine Dokumentation in drei Bänden*, Hamburg, 1969.

Redgrave, Michael, and Jean-Louis Barrault. 'Actors' Comments' (on Brecht's 'New Technique of the Art of Acting') in *World Theatre*, iv, 1, 1955.

Rowell, G. (ed.), *Nineteenth Century Plays*, Oxford, 1953.

Ryder, A. J. *The German Revolution of 1918, A Study of German Socialism in War and Revolt*, Cambridge, 1967.

Twentieth Century Germany: from Bismarck to Brandt, London, 1973.

Schoeps, Karl-Heinz. *Bertolt Brecht und Bernard Shaw*, Bonn, 1974.

Schumacher, E. *Die dramatischen Versuche Bertolt Brechts 1918–1933*, Berlin, 1955.

Sinn und Form, 'Zweites Sonderheft Bertolt Brecht,' Berlin, 1957.

Sontag, Susan. *Against Interpretation*, London, 1967.

Steiner, Gerhard, (ed.). *Jakobinerschauspiel und Jakobinertheater*, Stuttgart, 1973 (Texts of plays).

Stern, E., and Herald, H. *Reinhardt und seine Bühne*, Berlin, 1919 (Illustrations).

Taylor, John Russell. *Anger and After. A Guide to the New British Drama*, London, 1962.

Theater in der Zeitenwende. Zur Geschichte des Dramas und des Schauspiels in der Deutschen Demokratischen Republik, 2 vols., Berlin, 1972 (Illustrations).

Theaterarbeit. Sechs Aufführungen des Berliner Ensembles, Dresden, 1952 (Illustrations of Brecht's productions).

Thyssen, Fritz. *I Paid Hitler*, London, 1941.

Tobias, F. *The Reichstag Fire*, London, 1964.

Tucker, R. C. *Philosophy and Myth in Karl Marx*, Cambridge, 1967.

Turner, Michael R. *Bluff your Way in the Theatre*, London, 1967.

Tynan, Kenneth. *Tynan on Theatre*, Penguin, Harmondsworth, 1964.

Völker, Klaus. *Brecht-Chronik. Daten zu Leben und Werk*, München, 1971.

Waley, Arthur. *The No Plays of Japan*, London, 1921.

Weise, Wolf-Dietrich. *Die 'Neuen englischen Dramatiker' in ihrem Verhältnis zu Brecht,* Bad Homburg v.d.H., 1969.

Wellwarth, George E. *The Theatre of Protest and Paradox,* London, 1964.

Willett, John. *The Theatre of Bertolt Brecht,* London, 1959.

'Thoughts on Brechtian Theatre', in *Adam and Encore,* Brecht number, 1956.

'The Story of Brecht's Odes to Stalin' in *The Times Literary Supplement,* 26 March 1970 (see also *T.L.S.* 9 April 1970, 'Commentary', and letter on 16 April 1970).

Williams, Raymond. *Drama from Ibsen to Brecht,* London, 1968.

Wixson, D. C., Jr. 'The Dramatic Techniques of Thornton Wilder and Bertolt Brecht' in *Modern Drama,* vol. 15, 1972.

INDEX